Contents

Dedication iv

Acknowledgements v

Introduction to the fifth edition vi

Part 1
Early childhood education traditions: what they are and where they come from 1

1 Three different views of the child 2

2 Ten principles of the pioneers: the bedrock of the
  early childhood traditions 19

3 The first three years 43

Part 2
Applying the principles 59

4 Play 60

5 Schemas 74

6 Representation: children as symbol users 102

7 Communicating with and without words: the foundations of literacy 122

8 Learning how you and other people feel and think 148

9 People who matter to children 168

10 Diversity and inclusion 189

11 Observation that informs assessment, planning and evaluation 201

12 The way forward 214

Bibliography and references 216

Index 225

Dedication

To Sybil Levy.

> The gods did not reveal, from the beginning
>
> All things to us; in the course of time,
>
> Through seeking, men find that which is the better.
>
> But as for certain truth, no man has known it,
>
> Nor will he know it; neither of the gods,
>
> Nor yet of all things of which I speak.
>
> And even if by chance he were to utter
>
> The final truth, he would himself not know it;
>
> For all is but a woven web of guesses.

Xenophanes (c.570–475 BCE)

Early Childhood Education

5th edition

Tina Bruce

HODDER
EDUCATION
AN HACHETTE UK COMPANY

Orders: please contact Bookpoint Ltd, 130 Milton Park, Abingdon, Oxon OX14 4SB. Telephone: (44) 01235 827720. Fax: (44) 01235 400454. Lines are open from 9.00–5.00, Monday to Saturday, with a 24-hour message answering service. You can also order through our website: www.hoddereducation.co.uk.

British Library Cataloguing in Publication Data

A catalogue record for this title is available from the British Library

ISBN 978 1 4718 4669 4

First Published 2015

Impression number 10 9 8 7 6 5 4 3 2 1

Year 2018 2017 2016 2015

Hachette UK's policy is to use papers that are natural, renewable and recyclable products and made from wood grown in sustainable forests. The logging and manufacturing processes are expected to conform to the environmental regulations of the country of origin.

The Publishers would like to thank the following for permission to reproduce copyright material:

Photo credits page 1: © xavier gallego morell/Fotolia; p. 59 © Serhiy Kobyakov/Fotolia; all others © Tom Bruce

Every effort has been made to trace all copyright holders, but if any have been inadvertently overlooked the Publishers will be pleased to make the necessary arrangements at the first opportunity.

Cover photo © Imgorthand/Getty Images

Typeset by Integra Software Services Pvt. Ltd., Pondicherry, India.

Printed in Great Britain for Hodder Education, an Hachette UK company.

Acknowledgements

From the author

I give my heartfelt thanks to Tom Bruce for the photographs in this edition of the book. He is a joy to work with, as he tunes in to what is needed, seems to read my mind, and captures important moments. Thanks also to Gemma Bruce for her help in organising some of the opportunities for photographs. Without the help of Michele Barrett at Vanessa Nursery School and Children's Centre – and the quiet and enormously helpful support of Sian Thompson and all the staff, parents and children – the photographs would not have told the stories of how children flourish when they spend time with people who love them, and who strive to give them educationally worthwhile experiences. Thank you.

Thanks to Barbara Isaacs, Director of Studies of the Montessori Centre International, and Janni Nicol, Early Years Representative, Steiner Waldorf Education, for their insightful, helpful and fascinating dialogues with me in relation to Chapter 2. I am most grateful to Fran Pafford for her sensitively written and invaluable critical feedback.

My thanks also to Stephen Halder at Hodder Education for his understanding. I give my appreciation to the late Chris Athey, who has helped me more than I can ever say to enjoy thinking about and working with young children and their families and carers.

I have really appreciated discussions with Hannah Bruce and Jonathan Eato. I thank my parents, Margery and (the late) Peter Rowland, and my brother Marc, for being loving anchors, always there for me both physically and in spirit.

Most of all, my thanks to Ian Bruce, as we continue to move together from Ruby towards Golden times; you are my best (critical) friend, you give me real feedback and empower me, and I enjoy your friendship.

From the publisher

The publishers would like to thank the following for permission to reproduce these items: images on page 106 from Goodnow, J. (1977) *Children Drawing*. Harvard University Press: Cambridge; page 107 from Strauss, M. (1978) *Understanding Children's Drawings*. Rudolf Steiner Press: Sussex; and pages 133–4 taken from Ferreiro and Teberosky (1983) *Literacy Before Schooling*. Heinemann Educational Books, Inc.: New Hampshire.

Every effort has been made to trace all copyright holders, but if any have been inadvertently overlooked the Publishers will be pleased to make the necessary arrangements at the first opportunity.

Introduction to the fifth edition

Early childhood practice has undergone far-reaching changes since the first edition of this book was written in 1987, due to the impact of the Conservative, New Labour and Coalition Governments.

But although governments come and governments go, the situation remains that children, as they begin to meet people beyond their family, need adults who are mature, well educated, trained and qualified to a high level in their knowledge and understanding of child development. This will enable them to help children to learn effectively, to achieve, enjoy and make a contribution. Continuing professional development is fundamental to early childhood practice when working with other people's children. Across the years, I have found that early childhood practitioners of all different backgrounds want this. This book is offered in response to that spirit. It is heartening that this fifth edition has been requested.

In early childhood practice, we need to look to the future by building on the past. The core principles in the first edition, extrapolated from the writings of pioneer educators – especially Froebel, Montessori and Steiner – are, it seems, as important now, if not more so, as they were in 1987. In this fifth edition these principles are revisited in the hope that their practical implications will help early childhood practitioners of all kinds, to make progress in the important work that they do with young children and their families.

Chapter 1 looks at three different views of the child; Chapter 2 explores the work of three pioneer educators. Chapter 3 addresses the importance of the first three years, and Chapter 4 looks at the importance of play. Chapter 5 gives examples of schemas. Chapter 6 gives the child's journey into representation, while Chapter 7 focuses on communication, language and literacy. Chapter 8 shows how children develop understanding of their own feelings and thoughts and those of other people. Chapter 9 emphasises the role of the adult in development, as well as the importance of other children, as both matter to children. Chapter 10 is about diversity, inclusion and equalities, and Chapter 11 examines how observation informs assessment, planning and evaluation.

The book finishes with four action points comprising an agenda for change that emphasises the socio-cultural context in which children develop and grow up, together with the biological aspects of child development and learning. These guard against stagnation and enable the contribution of the early childhood traditions to be seamlessly integrated into a continually renewed and regenerated framework for early childhood practitioners.

Early childhood education traditions: what they are and where they come from

1 Three different views of the child

This book reaffirms traditional approaches to working with other people's young children and their families; it also explores the challenges of this. Until we are clear about the lenses through which we view children, we cannot begin to work effectively with them, nor is it easy to work in partnership with other practitioners or multi-agency colleagues, parents or carers. This is because our assumptions about the child are crucial in influencing our practice.

The most typical lenses through which early childhood practitioners have viewed, and continue to view, the child are:

○ **The empiricist lens** – looking through this lens, the child is seen as an empty vessel to be filled, or as a lump of clay to be moulded by adults into the desired shape. This approach derives from the philosophy of John Locke (1632–1704).

○ **The nativist lens** – this is the opposite of the empiricist approach. The nativist practitioner sees the child as pre-programmed to unfold in certain directions. This view is influenced by the philosopher Jean-Jacques Rousseau (1712–78).

○ **The interactionist view** – children are seen partly as empty vessels and partly as pre-programmed. There is an interaction within and between the two. Immanuel Kant (1724–1804) originated this approach.

We will now look at each of these approaches in more detail.

Empiricism – transmitting the culture

John Locke (1632–1704)

John Locke's father was a commander in the Parliamentarian army during the English Civil War, and Locke, who grew up near Bristol, was educated at Westminster School and the University of Oxford, sponsored by a senior officer under whom his father served. At Oxford he studied medicine and was interested in science. He believed in religious tolerance and freedom of belief, and that a lack of such tolerance results in more violence than does allowing diversity.

Locke pioneered the idea that humans have a self, which is in the body and is reached through the physical senses (hearing, seeing, smelling, tasting, touching, moving), and which has continuity throughout life. He put forward the notion that at birth the human is a *tabula rasa* (a blank slate) and that experience is crucial in influencing whether or not a person develops good or bad associations. He wrote about this in 'An essay concerning human understanding', which was heavily influenced – as the thinking of seventeenth-century philosophers often was – by Islamic texts from the twelfth century. It is not surprising that he emphasised the impact of education during childhood in his essay 'Some thoughts concerning education and of the conduct of understanding'.

The empiricist view of education sees the child as a *tabula rasa*, an empty vessel or a vessel to be filled. This implicitly subscribes to a deficit model of the child. The role of the adult is to identify experiences, skills, concepts and so on that the child is missing, and then to select appropriate experiences and transmit them to the child.

This orientation came to the fore during the compensatory education movement of the late 1960s, with Bereiter and Engelmann as clear proponents. This movement built on the work of psychologists such as Watson (1878–1958) and Skinner (1904–90). In 1925 Watson wrote:

> … give me a dozen healthy infants, well-formed, and my own special world to bring them up in and I will guarantee to take any one at random and train him to become any type of specialist. I might select doctor, lawyer, artist, merchant-chief and, yes, even beggarman and thief – regardless of his talents, penchants, tendencies, abilities and vocation, and race of his ancestors.
>
> (In Schaffer, 1996: 20)

This quote demonstrates how, in this approach, children are seen as something to be moulded into shape and given experiences that are appropriate and necessary for them to take their place in society. Habit formation is valued and learning is broken down into meaningful sequences. For example, children are taught step-by-step how to tie their shoelaces, hold a knife and fork correctly, sing songs that are part of their heritage, know their letters and numbers, and so on.

In the early childhood tradition, empiricism has always held a place. John Locke emphasised the importance of learning through the senses. His alphabet blocks can still be found today, with raised letters on the faces for children to hold, feel, see, suck, bang together, and balance, all of which give movement feedback through the body. But the empiricist approach has tended to become linked more with paper-and-pencil learning, rather than first experiences through the senses, albeit chosen, controlled and led by the adult.

The adult's role in working with a child will completely change depending on whether we support the view of the child as passive recipient of culture and knowledge, or as an active explorer and initiator of experiences,. In other words, there may be agreement that the child is shaped by events, situations, objects or people that he or she meets, but there is disagreement over the nature of these experiences.

> **CASE STUDY**
>
> The teacher decides to make bread with the children after reading the story of the 'Little Red Hen'. She collects the ingredients and equipment needed as part of her planning. She organises a rota of groups, so that each child has a turn making bread. She begins each group session by demonstrating a stage and then handing the bowl round for each child to have a turn. She comments on the key elements of successful mixing, measuring, etc. In this way the task is completed through simple steps. The children watch the teacher place the bread in the oven, and take it out when cooked. She cuts the loaf, and each child has a piece of bread to eat. Children say if they want butter or not. The story of the Little Red Hen is told again at the end of the week when all the children have had a turn at making bread. Children can take a recipe card home to make bread with their family if they wish.
>
> While a group of children is cooking, other children are involved in tasks set by the teacher. They complete these at a table, or work with the Teaching Assistant.
>
> The following week the teacher checks how much the children have remembered about bread making, by asking questions. Do the children know how to make bread? Do they know the story of the Little Red Hen?
>
> The teacher has chosen the topic, and leads the experience of the children. She checks on the knowledge that has been transmitted.

Empiricist approach – key aspects

- The child is likened to an empty vessel to be filled, a lump of clay to be moulded into shape, or blotting paper that absorbs ink poured on to it.
- Habit formation is seen as important, e.g. practising handwriting with correct pencil grip or lining up in an orderly way ready for playtime.
- Children are taught in small, simple steps and cannot proceed to the next step until each is mastered in turn.
- Learning is seen as a hierarchy, from simple to complex.
- Knowledge of the culture is seen as something that needs to be transmitted from adult to child.
- The adult is seen as needing always to lead the child's learning and to dominate and control it (guiding).

Nativism – biologically pre-programmed to learn naturally

Jean-Jacques Rousseau (1712–78)

Jean-Jacques Rousseau grew up in Geneva, but moved away in later childhood. He was a major influence on the thinking of the French and American Revolutions. He advocated that mothers should remove swaddling clothes and breastfeed their own babies, rather than sending them away to a wet nurse. This, ironically (for his own five children with Thérèse Levasseur were sent to a Foundling hospital), probably saved the lives of thousands of children. He believed that humans are happier when they are compassionate and show empathy for others, and when they show reason through seeing and acting on the consequences of their actions. This, he proposed, leads to the development of civil society.

The nativist, or biologically pre-programmed, view of the child suggests that humans are biologically pre-programmed with a propensity to unfold in certain ways. Bower (1974: 2) describes the nativist view as 'that human knowledge and human skill were built into the structure of the organism'. Rousseau also saw the desire to be good as part of this. Typical supporters of this stance include Gesell, Erikson (a psychodynamic theorist) and, more recently, Chomsky. For Gesell (1954: 13), growth is seen as being:

> … laid down by intrinsic patterning prior to and independent of actual experience … environment predicts preliminary patterns; it determines the occasion, the intensity and the correlation of many aspects of behaviour development, but it does not engender the basic progressive behaviour development. These are determined by inherent maturational mechanisms.

Sally (aged one year) begins to walk when she is ready, not before, holding the armchairs and moving further and further from one to the other in the room. This view is supported by Erikson (1963: 11), 'If we only learn to let live, the plan for growth is all there.' Chomsky reasserts this stance when he claims that we have an innate propensity for language. The environment dictates the kind of language learned, but the Language Acquisition Device (LAD) is, he argues, a genetic part of being a human.

In the nativist tradition there remains a feeling that adults might interfere in a child's learning by intervening in the wrong way at an inappropriate moment. Rousseau's concept of natural justice is evident; in his view, children naturally learn from their actions. The nativist approach emphasises that children need to play, to develop creatively and with imagination, uninterrupted by interfering adults. Adults can offer help, but in this approach they should never insist upon it. They need to be highly skilled in the way they approach children.

The home area in an early years setting is still often a sacrosanct area with walls around it so that children can be away from adults in a 'world of their own'. Inevitably this leads to a major emphasis on relationships between adults and peers, based on respect for the child's unfolding development. These assertions stem from the nativist influence on the early childhood tradition.

Every day, children can choose what to do from a carefully thought-through range of experiences. Cooking is one experience that is offered daily. Children choose a cookery book, and they gather their ingredients. They follow the pictures/instructions, so first they wash their hands and put on an apron. The adult is there in the background, and only intervenes if a child needs help. For example, when the bread needs to be put in the oven, the adult goes with the child to the kitchen to do this, and they set the timer together. They both go to take the bread out when it is cooked.

The children can choose whether to share the bread at group time, or take it home to eat with their family. RAKSHA chooses to take it home. The next day she asks to take a recipe book home so that she can make bread at home.

The teacher has made a display of bread making, having observed that Raksha is interested in a sustained way. There is wheat, photos of it growing in a field, and a range of breads. She places books, including the story of the 'Little Red Hen', on the display. Raksha asks her to read this to her in the book corner.

The teacher does not check what Raksha knows, because the interest shown and the conversations they have together give her all the information she needs to assess where she is in her learning. The teacher calls this 'knowing the individual child'. She records significant points about Raksha's learning in her file.

Nativism – key aspects

- The child is pre-programmed for development to unfold, and this unfolding is determined by genetically pre-programmed maturational mechanisms.
- Socio-cultural aspects influence, for example, the language(s) a child speaks. If a child hears Chinese, then the child learns to speak that language; but the mechanisms for learning language are a genetic part of being a human.
- In this approach, there is great emphasis on adults observing children and monitoring progress, with attention paid to milestones. Readiness checks are made, in relation to physical development or learning to read.
- The child is seen as leading his or her own learning, with the adult as the facilitator.

The inadequacies of extreme ve... nativism

Empiricism and nativism are two lenses that should, because the... so differently, lead to entirely different ways of working with young ch... In a sense, however, despite the great differences between them ideologically, they are often more polarised in theory than they are in practice (Bruce, 1984; Bruce *et al.*, 1995). This may well be because of the inadequacy of the theoretical support that either of these approaches alone can give to early childhood practice. In the practical setting, people have to get on with the job in the absence of satisfactory theoretical support for their work.

Both stances have, in fact, exerted strong influences over the early childhood traditions, but in many respects they present diametrically opposed views of the child. It is no wonder that there is confusion and lack of articulation about how the aims of each tradition can be reached in practice. If early childhood practice is to move forward, which it needs to do, more adequate ways of viewing a child's development and learning are needed, which are not embedded in culturally narrow, obsolete or incomplete theories.

Certainly the nativist view of the child has had its periods of ascendancy, especially in Europe, and empiricism has had its periods of dominance, primarily in the USA but also more recently in England. In reality, however, the early childhood traditions are capable of embracing a much more complex approach than either of these two polarised approaches. In fact, the early childhood tradition is too complex for one to say that it sees the child from either a dominantly empiricist or a nativist viewpoint.

Practical considerations

It is interesting that the first case study (page 4) does not reveal children's names. This is a class of children, and there is a 'one size fits all' feeling. Some children will complete tasks better than others, but all are put through the same tasks, with some made a bit simpler or harder depending on which group the child is placed in. It feels easier to teach in this way, and teachers might feel more confident that they have taught children certain things, but they also miss much of the learning that is happening or might happen. Children who are able to complete tasks easily may not be sufficiently stretched and will therefore underachieve, while children who find the tasks challenging will lose confidence and will not find learning a pleasure.

Raksha's education (page 6) depends heavily on her own initiatives. The experiences offered in the learning environment will need to be rich and fascinating for her, or she will become bored. She also depends on her teacher being such a good observer that she tunes in to Raksha's interests and needs.

...g conversations, music together

...who influenced Enlightenment ideas. He
...nd never went further than ten miles from his
...nd influence worldwide, including his contribution
...He emphasised the importance of understanding the
...r human knowledge, the structures of the mind, and
...rect and real experience in the development of thinking.
...noughts are the result of how our minds are structured to
th... ...y are also limited by those structures. These *a priori* structures give
the t... ...the mind, and are about time, space and reasons, in particular. He
gave an important place to causality (cause-and-effect relationships as aspects of
reasoning) and the development in understanding of time and space. These, he
believed, are central features of the developing intellect.

He developed the idea of concepts as categories of understanding. Through
these, people are able to be active and do their own thinking. Our experiences
(the content of our learning) are formed through the senses. He calls this
a posteriori learning, which means it depends on experience. Our minds process
what is experienced (through seeing, hearing, touching, tasting, smelling and
movement feedback), giving order and understanding through the concepts
in the mind. He wrote two books, which are landmarks in the history of
philosophy: *A Critique of Pure Reason* and *A Critique of Practical Reason*, in the
latter of which he wrote:

> Two things fill the mind with ever new and increasing admiration and
> awe, the more often and steadily we reflect upon them: the starry heavens
> above me and the moral law within me.

Kant saw people as active, rational thinkers about moral issues.

In the interactionist view of the child, which stems from the philosophy of
Kant, not only do the biological structures in the child's brain interact with
each other, but they also change in light of the people the child meets and the
cultural and physical experiences they have (Bruce, 2004a). There is interaction
with what is external, but there is also interaction within the child through the
senses and through the interconnectivity of different parts of the brain. This is
a much more sophisticated view of the child than that of either the empirical or
the nativist approach.

This view is gaining ever-increasing evidence to support it (Bruce, 2004a), through cognitive psychology (Mandler, Forman), connectionists (Bates, Karmiloff-Smith), the neurosciences (Greenfield, 2000; Trevarthen, 2002; Dennett, 2003; Damasio, 2004) and social constructivism (Athey, 1990). It is supported also by socio-cultural strands in the research (Rogoff et al., 1993). It places as much emphasis on the socio-cultural context in which children grow up, develop and learn, as on the biological path of their development. Damasio (2004: 37) gives the image of 'a tall messy tree with progressively higher and more elaborate branches coming out of the main trunks, and this maintains a two-way communication with their roots.' He calls this the 'nesting principle', through which 'parts of simpler reactions are incorporated as components of more elaborate ones, a nesting of the simple within the complex.'

In the interactionist approach, children are not seen as nativist sole instigators of their knowledge, pre-programmed to learn naturally, and held back or helped as the case may be by variations in the environment and culture. They are instead supported by adults and other children, who help them to make maximum use of the environment and cultural setting.

This implicitly reasserts the view of the pioneers of the early childhood traditions (see Chapter 2) that the role of the adult is critical. Adults are not seen as empiricist instructors giving out information and knowledge. Instead, they are seen as the means, the mechanism by which children can develop their own strategies, initiatives and responses, and construct their own rules that enable their development.

Jean Piaget (1896–1980)

Earlier highly influential theories and research also give support to the interactionist approach, and they chime with the philosophy of Kant in important ways. For instance, Piaget (1896–1980) trained as a zoologist, studying water snails and publishing many important scientific papers on the subject by the age of 21. He became interested in genetic epistemology, the study of how knowledge develops in human beings. He realised the importance of early childhood for later development.

His work resonates with Kant's ideas in that he realised that in young children there are schemas – structures in the brain that serve as windows on the world. These, as they develop, become concepts. Children absorb experiences into the structures (schemas) they already have through a process he calls 'assimilation'. Schemas adjust and expand and link with other schemas through a process he named 'accommodation'. Through this concept of self-regulation (which continues through life), children experience a range of feelings and thoughts. Recognising what is familiar, and repeating what is known and comfortable, brings enjoyment and the deep pleasure of play and humour; or, the boredom that comes from familiarity brings the need to move on and try new things.

The importance of the adult tuning in to the child's interests, and the way the adult supports and extends the child's learning into worthwhile educational directions is of central importance. There is a difference between adults intervening to help children, and adults interfering and constraining or frustrating the child's learning.

Like Kant, Piaget focused on the understanding of time, space and reasoning (causality) as being central to the development of thinking. He also emphasised the way children learn through the senses, and the way that the mind processes real and direct experiences, with the increasing possibility of thinking in ways less tied to the here and now.

Of the theories in this book, Piaget's is in many ways the most overarching, viewing human development as a matrix or network that is interconnected. To think without feeling, or to have feelings or relationships without thought, is not possible in the physical human body according to his approach to human life.

Lev Vygotsky (1896–1934)

Although Vygotsky was born in the same year as Piaget, he died of tuberculosis at an early age. His work was not translated into English until the 1960s. As such, his criticisms of the work of Piaget were out of date, as Piaget's work had moved on by then. Piaget regretted not having had the opportunity to meet Vygotsky. Piaget acknowledged that Vygotsky was right in his assertion that when children of about five years talk to themselves, they are engaged in private speech. Like Kant, Vygotsky saw real experience of the material world and people as feeding the mind, such that the interpersonal is first and then the inner life develops, with more abstract thinking becoming possible. He, like Piaget, places great emphasis on language as crucial for abstract thinking, but he places greater importance on language, seeing it as part of the child's early experience of the world and the culture. His work is in tune with Kant in that he investigates thought, reasoning and logical memory. There is a resonance with Kant in the Marxian attention Vygotsky paid to collectivism, co-operation and sharing. Kant explored the concept of duty, and the categorical imperative (which looks at the demands of moral law on individuals).

Vygotsky distinguishes between the 'buds of development', which are the 'functions that will mature tomorrow but are currently in an embryonic state' (Vygotsky, 1978: 86), and the 'fruits of development'. These are the matured structures that show what the child can do alone and without help. He places great emphasis on the zone of proximal development (the buds), which shows what the child can do when helped by the adult or by another child. The zone of actual development (the fruit) is the result of learning. He saw play as making an important contribution to the zone of proximal development:

> In play a child always behaves beyond his average age, above his daily behaviour; in play it is as though he were a head taller than himself. As in the focus of a magnifying glass, play contains all the developmental tendencies in a condensed form and is itself a major source of development.
>
> (Vygotsky, 1978: 102)

Jerome Bruner (born 1915)

Bruner is interesting because in many ways he bridges the work of Piaget and Vygotsky. Although there are differences between these theorists, they are all in the interactionist framework, making a powerful trio.

Bruner's work has resonance with Kant's philosophy. He sees the mind as processing knowledge, and as having structures through which to achieve this. Kant states that pure reason without experience is of no value, and that thinking requires a context based in real life, so that it is practical reasoning. Bruner has increasingly explored this aspect, emphasising the importance of culture and social relationships. Piaget is closer to Kant than either Vygostsky or Bruner in that he focuses more on the material, physical world of the senses and active movement. But they all agree on the importance of real and direct experience in social contexts.

Bruner's notion of the spiral curriculum (1977) remains useful in helping practitioners to make links between what is appropriate and relevant to the child in the here and now, and how this needs to have, nesting within it, the emergent essentials of later, more complex, abstract and sophisticated knowledge. Bruner states that:

> Any subject can be taught to any child at any age in some form that is honest.
>
> (Bruner, 1977: ix)

A baby in a high chair, who drops custard on the floor and watches it splat, and then crumbles biscuits over the edge, watching them fall, is learning about the physics of gravity, helped by the adult remarking 'Did it splat on the floor?'

Bruner suggests that practitioners should consider whether situations contain the seeds of later learning. If not, offering them to children can be regarded as 'clutter'.

> Learning should not only take us somewhere; it should allow us later to go further more easily.
>
> (Bruner, 1977: 17)

Finger painting is an activity in which children often participate, involving the transforming of powder into sludge. It helps children to learn the essentials of chemistry in ways appropriate for them. Can the sludge be changed back into powder again?

Bruner sees the adult's role as scaffolding the learning. In a famous article (Bruner *et al.*, 1976) the importance of identifying the child's 'incipient intention' was emphasised, in order to lead the child to worthwhile learning. The conversations the child has with the adult and the way the child tunes in to the child's interests while finger painting are key to this occurring or not.

The key to the interactionist approach in early childhood education lies in the notion of reciprocity (give and take). This means that sometimes the child leads and sometimes the adult leads

Colwyn Trevarthen (2003), over many years, has studied proto-conversations between adults and babies, and has shown the importance of give and take in these. Conversations are not monologues by adults, issuing instructions or asking children questions to which the adult knows the answer.

Both Damasio and Trevarthen emphasise the interactionist ways in which the brain communicates both with itself (internally) and with other people and situations (externally).

Work by Trevarthen (2002, 2003) and colleagues (Malloch and Trevarthen, 2010) with musicians shows how the musical rhythm of the conversation between babies and carers means that babies participate with a particular rhythm and beat with unerring accuracy when their mother talks with them.

The Effective Provision of Pre-School Education (EPPE, 2003) shows how important it is that adults tune in to what children say, and respond in the light of this, as happens when conversations feel good to those making them together.

Similarly, Siraj-Blatchford and colleagues (EPPE, 2003) have shown how important it is that adults do not dominate in conversations between adults and children, but are instead involved in shared focus and exchanges of ideas and feelings. They call these conversations 'shared, sustained thinking'.

These research and development studies support the views of the pioneer educators, which are examined in the next chapter. The aim in this book is not to preserve a 'one size fits all' approach to work with young children, using the banner of 'universals' to do so, which, as we shall see in the last part of this chapter, has been criticised by Dahlberg *et al.* (1999) and other postmodernists. Instead, the aim is to conserve that which is found to be worthwhile and effective, and to build upon it. This means conservation of what is effective, and not just romantic preservation of the traditional.

A group of two year olds had been growing pumpkins from seed in the garden of the nursery they attend (See Figure 1.1). One of the pumpkins fell to the ground, and was placed on the window sill to ripen into a golden colour in the autumn. Children were often observed touching and examining it. Children and adults had been involved in regular and engaging conversations about the growing of the pumpkin and what would happen next.

When the pumpkin looked ripe, the staff decided to scoop it out and cook the contents. The children were invited to come and see the practitioners cut a hole in the top, ready for the children to join the scooping out. Most children stayed throughout, and were focused from beginning to end, talking with the adults who helped them. One or two joined for a time and them went away, but often returned to check on things, and sometimes rejoined the group. One child left, but because he had shown great interest in the pumpkin during the period of it growing and ripening on the window sill, his Key Person sought him out in the garden and encouraged him to join. He did so, but did not seem to want to touch the pumpkin. He watched, and left. Perhaps the mulchy texture did not appeal. Other children enjoyed the slushiness, and smoothed the pumpkin seeds in their hands with pleasure and fascination.

The practitioners were skilled in taking these very young children through the planting and gardening process, with care taken to ensure that children were offered appropriate garden tools. They engaged children in conversations that were helpful in giving them the idea that the pumpkin would ripen (change colour) and they helped children to monitor this. There was daily attention paid to pointing out to children the ripening of the pumpkin on the window sill such that children began to initiate looking at it without adult prompting. Children began to point out to the adult the way the pumpkin was changing.

The practitioner cut the pumpkin open, because that would be dangerous for children to do, but did so in a way that involved them, with several of the staff talking children through what was happening at the same time as ensuring children did not lunge forward near the sharp knife. The adults gave the children an enjoyable opportunity to spend time examining in a fully sensory way (touch, smell, looking, banging to hear the hollowness, and tasting) the raw pumpkin and its seeds. There was conversation throughout. The cooking followed the next day, and the eating. This was so that children were not overwhelmed with too much all on the one day.

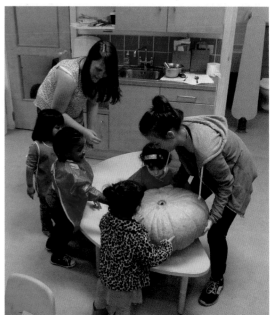

Figure 1.1 The interactionist approach

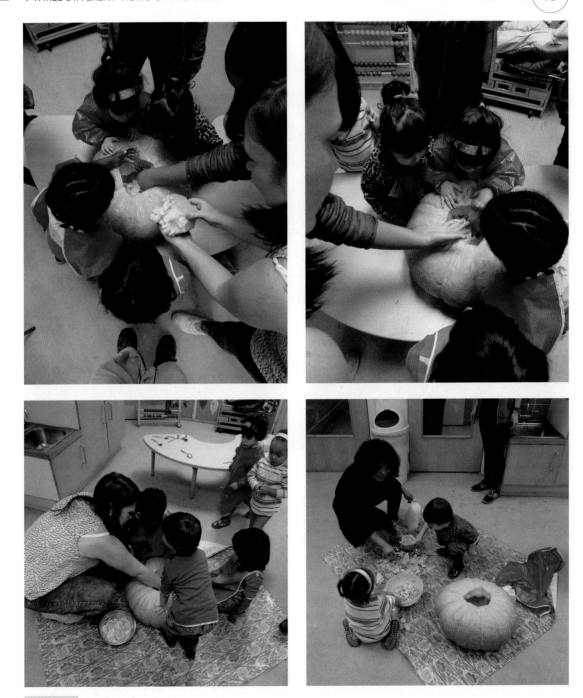

Figure 1.1 *Continued*

Figure 1.1 *Continued*

The EPPE research, directed by Kathy Sylva (EPPE, 2003), shows that in England the most effective provision is in integrated centres and maintained nursery schools. Since nearly 60 per cent of the integrated centres are adapted nursery schools, this really suggests that this traditional form of practice has sustained its record of excellence across a hundred years, and across constantly changing socio-cultural contexts.

It is also important to assess the heritage of early childhood work in different cultures and in different parts of the world. The interpretation of core principles will vary, for example in Finland, New Zealand, South America, the USA, Indonesia or India, in both the broad sense and also in the interpretation of individual early childhood specialists, who may vary in their outlook, even within a culture.

The interactionist view is a broad one within which there is inevitably a measure of debate and lack of agreement. It nevertheless gives present-day support to the early childhood traditions, both theoretically and through research evidence.

Interactionism – key aspects

- This approach integrates empiricism and nativism, recognising that there are biological pre-dispositions in children to develop movement, communication, language, representation, symbol use, attachment to people, etc. There is also a heavy emphasis on the socio-cultural context in which the child grows up, comprising the people, cultural and physical environments around them.
- The context is understood to be diverse in its range in different parts of the world, and in different families and communities.
- People are important, both children and adults. Sometimes one leads, sometimes another.
- Interactionism is a little like a conversation. Different people might start conversations, but the various speakers need to listen to each other and respond in the light of what the other person has said, appropriately and relevantly.
- Interactionism is also a little like dancing together or making music together. People have to 'tune into' each other, be sensitive to what others do and respond appropriately.

The postmodern disruption of the traditions of early childhood education

Dahlberg, Moss and Pence (1999) look at early childhood education and care through a postmodern lens. Debbie Albon (in Miller and Pound, 2010: 38) argues that:

> … the key contribution postmodernist thinking has made to early childhood education and care is in disrupting commonly held 'truths' about our understandings of children and how they develop and learn and, consequently, the curricula and pedagogical approaches practitioners employ in early childhood settings.

Theories and particular approaches are characterised as meta–narratives in postmodern language. These include challenges to the idea that play is a valuable aspect of childhood, or that there is no such thing as universal child development, because it does not take into account situations, race, gender, class, disability, etc., and so 'normalises' the child.

It is easy to attack and destroy traditional approaches to early childhood education, but postmodernists have not offered anything practical to put in its place. The question might be asked, 'So what will you do with the children on Monday?' It is perhaps significant that postmodern ideas did not develop from early childhood education. Postmodernism emerged from the arts, literature and philosophy. This may explain in part why there is not great emphasis on the practical application of its ideas.

Developmental psychology has always, as Debbie Albon (in Miller and Pound, 2010: 45) says, argued that children are not, when very young, as autonomous or competent as they are later able, with appropriate help and support, to become. They are therefore vulnerable and dependent when young. Postmodernism ignores this, in her view. There is also little acknowledgement of the physical, relational or developing self. Instead, it is argued that the self is ever-changing, which is different.

Postmodernism has certainly rocked the traditions of early childhood education, but it has not destroyed them.

The next chapter looks at the principles of the early childhood tradition and examines the work of three pioneers of early childhood education – Froebel, Montessori and Steiner – through the interactionist view, which gives current support theoretically to their pioneer work. It is necessary, however, to update the terminology that surrounds their work, which was undertaken in earlier historic contexts.

Ten principles of the pioneers: the bedrock of the early childhood traditions

This chapter looks at three of the most influential pioneers of early childhood practice in the UK and draws out commonalities between them that form some bedrock principles, both in the UK and beyond. The pioneers are Friedrich Wilhelm Froebel (1782–1852), Maria Montessori (1869–1952) and Rudolf Steiner (1861–1925). Each has:

- ○ an international reputation and influence
- ○ influenced schools in different parts of the world, which strive to use their approaches
- ○ established training colleges where practitioners can learn about their ideas
- ○ significantly influenced mainstream education in Europe and North America.

All three were skilled practitioners as well as being educational thinkers. Each was concerned, among other things, with world citizenship, respect for individual needs, poverty and the concept of community.

Other pioneer educators such as Pattie Smith Hill (USA, 1869–1946), Margaret McMillan (UK, 1860–1931) and Susan Isaacs (UK, 1885–1948), each working in the Froebelian tradition, have also been influential in contributing to these common principles and traditions, but not across all the criteria mentioned above. The same can be said of the Reggio Emilia approach, pioneered by Loris Malaguzzi (1920–94).

The work of these pioneer educators with young children and their families reveals a set of common principles that have endured and still have a useful future. The agreements (rather than the disagreements) between them have been fundamental in creating and developing our early childhood traditions. The emphasis in this book is on keeping the heritage in the spirit of conservation, not preservation or ossification.

The early pioneers used language that is difficult to understand today, and this means that their common principles have become obscured.

The commonalities between Froebel, Montessori and Steiner have been underemphasised by the vastly different practical interpretations of the principles in the 'demonstration' schools of each of these pioneers. Ironically, it is in mainstream schools where the principles and practices of the three have come together, but this has been largely through a process of osmosis and has often resulted in very confused practice and ill-defined principles. The need to revisit, rework and own the core principles of practice in early childhood work is demonstrated by reframing the wording that appeared in the first edition of this book (Bruce, 1987), which stated:

1 Childhood is seen as valid in itself, as part of life and not simply as preparation for adulthood. Thus education similarly is seen as something of the present and not just preparation and training for later.
2 The whole child is considered to be important. Health – physical and mental – is emphasised, as well as the importance of feelings, relationships, and thinking and spiritual aspects.
3 Learning is not compartmentalised, for everything links.
4 Intrinsic motivation, resulting in child-initiated, self-directed activity, is valued.
5 Self-discipline is emphasised.
6 There are especially receptive periods of learning at different stages of development.
7 What children *can* do (rather than what they *cannot* do) is the starting point in the child's education.
8 There is an inner life in the child that emerges especially under favourable conditions.
9 The people (both adults and children) with whom the child interacts are of central importance.
10 The child's education is seen as an interaction between the child and the environment in which the child finds him/herself – including, in particular, other people and knowledge itself.

The **ten bedrock principles** revisited and reframed are as follows:

1 The best way to prepare children for their adult life is to give them what they need as children.
2 Children are whole people who have feelings, relationships, thoughts, ideas, a sense of embodied self and relationships with others, and who need to be physically, mentally, morally and spiritually healthy.
3 Areas of learning involving the humanities, arts and sciences cannot be separated; young children learn in an integrated way and not in neat, tidy compartments.
4 Children learn best when they are given appropriate responsibility, are allowed to experiment, make errors, decisions and choices, and are respected as autonomous learners.
5 Self-discipline is emphasised as the only kind of discipline worth having. Reward systems are very short-term and do not work in the long term in developing the moral and spiritual aspects of living. Children need their efforts to be valued and appreciated.

6   There are times when children are especially able to learn particular things.

7   What children *can* do (rather than what they *cannot* do) is the starting point for a child's learning.

8   Through the inner life, diverse kinds of symbolic behaviour develop and emerge when learning environments conducive to this are created in the home and in early childhood settings, indoors and outdoors, working together. These include pretend and role play, imagination, creativity and representations through talking/signing, literature, writing, mathematics, dance, music, the visual arts, drama and scientific hypothesising.

9   Relationships with other people (both adults and children) are of central importance in a child's life, influencing the child's emotional and social well-being.

10 Quality and worthwhile education is about three things: the **child**, the socio-cultural and global **context** in which the learning takes place, and the **content** of the knowledge and understanding that the child develops and learns.

In the next section the ten common principles are each taken in turn, and supported through reference to the interactionist philosophies of Froebel, Montessori and Steiner. The differences between them are more like the fascinating, stimulating, energising conversations and lively discussions that take place between friends who have shared interests, concerns and values, rather than confrontations between opposing views of how children should be educated.

1: The best way to prepare children for their adult life is to give them what they need as children

Froebel, Montessori and Steiner agree that early childhood is not merely a period when children are prepared and trained for adult life. It is a phase of life that is important in its own right – although, as a by-product, giving children what they need during childhood is the best preparation for adulthood. Froebel saw the family as the most important first educators in the child's life. Joachim Liebschner (1985: 35) points out that Froebel believed women were important not only in their role as parents but were capable of teaching children too. This was a revolutionary idea at that time! The school was seen as a community, where home and school came together. Froebel (1887: 89) said, 'Let us live with our children, let them live with us, so shall we gain through them what all of us need.'

Children and adults learn from each other and enrich each other's lives. Children are not seen as being in need of instruction in how to achieve an all-knowing adulthood. Childhood is seen as a different state from adulthood, one that takes from and gives to the community in its own way (Bruce *et al.*, 1995: 18).

Montessori also recognised the different nature of childhood. Like Froebel, she did not see the role of the adult as preparing children for adulthood. Childhood is a state to be protected and allowed to develop without damage in a specially prepared environment. In *The Secret of Childhood* (1966) she describes this as a favourable rather than a prepared environment:

> … that protects the child from the difficult and dangerous obstacles that threaten him/her in the adult world. The shelter in the storm, the oasis in the desert, the place of spiritual rest ought to be created in the world precisely to assure the healthy development of the child.
>
> (Montessori, 1975: 13)

The name Casa dei Bambini (the Children's House) contrasts with Froebel's Kindergarten, symbolising a protected, predictable, contained environment as well as a controlled environment. It is cocoon-like, and may reflect her relationship with her son. She wants other children to have what she had not been able to give Mario in his early years. Mario's father was Giuseppe Montesano, a doctor who worked with Maria Montessori. The relationship was kept secret, and he subsequently married another woman. Mario was brought up in the countryside with a foster family until he was reunited with Montessori as a teenager.

She argued that 'the child is a personality separate from the adult'. Children need different treatment but not, for Montessori, in the Froebelian sense of community where adults 'live with their children'. Montessori argued instead for a favourable environment where adults do not enter the child's world, except for the trained directress who 'liberates' the child. Childhood is seen as a state with needs quite separate from adult life, one that exists in its own right.

For Steiner, childhood exists as a period of life in its own right. In his philosophy, life after death is seen as another aspect of life before birth. There is therefore no question of childhood being 'preparation for life', instead there is the idea of helping the child to find his or her way in this life. Janni Nicol, who is the Early Childhood Representative for the Steiner Waldorf Schools Fellowship, emphasises that Steiner talks of three phases of childhood.

> In the first (birth to seven years), the child is inclined to respond to his world through the 'will' (directed movement) and is highly sensitive to his/her environment. The spirituality of the child is held in the highest regard, therefore the child's entry into the world needs to be protected and the environment is therefore carefully planned. While the adult can offer a certain resistance to his environment, the child accepts it, drinks it in. Thus the whole environment of the child should be a positive, harmonious one.
>
> (Wilkinson, in Bruce, 1997)

In the second phase (7–14 years), children live strongly in the emotional realm, and the teaching methods address their feeling for life. In the third phase (14–21), the adolescent enters the realms of ideas and ideals. This is a fusion of head (thinking), heart (feeling) and will (doing) – an education of the mind, body and spirit. This 'threefold-ness' of body, soul and spirit is acknowledged.

Steiner, like Montessori, separated the child from the world during the first seven years and placed him/her in a carefully planned environment. Both differ from Froebel who, while he also saw childhood as a stage with its own needs, and as distinct from adulthood, nevertheless saw the child as being in the community and the school as being within that community. None of them saw childhood simply as preparation for adult life.

2: Children are whole people who have feelings, relationships, thoughts, ideas, a sense of embodied self and relationships with others, and who need to be physically, mentally, morally and spiritually healthy

Froebel, Montessori and Steiner all considered the development of the whole child to be of enormous importance.

They all saw the whole child as including the physical, spiritual, feeling and intellectual aspects of the person. They gave a great deal of thought to how the whole child could be developed through an appropriate curriculum.

Froebel innovated and developed the 'kindergarten' (Bruce, 2012). He addressed the physical needs of the child through the 'forms of life', which involved the senses and first-hand experiences; the feelings and imagination of the child through the 'forms of beauty' – music, arts and crafts, nature and mathematics; and the thinking of the child through the 'forms of knowledge'. The moral and spiritual pervades everything through the concepts of Unity and Interconnectivity (Liebschner, 1991, 1992). These develop through the 'Mother Songs', 'Gifts', 'Occupations', 'Movement Games' and the garden. Every experience presented to the child is presented first as a whole. The first Gift is the soft sphere, the second Gift is the cube, cylinder and wooden sphere. The third, fourth, fifth and sixth Gifts are cubes divided in different ways comprising small wooden blocks (bricks) that can be built into a larger one. Only after being presented whole are they broken down into parts. The whole precedes the parts.

Seeing how adults constrained children's use of the Gifts through rigidly prescribed interpretations of his suggestions of how to present them to children, Froebel increasingly moved away from a set curriculum. He became more interested in the process of play in the child, which he began to see as the mediator between opposing forces: the natural and spiritual, the emotions and intellect. In other words, he saw play as a means by which the child maintains the wholeness of his or her experiences (Bruce, 1987, 1991, 1996). Play is a unifying mechanism and, for this reason, for Froebel it was the child's most spiritual activity. For him, no single aspect in development was more important than any other. The whole child is the child where all aspects of development are enabled. This included the child's relationship with nature and the freedom to move. Froebel observed how children used the kindergarten experiences of nature and indoors.

> The garden is the essence of a Froebelian early years setting.
>
> (Tovey, 2013: 62)

While Montessori believed equally strongly in the whole child, she approached the concept quite differently. She created a simple-to-complex hierarchical model. Each sense is developed separately and in isolation (visual, aural, baric [weight] learning, and so on) through a sequence of carefully graded, simple-to-complex sensorial exercises. She considered that, as children master each step and arrive at the end of a sequence, they are then in a position to use, in a general way, the skills acquired:

> … but, once the handicraft leading to the construction of vases has been learned (and this is part of the progress in the work learned from the direct and graduated instruction of the teacher), anyone can modify it according to the inspiration of his aesthetic tastes, and this is the artistic, individual part of the work.
>
> (Montessori, 1912: 22)

Montessori took each part of the child's development and built it to make the whole through her simple-to-complex model (Bruce, 1984). Barbara Isaacs sees 'her preoccupation with carefully structured activities as based on her belief that the child "scaffolds" his/her learning through these activities' (personal communication, 2004). She suggests that Montessori sees the role of the adult as fundamentally different in practical life and sensorial aspects from the adult's role in mathematics and literacy, which 'reflects the child's growing ability to communicate his/her ideas, and have a discussion or follow instructions, whereas in practical life and sensorial exercises the child finds it easier to learn by imitation.'

In most respects, Montessori's view of working with the whole child contrasts with that of Froebel. Barbara Isaacs sees some inconsistency in Montessori's approach, however, in that, although in the main she advocates working from the simple to the complex, when looking at the world she embraces the 'cosmic' approach (a term borrowed from Froebel) (in Standing, 1957: 362; Montessori, 1932, 1972). In this she wanted the child to feel part of the whole cosmos and to learn about the planets and Earth, before learning about continents and countries. This global perspective supports her argument for Peace education (Montessori, 1932, 1946).

In their different ways, both Froebel and Montessori stressed the 'whole child'. Steiner was also concerned with the whole child. He believed that we bring various qualities with us into life. The whole child emerges as the four-fold picture of man (Steiner, 1965: 21), involving the physical body, the life body, the soul element and individuality. Uneven development is seen as damaging.

Steiner saw the child as a visible entity, possessing an invisible, inner soul life and an eternal spiritual nature. Steiner was like both Froebel and Montessori in that he placed great emphasis on processes in the child. Steiner considered the whole as reflected in each of its parts. In this respect he was more like Froebel than Montessori. The whole comes first. Nevertheless, Froebel, Montessori and Steiner all emphasised the whole child and the whole cultural environment of the child, which is considered in the next section.

3: Areas of learning involving the humanities, arts and sciences cannot be separated; young children learn in an integrated way and not in neat, tidy compartments

In the last section, emphasis on the whole child was highlighted. In this section, the wholeness of knowledge and the fact that everything connects is stressed. Nothing can be compartmentalised. Froebel (1887: 128) believed that:

> The school endeavours to render the scholar fully conscious of the nature and inner life of things and of himself and to teach him to know the inner relations of things to one another, to the human being, scholar and living source and conscious unity of all things.

The 'conscious unity of all things' was central to Froebel's philosophy. He saw a unity between home and school, and community and nature, and between different areas of knowledge. We saw in the last section the links between different aspects of the child's development. Froebel (1887: 134) said:

> Never forget that the essential business of the school is not so much to teach, but to communicate the variety and multiplicity of all things as it is to give prominence to the everlasting unity that is in all things.

The soft ball (the first Gift) contrasts with and contradicts the wooden ball (the second Gift). In Froebel's notion of a sequence, this is not a smooth progression but represents slight changes in the familiar, since learning involves challenges to what is already known. This has important implications when differences and common features in people are focused upon (Bruce *et al.*, 1995) (see Chapter 10).

In both this section and the last, Froebel's approach to the whole and to unity across different aspects of the whole is stressed. Everything relates and connects. In the same way the simple–to–complex aspects of Montessori's approach (presented through the sensorial and didactic materials and the exercises of practical life) can be applied both to her view of the whole child and to links within and between knowledge. For Montessori, the links are gradually built, step by step, and a complicated world is thereby carefully made comprehensible. For example, through the use of didactic materials, or the carefully sequenced exercises of practical life, she emphasised imitation. She isolated each sense, and developed each sense independently – baric, thermic, visual, and so on – 'from the education of the senses to general notions, from general notions to abstract thought, from abstract thought to morality' (Montessori, 1912: 4). In her approach to mathematics and literacy she emphasised discussion, which leads the children gradually to link with the wider world. Both Froebel and Montessori saw the whole, and the ways in which different parts link, as important features in early childhood.

Steiner's notion of unity is more like Froebel's in that he wanted to help children towards the essential unity by formulating a network across different areas of knowledge and different stages of development, which would illuminate unifying concepts in different contexts.

Lynne Oldfield (2003) emphasises working with ecology, rhythm and repetitions as aids to learning about the seasons and festivals, and embracing diversity and the outdoors. For instance, justice was explored in early education through the child's temperament balanced by activity and imitation. This is achieved with the help of the early years practitioner, who is a warm parent figure. Later, justice is explored through the history of the Romans, and later still through the notion of justice as an idea, with the Romans as one example of a culture to be compared and analysed alongside others. For Steiner, natural science, literature, mathematics – indeed all areas of knowledge – link and (as seen in the previous section) so do the different facets of the child's development.

Barbara Isaacs points out that 'Montessori, like Froebel, advocated that adults need to develop the skill of knowing how and when to intervene in the child's learning … Her hierarchical model, however, encourages some adults to work with children in a more controlling manner' (personal communication, 2004). This, however, is something that can be addressed through the training of Montessori practitioners. Montessori and Steiner helped the child towards links between knowledge and unity within themselves through an interactionist approach, with a clearly set down curriculum that has tended to lead to a more formally structured approach, although this is something both Montessorians (Isaacs, 2007) and Steinerians

(Nicol, 2006) are engaging with in developing current approaches to their practice. By contrast Froebelians are only now, since the Revisionist Movement of the 1920s, beginning to revisit the traditional Froebelian practices instead of focusing mainly on the principles of practice. This has led to a gradual erosion of an identifiable Froebelian approach to the early childhood curriculum because of an ever-broadening approach.

It is of central importance that Froebelians, Montessorians and Steinerians continue to explore, question and develop the curriculum approaches they embrace, in order that stagnation does not destroy the possibilities they have of giving children and families today and in future good moral, inclusive and high quality education. This means that the topics and content of the curriculum must be worthwhile and that interconnection should occur between the different aspects of each child's continual process of development and learning.

4: Children learn best when they are given appropriate responsibility, allowed to experiment, make errors, decisions and choices, and are respected as autonomous learners

Froebel, Montessori and Steiner agreed that children are self-motivating. There is no need for adults to find ways to motivate them. The difficulty lies in adults' tendency to cut across the child's self-motivation because of an inclination to be too dominant.

Froebel came to the view that childhood play gives children the opportunity to learn to take responsibility, to make mistakes safely and to experiment with different ways of dealing with things. He made the distinction between play and work. Play is what children are involved in when they control the task, and work is what they do when they fulfil a task required by an adult. If the child is required to work rather than to play, he or she follows a task presented to him by another, and does not reveal his or her own creativeness or possibility to make decisions, or resolve errors and work out how to deal with conflicts. Through play children are able to develop in themselves the resources to transform what is important in childhood play into what is important for inspired, worthwhile, creative adult work (Brehony, 2006). This is why Froebelians have traditionally said that play is a child's work.

The skill of the adult educator is in tuning into and joining the child's interest and going with them into an episode of play, as a partner who shares the process. The adult may intervene sensitively (not interfere) when appropriate, meaning that the child is not dominated by the adult, but equally is not left to flounder. Adults can support and extend children's play. There are moments when children do not require help and moments when they do. The skill of the adult, in Froebel's view, lies in knowing how and when to intervene. In a personal communication, Kevin Brehony (2008) wrote:

> Schrader-Breyman (1827–99), one of Froebel's students and spokesmen, is often referenced in this regard. She claimed that a kindergarten leader should be *'Ausserlich passive und innerlich aktiv,'* i.e. 'externally-passive' and 'internally-active'.
>
> (quoted in J.-E. Johaansson, 1994: 43)

Froebel did not stress play as the only aspect of self-directed, self-motivated activity. He also emphasised the arts, natural science, mathematics and all the areas of knowledge in the curriculum. He saw these as another mechanism through which children would make 'the inner outer and the outer inner'. As seen above in Principles 2 and 3, processes in the child's development, and encounters with different areas of knowledge, emphasise and affect the child's ability to initiate, self-direct, self-regulate and self-manage (Robson, 2010).

Montessori also stressed the importance of intrinsic motivation and the self-directed child initiative that results. Her 'favourable environment' was designed to encourage self-chosen tasks. In Montessori's approach, self-direction is encouraged by 'real' tasks, or apparatus that is based on Montessori's observation of children's natural concerns – for example, the way children love to put objects into rows or to build towers. Montessori did not value play, however (O'Donnell, 2013: 122–23); she saw it as an insult to the child. 'If I were persuaded that children need to play, I would provide the proper apparatus, but I am not so persuaded' (Kilpatrick, 1915: 42). She felt that children search for a real life. Rather than toys, Montessori argues:

> We must give the child an environment that he can utilise by himself: a little wash-stand of his own, some small chairs, a bureau with drawers he can open, objects of common use that he can operate, a small bed in which he can sleep at night under an attractive blanket he can fold and spread by himself.
>
> (Montessori, 1975: 116)

Her exercises of practical life were geared towards real household tasks. Her rejection of play, however, does not mean a rejection of self-direction. She argues we should:

> … take certain objects and to present them in a certain fashion to the child, and then to leave the child alone with them and not to interfere.
>
> (Montessori, 1949: 253)

Her materials offered children choices of a different nature, within a prescribed sequence. For Montessori, children need a prepared environment in which the complicated world is simplified by means of a set sequence for the children to move through, with the tranquillity that develops concentration. The highest moment is the silence that attends the 'polarisation of the attention', when the child is so absorbed that he or she is not in communication with others. Self-motivation is fed most by isolating children from the world, and its height is reached by their choosing to isolate themselves within a favourable environment that is designed so that they may be enabled and free to do so (Bruce, 1976). Marion O'Donnell (2013: 123) suggests that Montessori believed the universe needs to be presented to children in the right way, so that instead of wandering unfettered through fantastic ideas, the mind is able to fix and work in self-managed and fruitful ways.

Steiner dealt with self-directed activity differently. He describes how during the early years, the child lives mainly in the 'will' element, where he or she learns through doing, through movement and activity. The head is the physical base for thinking, the rhythmical system (breathing and circulation) is the centre for the feeling life, and the limbs provide the physical means for expressing the will.

During the period up to seven years of age, teachers take care to ensure that nothing is done that will weaken or otherwise compromise the child's physical constitution. Warm clothing, organic food, carefully chosen sensory experiences, and a general protective gesture toward the child's physical well-being are central features of the child's care.

The challenge for the Steiner early years/childhood teacher is 'How do I work with the unconscious will forces of the child under seven so that these forces gradually become self-directed responses?' There is an additional responsibility arising from accepting that in early childhood:

> … the foundation is laid for the development of a strong and healthy will.
> (Steiner, in Oldfield, 2003: 53)

Oldfield stresses that Steiner believed children reach stages of development in the first seven years at different times. The key to the next stage is when the child actively wants to do things on their own initiative, usually around six or seven years, when the teacher understands and begins to work with the temperament of each child.

Self-directed activity varies according to the different approaches. Froebel emphasised the value of play and language, actions, feelings and thoughts. Montessori emphasised the value of real tasks, and Steiner emphasised the different needs of the stages he identified. All three, however, stress self-directed, child-initiated activity as aspects of intrinsic motivation. Intrinsic motivation is fundamental to all three philosophies.

> ## 5: Self-discipline is emphasised as the only kind of discipline worth having. Reward systems are very short term and do not work in the long term in developing the moral and spiritual aspects of living. Children need their efforts to be valued and appreciated

The development of self-discipline is closely linked with intrinsic motivation, and with the need to promote it by allowing children to initiate and self-regulate tasks, activities and ideas. Self-discipline is probably one of the most important elements in life. Without it, no matter how imaginative, creative, logical or skilful a person is, there will be no development towards the completion of the work. Froebel, Montessori and Steiner all agreed that self-discipline emerged from keeping intrinsic motivation intact.

We saw how Froebel emphasised play as a means by which the child willingly sees things through to completion. This sort of environment is conducive to the development of self-discipline – the strong, confident self with sufficiently high self-esteem not to be distracted from fulfilling an objective, or working towards ideals. Froebel (1887: 131) said:

> The faith and trust, the hope and anticipation with which the child enters school accomplishes everything.

The early childhood practitioner must not destroy this, but a dialogue with and respect for the child will help self-discipline to emerge – a discipline that is an inner influence rather than an external force. The partnership element of the relationship between adult and child is stressed. The adult helps the child to articulate and understand events in which he or she has participated, through language, play and activities. Inner influence rather than external force is the key to the emergence of self-discipline. Froebel would shudder to see any kind of extrinsic reward.

At the centre of Froebel's approach to discipline was his belief that the child's intrinsic motivation should not be damaged. This is encouraged by his belief that humans are basically good. He rejected the notion of original sin. He said:

> … the only and infallible remedy for counteracting any shortcoming and even wickedness is to find the originally good source, the originally good side of the human being that has been repressed, disturbed or misled into the shortcoming, and then to foster, build up, and properly guide this good side. Thus the shortcoming will at last disappear, although it may involve a hard struggle against habit, but not against original depravity in man.
>
> (Froebel, 1887: 121–22)

In the disciplining of the child, Froebel placed emphasis on discussion between the adult and the child in bringing to light this good tendency. Discussion helps the child to analyse and reflect, to come to an understanding of the implications of actions and so to work out a solution to problems.

Froebel emphasised mutual respect, and a truly reciprocal partnership between child and adult is central to his philosophy. Froebel's attitude to self-discipline leads towards an informally structured interactionist curriculum. Montessori also asserted the importance of self-discipline. She did so by stressing the child's need for protection from the over-dominating adult, thus allowing space for self-regulation. The child who is separated from the 'over-directive, cacophonic' inputs of adults, and in tranquillity is allowed to fulfil his or her individual inner needs, is able to develop self-discipline.

> The child needs rest and a peaceful sameness in order to construct his inner life: yet, instead, we disturb him with our continual, brutal interruptions. We hurl a quantity of disordered impressions at him that are often sustained with such rapidity that he has not time to absorb them. Then the child cries in the same way that he would if he were hungry or had eaten too much and was feeling the first signs of digestive disturbance.
>
> (Montessori, 1975: 127)

There are limits to self-discipline. Montessori (1912: 87) said: 'The liberty of the child should have as its limit the collective interest.' The disciplining of the child is approached by isolating the child who transgresses, so that he or she can experience the tranquillity of the favourable environment by observing other children.

> This isolation succeeds in calming the mind: from this position he could see the entire assembly of his companions, and the way in which they carried on their work was an object lesson much more efficacious than any words of the teacher could possibly have been.
>
> (Montessori, 1912: 87)

It is important to note that the isolation leading to a calm state in which children can think more clearly is not a punishment in the way that a naughty chair or step is. Naughty chairs have no place in Montessori's favourable environment. Montessori makes this clear:

> If a child has to be rewarded or punished, it means he lacks the capacity to guide himself.
>
> (Montessori, 1939, 1967: 245)

Froebel and Montessori encouraged self-discipline in different ways. Froebel stressed play and discourse with adults and other children. Montessori stressed tranquillity in the 'favourable environment' and observing others. Both Froebel and Montessori agreed that self-discipline was of central importance in the development of the child. Neither would subscribe to the notion of behaviour management using extrinsic rewards through which the adult controls and moulds the child's behaviour to conform with what they want the child to do.

Steiner also asserted the importance of self-discipline. Like Froebel and Montessori, he saw it as emerging from allowing the child's natural willingness to learn, imitate, and create an ability to self-regulate during development. He emphasised the need to have a broad understanding of the world that will awaken human potential. Like Froebel, he stressed the community as a powerful influence in the development of self-discipline.

In a Steiner education the aim is to help each person find his or her right place in life, to fulfil his or her destiny. Self-discipline is a part of this. In contrast to Froebel's emphasis on conversation and language, in the Steiner approach discussion is not introduced until much later. In this respect, Steiner and Montessori are closer to each other. They see the child as absorbing the environment in the early years. Discussion is not seen as a mechanism through which children begin to reflect on situations in the development of self-discipline. Steiner's children first develop through the atmosphere created by the parent/teacher in the first seven years. Then their temperament is supported, in the middle years, by the authority of the teacher who extends them further – for example, with stories, songs and history. Only later does discussion relating to ideas and knowledge dominate the approach to self-discipline.

Froebel and Steiner emphasise the importance of the community of adults and children in the development of self-discipline. Froebel stresses the need for discourse as an aspect of this. In contrast, Montessori requires a tranquil setting, free from over-dominant adults or children who cut across the self-disciplined work of another child. Steiner and Montessori stress the way in which children imitate their surroundings, and construct prescribed environments in which to set children, where they can be protected from damaging external influences.

Through the shared focus of Froebel, Montessori and Steiner on the interactionist ways in which adults can help and support children in developing self-discipline and self-management, these pioneers take a difference path to the empiricist approach.

None of these three pioneers controlled a child's behaviour through extrinsic rewards – with stickers, branding with a stamp on the hand, stars, and Golden hours and group outings as treats for good behaviour being extensions of these. This kind of behaviour control rarely generalises to other contexts. It is specific to an incident. The development of self-discipline is an inner process, built through engaging with the consequences of actions and the child's understandings and reflections on situations and relationships.

6: There are times when children are especially able to learn particular things

The end of the last section leads to the need for some consideration of stage theory in the philosophies of Froebel, Montessori and Steiner. Both Montessori and Steiner prescribed set procedures to deal with each stage in the child's development. In other words, stages in the child are closely linked with curriculum content and the environment in which the child is set. In Froebel's later philosophy, curriculum content and the child's environment are not prescribed.

Froebel's statement, 'At every stage, be that stage', summarises his view. He designed the Gifts and Occupations to make use of each stage in development. For example, the soft sphere is the first Gift, the wooden sphere, cylinder and cube the second; while the Occupations include paper-folding, plaiting, cutting and pricking paper, and stick-laying.

The message he gave was to allow children fully to experience within the level at which they are functioning, rather than to attempt to accelerate them on to the next stage. He argued for activities that are broad, rather than narrow and designed only to reach the next step in the hierarchy of knowledge as quickly as possible. The skill of the adult lies in observing the child and, acting in light of observations, extending at that level (Bruce, 1978, 1984, 1987).

'At every stage, be that stage' was for Froebel optimised by paying attention to physical activity, aesthetic knowledge (feelings) and scientific knowledge (thought). In this way the child fully experiences each stage. This links with his view that every stage exists in its own right. Speedy acceleration towards adulthood cuts across breadth of knowledge and experience. A richly developed person is more likely to emerge if children are encouraged fully to experience the stage at which they are.

Montessori's notion of the 'sensitive period' (which she took from the Dutch biologist Hugo de Vries) is probably her most important contribution to the education of young children (Bruce, 1976; Bruce et al., 1995). Sensitive periods occur when 'an irresistible impulse urges the organism to select only certain elements in its environment, and for a definite, limited time' (Montessori, 1949). She was very specific about the way with which these sensitive periods should be dealt, and here she parts company with Froebel. She lays down precisely, in what she called her 'scientific method', how her didactic materials, exercises of practical life and potters' arts should be used to get the most out of such periods. They allow for the practising of maturing skills during sensitive periods and they contrast with Froebel's more open-ended approach.

Steiner also saw certain stages in development as particularly receptive and requiring certain attention – for example, at 12 years old Steiner believes it is right for children to start physics, chemistry and mechanics. Steiner was more like Montessori in his reaction to stages of development, as he set down precisely what was appropriate in his method.

Although there has been a tendency to interpret Montessori's approach in a prescriptive way in the training colleges, in fact it is only in the use of Seguin's 'Three Period Lesson' that her instructions are specific. Barbara Isaacs (personal communication, 2004) points out that in *The Discovery of the Child* (1948) Montessori discusses 'the limitations of prescribed presentation, as she is aware of the dangers in limiting the child's exploration and self-learning.' Froebel was less precise about what ought to be done during sensitive periods, in terms of the exact knowledge children should meet or experiences they should encounter. His concern was for adults to recognise stages of order through observing a child carefully, and work out their own ways of acting upon their insights. At one stage he began setting out more specific instructions, but later moved away from this more curriculum-based and adult-focused approach in favour of his earlier child-focused work. This was probably because he found that adults used his Gifts and Occupations too narrowly (Liebschner, 1991, 1992). Montessori and Steiner prescribed specific actions that left the adult with less choice.

These different views of how to build on the developmental sequences or sensitive periods led to important practical differences in approach that are still seen today. Froebel's view led to an indirectly structured approach. This relied heavily on sound initial training and later good quality in-service training for teachers, studying child development and acquiring knowledge of the subject to be taught. Froebel's is an open system, with incompleteness (an unfinished state) an important ingredient for ensuring development – with great responsibility devolving upon the practitioner. In contrast, Montessori and Steiner led to a more internally, though still indirectly structured, approach that was a complete system in itself.

Froebel, Montessori and Steiner all believed, however, that there are definite developmental sequences that require appropriate, sensitive tuning in to the child and that they should be not accelerated, but enriched instead.

7: What children can do (rather than what they cannot do) is the starting point for a child's learning

The idea of starting with what children *can* do, rather than with what they *cannot* do, is common to Froebel, Montessori and Steiner. Froebel's belief in this principle is encapsulated in one of his most famous remarks: 'Begin where the learner is.' For Froebel, play alerts the adult to what the child is able to do (see Chapter 4) and what is needed in order both to support and, very importantly, to extend learning at that stage. He saw play as a mediating factor between the knowledge the child is acquiring, be it aesthetic or scientific, and the natural and spiritual development within the child.

Like Froebel, Montessori stressed observing children in order to see what they can do and building on this. Her approach was based on the observations she made of children, many of them with special needs. These observations may account for the particular emphasis her method placed on action and the lack of emphasis on imagination and language. She developed didactic materials, exercises of practical life and graded sequences to exploit what the child could do, and to help each child develop at his or her own pace in carefully spaced steps. Her Three-Part Language Lesson demonstrates her desire to build on success, rather than to emphasise weakness. At the point of failure, the sequence is stopped. The child is not left overwhelmed with a 'can't do feeling', but instead with a memory of the success they experienced and enjoyed.

> Then in order to teach the colours, she says, showing him the red, 'This is the red', raising her voice a little and pronouncing the word 'red' slowly and clearly; then showing him the other colour, 'This is blue.' In order to make sure that the child has understood, she says to him, 'Give me the red, give me the blue.' Let us suppose that the child, following the last direction, made a mistake. The teacher does not repeat, and she does not insist: she smiles, gives the child a friendly caress, and takes away the colours.
>
> (Montessori, 1912: 109)

In order to assess the point in the sequences at which the child has arrived, and to use the materials or sequences properly, the directress must be a proficient observer of children. Froebel and Montessori also stressed the importance of observing children and building on what they can do, in order to make the most use of each stage of development.

Steiner also subscribed to this view. In the early years (up to seven years of age), the will is dominant as the child works actively in the limbs. Steiner's belief in reincarnation led him to suggest that the adult needs to observe the child and work at providing a suitable environment that provides for the needs of each child at their particular stage of development. In this way the environment can be structured for the teacher to build on the child's strengths by using what the child can do; this encourages physical activity (baking, painting, planting a garden, for example) and allows for imitation as the child absorbs his or her surroundings. The aim is to go with the child's abilities, not against them.

In different ways, Froebel, Montessori and Steiner emphasised what the child can do now, in the present. All three asserted the importance of building on strength because this does not damage the intrinsic motivation or developing self-discipline of the child.

Through careful observation, based on knowledge of the stages of child development, the adult can work *with* the child, rather than against what is natural.

In this way, children are more likely to be prepared to struggle and persevere when difficulties in learning are inevitably encountered. The message that Froebel, Montessori and Steiner give is that self-esteem and emotional well-being lead to success.

8: Through the inner life diverse kinds of symbolic behaviour develop and emerge when learning environments conducive to this are created in home and early childhood settings, indoors and outdoors, working together.

These include pretend and role play, imagination, creativity and representations, through talking/signing, literature, writing, mathematics, dance, music, the visual arts, drama and scientific hypothesising

The inner life of the child was deeply valued by Froebel, Montessori and Steiner. It featured especially in children's imagination, creativity, symbolic functioning and language. Froebel stressed that children need help in absorbing and transforming knowledge into clear ideas, feelings and knowledge. He emphasised physical knowledge, aesthetic knowledge and scientific knowledge, and helped children to develop these through the Mother Songs (Froebel, 1878), Gifts, Occupations and Movement Games (Liebschner, 1991, 1992), and direct experience of nature (for example, in gardening). He saw conversations as an important part of this process, and stressed play as an integrating mechanism (Froebel, 1887: 55). Children also need to share these learning experiences, and to use the knowledge they have 'processed' and 'transformed'. The activities mentioned also have this possibility. Children paint and fold paper (the Occupations), use wooden blocks (bricks) and the Gifts, and work in the garden. Froebel aimed 'to make the outer inner and the inner outer' through a wide range of experiences.

He emphasised that play, the imagination and the ability of the mind could make the 'inner outer', to transform knowledge, 'to associate facts into principles'. He stressed the importance of images through the Mother Songs (Froebel, 1878) and through interacting with nature. He said that the child needs help in sharing his or her knowledge through using paint, clay, music, dance, drama, written work, conversation, mathematics and many other means. The inner life of the child is fed through imagery, imitation (in the sense of reconstruction and transformation by the child, rather than passive copying), and the child's developing ability in language and non-verbal representation (the symbolic mechanisms) (see Bruce *et al.*, 1995). Physical activity, language, the arts and natural sciences are all of critical importance in Froebel's approach. They feed different aspects of the transformation between inner and outer.

Montessori uses Seguin's three-period vocabulary lesson as the basis of her approach to language work. She drew on Seguin's work because he had achieved remarkable results with children with learning difficulties, and she had also begun her work in education with these children (Lane, 1977). Her use of Seguin's three-period vocabulary lesson, which involves giving vocabulary that is first imitated by the child, then spontaneously produced by the child, does not emphasise the transformational aspect of the inner life of the child in the way that Froebel does. For Montessori, knowledge, as it stands, is absorbed and used. For Froebel, knowledge is absorbed, but transformed in the process and, after acquisition, stored in the imagination. For Montessori, tranquillity is the key to the inner life. She describes her lesson with the seriated cylinders:

> These lessons may appear strange, because they are carried out in almost complete silence, while one thinks in general that a lesson signifies an oral recitation, almost a tiny lecture. The teacher never encourages this tranquillity with words, but with her own quiet sureness. Thus, we can say that our own 'tranquillity lessons' are symbolic of our method.
>
> (Montessori, 1975: 137)

The child absorbs the teacher's tranquillity. It is the practitioner's skilled contribution to the tranquillity in the 'favourable environment' that is of fundamental support for the child's self-motivation and the development of the will and subsequent inner life, which help the child to directly absorb what is before him or her. The seriated cylinders are copied within the child, and so the outer becomes inner. Language does not feed the inner life in the way that it does for Froebel. Imitation is copy rather than reconstruction.

Steiner, on the other hand, like Froebel, stressed the inner life as the child transforms experiences through the imagination, but not during the initial stages of childhood. In the early years, the Grimms' fairy stories are sometimes told (amongst other stories) and these present wisdom in picture form, giving a pictorial understanding of the world and developing the moral sense. Most important, according to Janni Nicol (personal communication, 2004), is the use of imitation of the teacher, who provides a loving moral example for the child.

In approaching the first seven years, Steiner is in some respects closer to Montessori than to Froebel. The emphasis is on imitation as absorbing or copying, rather than Froebel's emphasis on reconstruction. Children speak, sing, model, paint, and perform household duties (including gardening), absorbing what surrounds them like blotting paper. Imagination is stressed through fairy stories (wisdom in picture form), but a child is seen to drink in and absorb the environment without at first much transformation.

The child needs sensory protection from the world outside the early childhood setting (for instance, the wrong colour scheme in rooms, inappropriate toys, or TV and electronic media), and this continues to some extent into middle childhood. In other words, the emphasis in the first two periods of life is on the outer surroundings becoming internalised through absorbing that which surrounds the child. It is not until the last period that independent thinking is considered to emerge and the inner transforms and uses what has been absorbed.

The inner life of the child is directly helped through graded sequences and experiences in a favourable environment by Montessori's method. Steiner also created a community where the child meets carefully selected experiences, led directly by the adult. Both offer direct, formally structured curricula. For Froebel, the curriculum was informally structured. The adult, using the tools of the child's burgeoning symbolic processes – the imagination, language, objects, people, places, events – works informally with the child, often indirectly. The adult still controls and manipulates the situation but less tangibly. In recent years, however, a specific Froebelian approach has often become unidentifiable and has merged into the mainstream with its inevitable ebbs and flows of different educational fashions. Froebelians are now beginning to revisit once again the traditional Froebelian practices and principles in more organised ways through local Froebelian networks and courses.

Froebel, Montessori and Steiner all stress the inner life of the child. Steiner and Montessori are alike in their approach to the early years of education in that they stress children's ability to absorb into themselves their experiences of their surroundings. In the later years, Steiner and Froebel emphasise throughout the child's development the child's ability to transform experiences as they are taken in so that they fit with previous learning, or cause modification in what has previously been learnt. For all three, the inner life is one of the most important aspects of the child's development.

9: Relationships with other people (both adults and children) are of central importance in a child's life, influencing emotional and social well-being

Froebel saw the mother as the first educator in the child's life – a revolutionary view at a time when only men were seen as capable of teaching children. The adult is a partner in the child's learning, not a threat to it. First the adults in the family, then the teacher, help and guide the child into the wider community. Through play, children manipulate, reflect, extend and experiment with their learning about social relationships, feelings and ideas. The adult is the child's helper, through conversation and provision of appropriate materials; the arbitrator in quarrels; and the orchestrator of the child's learning with other children and adults, objects, places and events. Children have different needs at different times in terms of social interaction. Sometimes the adult leads and the child follows, sometimes the reverse. The Mother Songs (1844) were Froebel's last writings (Powell, Werth and Goouch, 2013). They developed the finger plays and action songs that are still widely used in homes by parents and grandparents with their children, as well as in group settings. These transform into a later love of engagement with literacy and literature (Bruce and Spratt, 2011).

Similarly, the child interacts with other children. At times children need to be alone, at times together. Other children are an essential part of Froebel's philosophy. They need to play together, to learn to negotiate, lead, follow, to learn about the results of quarrels, to experience making music and to dance as a group. Montessori saw adults, including parents, as a threat to the child's freedom, in the sense that they need to be, according to Barbara Isaacs, 'a controlling influence in the child's life, as are other children. Montessori's approach enabled the child to escape into independence, concentration and tranquillity. She advocates adults taking responsibility for their actions, and respecting and trusting the child's inner motivation and driving force' (personal communication, 2004). Barbara Isaacs points out that in *The Discovery of the Child* (1948) in the chapter on 'Walking on the line', Montessori writes about the importance of letting children resolve their own conflicts rather than intervening.

The practitioner organises the favourable environment so that at times the child can do things alone without help. Barbara Isaacs (personal communication, 2004), however, shows how in the chapter on 'Cohesion of the social unit' in her book *The Absorbent Mind* (1949), Montessori writes about the importance of allowing the child's natural interest in other children to foster social awareness in the group.

Froebel, Steiner and Montessori felt mixed-age groups of children encourage social development. Montessori designed the more advanced materials in the sensorial areas to encourage shared use and recognise the child's growing ability to think from other people's points of view.

Steiner and Montessori, in different ways, like Froebel, emphasised the adult, peers and family. Montessori saw the child as guiding not simply him/herself, but also the practitioner, towards self-mastery in life. Barbara Isaacs suggests that Montessori included in this both social interactions and growing awareness of the group. Although the 'favourable environment' was tranquil, this does not mean there was silence in it. Children are free to speak, although there is less emphasis on language and discussion than in the Froebelian approach.

For Steiner the emphasis on the adult, other children and family is especially important initially, when the child absorbs the moral atmosphere projected by the family and school: 'What is of the very greatest importance is what kind of men we are, what impressions the child receives through us, whether it can imitate us' (Steiner, 1926: 22). Social interaction generally is greatly encouraged – for example, through emphasis on free imaginative child-led play, self-initiated creativity, language and caring for each other.

10: Quality and worthwhile education is about three things: the child, the socio-cultural and global context in which learning takes place, and the content of the knowledge and understanding that the child develops and learns

The previous two principles led us to the interactionist stance of Froebel, Montessori and Steiner – in Principle 8 from the emphasis of the child and his or her inner structure, and in Principle 9 from the acknowledgement of the external environment, primarily in the form of other people.

Froebel's acknowledgement of the interaction between the inner development of the child and the environment needs some justification, because some theorists have put him in the nativist camp. The following statement by Froebel exemplifies his position:

> Mothers know that the first smile marks an epoch in child development; for it comes, not from a self feeling only, but from a social feeling also.
>
> (Liebschner, 1985: 38)

In other words, the smile is not simply maturational unfolding, but is encouraged by the mother's impact on the child. Liebschner (1991, 1992), a leading Froebelian scholar, says to those who:

> … maintain that Froebel's model of education underestimates social influences and those aspects we inherit from tradition [that] … such an assessment cannot be sustained at the level of his philosophy nor at the level of his educational theory nor at the level of his practices.
>
> (Liebschner, 1985: 30)

Froebel also stressed that education must be based on the natural stages of development. His view of development is that of the law of opposites. The wooden ball contrasts with the soft ball. New experiences challenge old ones. In this way, maturation and experience constantly interact with each other.

Montessori's view stressed the interaction between the maturational processes in the child, the experiences the child has, and the environment he or she is in. She describes this view in an analogy with nature:

> Many species of palm tree, for example, are splendid in the tropical regions because the climatic conditions are favourable to their development, but many species of both animals and plants have been extinct in regions to which they are not able to adapt themselves.
>
> (Montessori, 1912: 5)

Her prepared environment provided the best conditions for growth. The interaction is straightforwardly between maturing structure and experience. For her, people are not central. Even the directress must aim to become like the wallpaper and not interact with the child unless necessary. Steiner's interaction operates differently. He stresses the way in which the spirit takes hold of the body of the child, first through the limbs, then the rhythmic breathing system, then the head. During the first seven years, the period of the 'will', the child is involved through his or her limbs (action) and senses in absorbing the environment through imitation and activity.

Froebel, Montessori and Steiner all emphasise the interaction between maturing structures in the child, and the experiences and environments he or she encounters. For Froebel and Steiner, the people and community are as important as the physical experiences. For Montessori, the prepared environment is mainly physical and she stresses the education of the senses.

Conclusion

In this chapter, we have explored the pioneer influences on early childhood education where there are areas of fundamental agreement. The practical interpretations of these approaches are at times fundamentally different. The impact of the philosophy of these pioneers is still felt today, and in terms of moving early childhood education forward, these areas of agreement are of central importance. They help us to put into historic context recent developments and research evidence into the early childhood curriculum.

The disagreements are also of enormous importance. They help us to see how even within a strong tradition, diversity of practice emerges, especially if the ten principles are to be continually reassessed and so invigorated. One significant difference has proved crucial. Steiner and Montessori fused their educational principles with their educational methods and content. This has facilitated the practical handing-down of the 'methods' through Montessori and Steiner schools. But this fairly close definition of method and content has worked against their absorption into mainstream schooling.

Froebel experimented with fusing his principles with a closely defined method and content, but subsequently rejected this. Consequently, increasingly his principles became the driving force behind what adults might do with children, but did not dictate precisely what should be done. Nowhere is this seen more clearly than in the curriculum.

Of the three approaches, Montessori's and Steiner's are found to be formally and directly structured curricula, while Froebel's is informally and indirectly structured. For all its intangibility, the informally structured curriculum has stood the test of time to a remarkable extent. In recent years, however, it has become increasingly mainstream to such an extent that it is in danger of losing its identity.

This more open-ended Froebelian interpretation of the ten principles has proved particularly receptive to the findings of later educationalists, especially those working from the interactionist standpoint. But it has also been eroded to such an extent that there is now the need to revisit the interconnectivity between the Froebelian principles and original Froebelian practices, and how they resonate with current research and official government curriculum frameworks.

Froebel, Montessori and Steiner followers, each in different ways, need to continue to explore their close agreements and also the lively arguments they have with each other, as close friends always do. This will help each to develop the principles and take forward the traditions of their practices so that their identifiable and dynamic approaches to early childhood education continue to be reasserted and extended, to the benefit of children and their families, now and in the future.

The first three years

Beginnings

Babies, and their parents, experience pregnancy and birth in many different ways. Some are born in hospitals, some at home. Some are forceps deliveries, others are born by Caesarean section. Some are born at night, some during the day. Some need to be put in incubators. From the beginning each baby is a unique person, and the relationships with mother and father will have a great influence. Position in family is not something greatly explored in current research, but if a child is the first born, or remains an only child, this will lead the child to an entirely different life from that of a child with siblings in a large family. Having all brothers or all sisters makes things different, compared to the child who is the first-born boy with a younger brother or sister, or the middle child of three. The variety of combinations of brothers and sisters is huge. In the UK there are now more only children than in previous times. Statistics suggest that people are becoming parents later than previously. There are more children of mixed heritage, and fewer children are born with a single disability (such as blindness or deafness). They are more likely to have complex needs. Premature babies are more likely to survive with modern medicine practices.

There continues to be debate about the extent to which we are born with a definite personality, and whether that can be altered though life experiences and relationships. Work on temperaments suggests that the socio-cultural climate plays an important part. The temperament of both baby and mother forms an interesting and influential equation. An anxious baby and an anxious mother will get on differently from an anxious mother and a calm baby. Babies influence their parents as much as parents influence their babies.

Parents may or may not live near their own parents. This affects them. In traditional communities throughout the world, the grandparents play a greater part in the child rearing. Nowadays, with globalisation and the nature of job availability, it is often the case that parents do not have the support of their own parents on a daily basis. This still remains the preferred option for families though, and many children are child minded by grandparents or other members of the family while their parents work. In 2000, Margaret Hodge, the first Minister for Children, Families and Young People, set up a group of experts in their own right (unattached to any organisations) to discuss early childhood education with her and her civil servants at regularly scheduled meetings. One of the issues that arose was the distress to families, babies and their parents, when mothers return to work at five months. As a result, Margaret Hodge, together with Patricia Hewitt (the Secretary of State for Health), made it possible for mothers to stay with their babies at home for a year on maternity leave. There is still some way to go before the UK offers families the possibility, as in Nordic countries, for both parents to have shared maternity/paternity leave for three years.

There are several options for parents if mothers return to work, usually now after the first year. One is for family to look after the baby, another is to engage a trained nanny (but this carries high costs), or to find a registered child minder who belongs to a child minder group for support and training, or for both parents to work part-time, or to find a day care setting of quality. Different forms of provision appeal to and suit different families.

Education begins at birth

There are some very useful publications about how to help babies flourish in their first year of life. Some are aimed at professionals working with babies, such as midwives and health visitors, or those working in day care settings, or child minders. Other texts are aimed at parents. Some texts focus only on the physical care of babies, or only on developing relationships, while others look at education, a concept that involves every aspect of the whole child.

For instance, Murray and Andrews (2000) give helpful advice on the first three months, such as demonstrating the way some babies like to be swaddled, while others prefer to be able to lie on their backs when they have 'conversations' with people. They focus on the development of social relationships. Because the book is full of photographs, it helps parents to tune in to their baby. Sue Gerhardt (2004: 121) also emphasises the importance of babies receiving love and affection. She explores the way that the development of a sense of agency and control is necessary for babies as they learn to anticipate affirmation and acceptance from other people with whom they spend time. For babies who learn not to expect this, and do not feel they have any control in this, the levels of the chemical cortisol increase in the brain.

Intellectual development is the focus of the work on schemas (see Chapter 5) and their development in children under three years of age by Atherton and Nutbrown (2013: 189). They point out that many of the observations in earlier books on schemas are of children over three years of age. Stella Louis (2012,

2013) has included examples from toddlers in her observations. Detailed examples of early schemas are presented in this edition of this book. The transporting schema in a two-year-old is given in Chapter 5, and in Chapter 8 the example of 10-month-old Stevie is given using the schema of enclosure (circles and spheres as the three-dimensional rotational form). Schemas open up the possibility for early childhood practitioners and parents to develop a vocabulary of observation. Atherton and Nutbrown (2013: 109) write, 'A knowledge of schema theory can be enlightening. It allows for previously unfathomable behaviours to be understood for the conceptual exploits they actually are.'

A broader discourse on the intellectual lives of babies is given by Gopnik, Meltzoff and Kuhl (1999: 133). They point out that, 'We know more about what children learn than about how they learn it. The mechanisms of learning may be quite different for different problems.' They argue that our brains physically change because of our experiences of the world. Early experiences during babyhood and the first five years are an important part of this coming about. The brain is not a fixed entity. It is dynamic and constantly active, with different parts of the brain interacting with other parts in a co-ordinated way. There are, of course, structures in the newborn brain, but these are built on through social, cultural and physical experiences, which actually alter the structures of the brain, building connections between brain cells. Gopnik, Meltzoff and Kuhl (1999: 184) quote the saying used by neuroscientists: 'Cells that fire together, wire together.' They go on to say (page 186), 'By three, the little child's brain is actually twice as active as an adult brain. This bristling activity remains at twice the level of an adult until the child reaches the age of nine or ten. It begins to decline round then but reaches adult levels only at about eighteen.' Neuroscientists such as Colin Blakemore argue that the best time for children to learn languages additional to their home language is in the first five years, rather than waiting until secondary school education begins.

Colwyn Trevarthen has pioneered work on 'proto-conversations', which have the characteristics of verbal conversations but do not yet use words. He has also worked with musicians to explore the rhythms and musicality of early language and relationships through mother–baby 'dialogues'. Adam Ockelford (2008: 78–9) undertook groundbreaking work in a project, 'Sounds of intent', at the University of Roehampton. This explored the way in which children with complex needs begin to recognise and understand musical structure. It is likely that this work has useful messages for those spending time with babies who present 'typical' development as well as those with complex needs. This research established five broad levels of recognition and understanding:

○ No awareness of sound (corresponding to 'typical' development five to four months prior to birth).

○ Developing awareness of sound, including musical sound (corresponding to 'typical' development four to three months prior to birth).

○ Development of awareness of the variety of sounds that are possible (corresponding to 'typical' development in the first few months after birth).

○ Developing awareness of simple patterns of sound brought about through repetition, with clusters and groups of sound (corresponding to 'typical' development two and a half to five months after birth).

○ Developing awareness that groups of sounds can be repeated and varied and are connected to form 'short pieces' (corresponding to 'typical' development at 7–11 months).

(Ockelford (2008) *Sounds of Intent*)

The Froebelian pioneer, Elinor Goldschmied

Key aspects of her work

All of this research resonates with the work of the towering figure and Froebelian pioneer, Elinor Goldschmied (1910–2009). More than anyone else she has helped practitioners working with babies in residential care and group day care settings to offer babies and toddlers educationally worthwhile experiences. She has quite literally transformed day care through her work in three areas:

○ Treasure Baskets
○ Heuristic Play
○ Key Person

Of these, the most important to her was the development of the Treasure Basket. She explains this in her conversation with Anita Hughes (2012), with whom she worked on the first chapter of her book, *Developing Play for the Under 3s: the Treasure Basket and Heuristic Play.*

Key figures who worked with Elinor and have kept her work alive in the UK are Jacqui Cousins, Sonia Jackson, Anita Hughes, Dorothy Selleck, Peter Elfer and Ruth Forbes. All have published books and articles across the years with her co-authorship or with her endorsement, exploring and illuminating her work. As Anita Hughes points out, Elinor Goldschmied's main concern was to promote practice that would lead to babies and toddlers having educationally worthwhile experiences. Education is a concept that embraces and includes the physical, health, emotional, social, cultural, intellectual and moral developments of the child. In this she was a typical Froebelian. The only publications she was interested in were those that promoted good practice. Academic tomes gathering dust on shelves were not for her. Froebelians have tended to focus their publications on the development of good practice, illuminated and underpinned with current theory and research. Goldschmied is a shining example of this.

The Elinor Goldschmied Froebel Archive Project, funded by the Froebel Trust

Anita Hughes (2012, Chapter 1) has written eloquently about the emergence of the Elinor Goldschmied Project, which is a groundbreaking gathering together of the life's work of Elinor Goldschmied. In 2006, Goldschmied offered her entire collection of films to Dr Jacqui Cousins, her friend and colleague. Jacqui felt that this generous gift was a great honour, but also a great responsibility. As Goldschmied had trained at the Froebel Educational Institute she readily agreed to the suggestion that the work might be given to the Froebel Archive Special Collection in the University of Roehampton, and this was facilitated through a link with the author of this book. In 2011, the Elinor Goldschmied Project was established, with funding coordinated by David Stanley from the Froebel Trust. Jacqui Cousins led the work, with a team consisting of the archivist Kornelia Cepok and co-authors Dorothy Selleck and Anita Hughes, with advisors Peter Elfer and Sonia Jackson, Italian translator Michaela Delamere, and the author of this book as project advisor.

The team transcribed all the films during 2011–13. A DVD was made that shows Elinor Goldschmied's Froebelian approach with its emphasis on the importance of play, and in the Froebelian tradition, teaching alongside practitioners and afterwards engaging them in analytical reflection. In the DVD's accompanying illustrated booklet she says, 'I had the good fortune to go to the best training college [the Froebel Educational Institute] at that time ... there were contacts with outstanding people and practices in early childhood like Margaret McMillan and Susan Isaacs ...' The DVD shows her with the team in discussion about Key Person, Treasure Baskets and Heuristic Play, as well as fascinating archival film footage of babies using Treasure Baskets and groups of toddlers with the Heuristic Play materials. Some of the films shown have never before been available to the public. This is a rare opportunity. The DVD with booklet is available from the Froebel Trust at a subsidised rate (see Bibliography). A day conference at the University of Roehampton (sponsored by the Froebel Trust and chaired by the author) launched the DVD. The speakers were Jacqui Cousins, Anita Hughes, Dorothy Selleck, Sonia Jackson and Peter Elfer.

Treasure Baskets

Once a baby can sit unaided, Treasure Baskets become a wonderful opportunity for developing learning and enjoying the process of doing that. Elinor Goldschmied had grown up surrounded by nature, playing with her brother and sister, climbing trees, playing in the stream, collecting stones and shells. This explains her enthusiasm for gathering natural materials to place in the Treasure Basket. It also gave her an eye for detail, which is a crucial component in developing observation skills. In Chapter 11 the importance of observation in helping practitioners and parents to understand children and their development is explored. Being a good observer, and knowing about and studying general child development, are processes that feed off and into each other, each strengthening the other. Good observation also helps in planning what the baby needs that will be interesting, fascinating, engaging of the baby's concentration, and educationally worthwhile.

The Treasure Basket developed out of Goldschmied's work in Italy after the Second World War. Here she saw in the institutions where illegitimate and abandoned babies were left, with babies isolated in their cots, nervous at first to take objects offered to them. She began to collect objects that appealed to the senses and before long, as she worked alongside the staff, the practice was transformed. She wanted the babies to experience a rich range of materials in the Treasure Basket, which she designed so that they did not tip up when a baby leaned on the edge, and so that a little arm could stretch into the middle to select what they saw and wanted to retrieve. The willow Treasure Baskets in the photographs in this book were made by Roy Yawsley using the dimensions provided by Ruth Forbes, who trained with Elinor Goldschmied.

It is no good simply to leave a baby with a Treasure Basket while the practitioner or parent gets on with chores, however, and this chimes with the current research and theory on the development of babies. Babies need a Key Person or their parent to sit close by, interested but what Froebel would call 'externally passive and internally active' (quoted in Johansson 1994: 43). The baby needs the adult to 'contain' any anxiety about interacting with the objects in the Treasure Basket, so that:

> The Key Person or parent 'contains' the infant's curiosity and releases the curiosity as he or she explores new and unfamiliar items.
>
> (Cousins, Hughes and Selleck, 2013: 13)

This enables the adult to observe and work out what the baby has most enjoyed and found of interest. It gives clues to what else the baby might appreciate.

In Chapter 8 we will see Stevie concentrating deeply on her Treasure Basket, and her consistent selection of spherical, cylindrical or circular objects. The metal sphere was a childhood object of Stevie's father, and it has a bell in it. The soft material spheres on a string are from the Maori traditions of dance and song in New Zealand, bought as a gift for Stevie. Froebel's first Gift, the soft string sphere on a string is there because her grandmother is a Froebel-trained teacher and bought a set at an International Froebel Society Conference long before Stevie was born. The circles are household objects, a metal jam jar lid, a brown plastic coffee jar lid. Occasionally plastic does creep in. After all, artists such as Kapoor have found beauty in plastic, and the helix of the screw top is fascinating to touch. The cylinder is a bobbin from a closed-down factory in Yorkshire.

Babies sometimes enjoy the companionship of another baby at the Treasure Basket, and Stevie's mother and Cecilia's mother sit quietly by, not talking, but observing how their babies use the joint time spent with the Treasure Basket.

Cecilia has entirely different interests to those observed in Stevie in Chapter 8. She selects spoons – wooden, plastic, metal. Elinor Goldschmied was concerned that every object should be emotionally important to the adult who chooses to place it in the Basket. This goes back to her childhood with her precious, lovingly collected stones and shells. She wants the outside natural beauty of the world to be offered to babies in a Treasure Basket. Two wooden spoons in this basket were hand carved in Lithuania, and bought in a market in Vilnius. Another wooden spoon was for picnics, and chosen because it represents an attempt to use recyclable cutlery rather than 'throw away' plastic that pollutes the environment. There are two more metal measuring spoons for cookery, one bigger than the other, with patterns on them. They were purchased in San Diego as a link with close friends there.

Elinor Goldschmied did not order objects from commercial catalogues for the babies she worked with in Italy. She gathered objects with loving care, increasingly, as she got to know them, with particular babies in mind. She encouraged the staff to do this, too. Ruth Forbes (2004) suggests that if a parent or practitioner feels hesitant about placing an object in a Treasure Basket for reasons of safety, they should not do so. The anxiety will spoil the impact of the Treasure Basket by creating an atmosphere of anxiety. The same principle applies to Treasure Baskets in home situations. Busy parents who are only just learning about Treasure Baskets find it difficult to gather materials, but grandparents delight in doing so, and know the culture of the family, and so are already tuned in to what might work for the baby in that particular family. Julia Manning Morton and Maggie Thorp remind us that no two families are the same; no two Treasure Baskets will have the same objects in them for this reason.

Early friendships begin to develop, as Julia Manning Morton and Maggie Thorp point out (2014). A feeling of togetherness and trust is part of friendship, and so are shared interests.

Figure 3.1 Maya stands at the table, briefly observed by the other two babies. She takes a pinwheel to the Treasure Basket, and tries to join in by selecting the pastry brush. These two objects have elements of the core and radial schema, which is discussed in Chapter 5.

Maya is already one year old, and beginning to walk. She has outgrown the Treasure Basket, and could have been a disruptive influence on the two babies in their Treasure Basket explorations. She cruises round the edge of the room, and stands for a time at the coffee table examining objects. Her mother sits with the mothers of Cecilia and Stevie and observes. Maya brings objects to Cecilia and Stevie at the Treasure Basket, such as the pin wheel. They look up, but quickly return to explore their own chosen objects. They also look at her standing, and contemplate with interest, before returning their focus to their selected objects. There is both a biological and socio-cultural interest in seeing her walking.

Maya notes that Cecilia has fallen in love with the wooden spoon, and for a moment it looks as if she is going to take it from Cecilia. But she doesn't. Instead, she selects the metal measuring spoon from San Diego. Rubin (1983) looked at leadership in children a little older than Maya, but here we see Maya presenting leadership characteristics. She adopts a side-by-side strategy, which shows companionship and a friendly overture, rather than a disruptive action of snatching an object from Cecilia. In early friendships there are plenty of quarrels, as children explore what works and doesn't work well in relating to others, but when children meet each other regularly from near the time of birth, as these three children have done, this builds a feeling of trusting each other and togetherness.

Figure 3.1 *Continued*

When Cecilia and Stevie have finished their Treasure Basket session (which lasted for about 40 minutes, and the mothers had sense of when to finish), they go into the kitchen while food is prepared. Cecilia does not want to be parted from her spoon, which she takes with her in a determined way. This is where rigid use of the Treasure Basket would not be appropriate. The main idea is that objects should be in the Treasure Basket, returned, and at

Figure 3.2 Cecilia picks up one spoon and explores it fully. She then picks up a second spoon, putting them together and apart.

the end of the session the basket should be put away. But here Cecilia needs to keep the Lithuanian spoon after the Treasure Basket session has come to an end.

To gain a broader view of the way Treasure Baskets can be offered to sitting babies, the DVD and booklet *Discovered Treasure* give excellent guidance (see Bibliography).

Heuristic Play

Once babies become mobile and crawl, cruise and walk, Heuristic Play becomes the emphasis in Elinor's work. The thinking for this came later than that of the Treasure Basket, as she developed the practice during the 1980s. Once again the objects are not from any catalogue. They need to provide possibilities for exploring how objects work and fit together. Excellent footage of this kind of work can be seen in the DVD showing archive footage from the work Elinor Goldschmied developed with the National Children's Bureau. Heuristic Play can still be offered to children from three to four years provided the objects are sufficiently fascinating to explore and to see how they work. Observations of children filmed at Eastwood (in the Froebel Trust DVD *Discovered Treasure*) demonstrate how older children begin to verbalise and to use symbolic representation as they engage. Just as it is important when using the Treasure Basket for the Key Person or parent to sit quietly, observing and interested, 'externally passive and internally active', so it is with Heuristic Play. It creates an atmosphere of calm and children show a sense of purpose.

The Key Person

Elinor Goldschmied, through her Froebel training, understood the importance of the interconnectedness of emotional security, play, freedom of body movement, reasoning and understanding. She developed a Triangle of

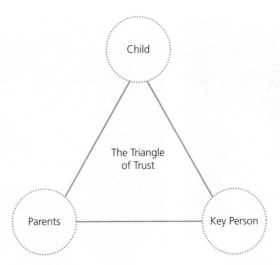

Figure 3.3 The Triangle of Trust (source: Goldschmied and Selleck, 1996: 12)

Trust, which has been taken forward and used in the English national and legally enshrined framework (EYFS, 2011; Elfer, Goldschmied and Selleck, 2012).

In a day care setting, the Key Person is important in developing trust in the child and in the parent. Peter Elfer has been developing important 'Work Discussion' sessions (funded by the Froebel Trust, 2013), which give support to practitioner managers, who find their staff are often anxious about this. Through the Work Discussion sessions they can assist practitioners in engaging more closely with children. It is easier in many ways to receive a baby or young child when they join the day care community than it is to, as Cousins, Hughes and Selleck express it (2013), 'relinquish the babies and children in their care'. The Key Person needs to feel trust and confidence in the parent to whom she or he gives up the child. There are overwhelming emotions sometimes, involving jealousy or even rivalry. A very useful film produced by Siren Films on two year olds helps practitioners in this important part of their work (see Bibliography).

The Key Person provides the personal care for the child. This involves mealtimes, sleep times, changing and toileting. It is important for the Key Person or the parent to know that when Stevie has yawned twice and begun to rub her eyes when at her Treasure Basket, that she is ready for a sleep. The tuned in Key Person or parent will know that she enjoys a Treasure Basket session after lunch, but after around an hour will need a sleep. There is no rigid timetable in this, but there is a predictable

Figure 3.4 Stevie seems to be enjoying her time with the treasure basket. She has been concentrating for about 45 minutes, which is not unusual as she is leading and feeling in control of her experience, and has interesting objects to explore and examine. But she is showing signs of becoming tired. The session needs to end before she becomes too tired.

framework, and the adult needs to be tuned in to how Stevie is navigating her way through the day.

Children need their Key Person to support them as they move through the day. For example, in Chapter 1 we saw a group of two year olds experiencing the interactionist approach to the curriculum and pedagogy. With some of the staff, they were helped to discover what the inside of the pumpkin they had been growing in their garden looks like. One little girl was anxious about joining the group (see Fig. 3.5). Her Key Person saw that she was on the edge of the group, not participating.

It is also important for young children to spend time with their Key Person and the other children in the group. Because of difficulties with shifts, holiday leave and sickness or training day absences, Key Persons often work in pairs. The Key Person will collect objects and books, which are shared with her group. Elinor Goldschmied called these group times 'Islands of Intimacy'.

Figure 3.5 The Key Person noticed that the little girl wishes to join the session but needs her to hold and support her.

Recent developments in Froebelian research and practice – Mother Songs in day care for babies

This pilot study by Powell, Werth and Goouch (2013) (with a further study underway, also funded by the Froebel Trust) was undertaken at Canterbury Christ Church University. As the research report says, 'While the project was primarily research-orientated, a strong ethos of professional development was maintained throughout.' As always, the legacy of the Froebelian approach in supporting as a central feature the development of educationally worthwhile practice has been maintained.

The work began with a review of Froebel's writings, and these were presented to the practitioners participating in the study. This gave the opportunity to investigate the relevance of Froebel's ideas and beliefs in the practice of the baby room today, and also encouraged practitioners:

> to reflect on and discuss their own ideas about singing in the light of Froebel's words.
>
> (Powell, Werth and Goouch, 2013: 7)

What emerged is the finding that:

> Reflecting on Froebelian principles has allowed those involved to spend time 'attending' to babies and their responses, and supported us in nurturing positive, interactive relationships in the process.
>
> (Powell, Werth and Goouch, 2013: 54)

Unstructured introductory research conversations were conducted by phone or in person. Films were taken observing baby room practice, and semi–structured interviews took place using film clips and Froebel quotes as discussion prompts. Finally there was a two–hour workshop at which participants were invited to discuss the data gathered, the ideas of Froebel and to think more about research on singing with babies. There was also a 'Song Audit'.

Four propositions had emerged from the previous work of Powell and Goouch with the 'Baby Room Project'. The four propositions were juxtaposed with four quotations from a review of Froebel's writings on singing. Froebel's ideas concurred and resonated with them all. The four propositions (Powell, Werth and Goouch, 2013: 8) were:

- ○ Singing promotes intimacy and connectedness.
- ○ There are educative effects of singing.
- ○ Singing connects families, babies and practitioners.
- ○ Singing supports practitioner well-being.

Neither parents nor practitioners knew about Froebel's ideas and thoughts on singing. They paid more attention to the sounds and musicality of the songs than the words, unlike Froebel who stressed the possibilities for language development, symbolic representation, moral development and musical development. He emphasised the way in which singing promotes intimacy and an expression of warm affection, as well as enhancing the well-being of adults who sing to babies.

Developing a sense of self, others and the universe

In the first three years, babies and toddlers are on a journey during which they develop a sense of self in relation to others. They begin to experience a wider world and a sense of awe and wonder. At first they see others as having the same thoughts as they do, but gradually they develop what psychologists call 'theory of mind' (Manning Morton and Thorp, 2014). Toddlers realise that while they might like banana cake, their friend does not. Abbott and Langston (2005) identify three questions that help practitioners to understand what is important to toddlers. Other chapters in this book explore these questions in practical ways.

- ○ Who am I?
- ○ What can I do?
- ○ Where do I belong?

The realisation that people look different and are not all the same is part of what is termed 'stranger fear'. At seven months Hannah was terrified at seeing her uncle, who was bald. As she began to meet him regularly, she greeted him with enthusiasm. She also cried with fear when she met the first Afro-Caribbean person she had seen, but once familiar with her, the stranger fear went. Manning Morton and Thorp (2014) call this 'discovering diversity'. It is now thought that originally stranger fear was a survival mechanism in evolution, but that it now carries the seeds of racism and disablist behaviour in damaging ways. It is important that parents and carers address the issue of stranger fear with sensitivity so that they 'contain' the baby's fears with a calm approach, and help the baby to see that they are warm and friendly to the person who looks different to those familiar to the baby.

Toddlers are helped to understand the differences as well as the commonalities between people through the introduction of Persona dolls (Brown), literature and through living in and meeting mixed communities.

It is useful to bear in mind, however, that when we see babies grabbing their toes, or taking off their hats, they are working out where they begin and end, which contributes to their developing sense of identity. In the same way, hand gazing and stretching out the arm to point gives a sense of the body and its space. The work of Penny Greenland (2010) explores early developmental movement and its importance. Naturally babies cannot be allowed to explore without restraint when they begin to crawl. They need constant supervision at this potentially dangerous stage. The same is true when they begin to show interest in changing levels of floors and to experiment with going up or down a step. But this does not mean that they have to be prevented from doing so.

> **STEVIE** (11 months) discovered a step between the kitchen and the dining area in her great-grandmother's house. She crawled to the edge and peered over, but did not dare to go further. Her father showed her how he could do it. She thought this amusing. After a while she had a go, cautiously, but appreciating the attention and support of her father. She was taught how to go up the step and down. She tired quite quickly, and her father removed her when she was on the brink of frustration, before she became upset. The next day she was taken to visit her maternal grandparents, where there is a similar step in the hall. She spent a joyous time going up and down the step without needing her father's deeply focused support.
>
> When she arrived home, she made a beeline for the staircase of the house, and again needed her parents to support her as she went up and then down, up and then down, for as long as her energy and strength would allow. Her parents made the decision to put in a stair gate, but they treated the stairs as they had done the Treasure Basket. They made time for 'stair sessions' (a bit like going to the gymnasium). Stevie began pointing at the stairs or the door leading to the stairs at times, and they tried to respond to this by taking her there for a session when practical. Just as she had been taught to go safely up and down one step, so she was taught how to go round the corner of the stairs on the wider section and not the narrow part. Her joy in this was intense, and so was that of her parents.

So far in this book different ways of working have been explored (Chapter 1), and the legacy of the early childhood principles and practice of the pioneer educators Froebel, Montessori and Steiner examined (Chapter 2). In this chapter there has been a brief dipping into some key aspects of the first three years. Many of the aspects explored in Chapter 3 will be expanded in subsequent chapters. In the next chapter the importance of play is given a central place in the development of learning.

Applying the principles

Play

4

| The 12 features of free-flow play

The 12 features of play (Bruce, 1991, 1996, 2001, 2011a, 2011b, 2014) emerged from the wealth of literature that exists on play, either in English or translated into English. They have at times been called indicators for quality play (Bruce, 1996) and were reflected in the English framework (Curriculum Guidance for the Foundation Stage, QCA, 2000), EYFS (DfES 2002; DfE 2012), Welsh Foundation Phase, 2008 and Scottish (Curriculum for Excellence 3–18) curriculum framework documents. The features are used in Scotland (Building the Ambition, 2014: 28) to train practitioners in giving good support to children in developing their play. They are a navigational tool through which to think about play as it flows along in the home or group setting, indoors or out of doors, across the world. The 12 features of play draw on the solidarity between theories and diverse disciplines and the converging evidence available about how to give holistic, consistent and coherent help to practitioners in developing play in ways that respect the depth of involvement children show in play.

The 12 features of free-flow play (adapted from Bruce, 1991) are:

1 In their play children use the first-hand experiences they have had in life.
2 Play does not bow to pressures to conform to external rules, outcomes, targets, or adult-led projects. Because of this, children keep control as they play.
3 Play is a process. It has no products. When the play ends, it vanishes as quickly as it arrived.
4 Children choose to play. It is intrinsically motivated. It arises spontaneously when the conditions are conducive, and it is sustained as it flows.
5 Children rehearse their possible futures in their play. Play helps children to learn to function, in advance of what they can do in the present.
6 Play has the potential to take children into a world of pretend. They imagine other worlds, creating stories of possible and impossible worlds beyond the here and now, in the past, present and future, and it transforms them into different characters.
7 Play can be solitary, and this sort of play is often very deep. Children learn who they are and how to face and deal with their ideas, feelings, relationships and physical bodies.
8 Children and/or adults can play together, in parallel (companionship play), associatively or co-operatively in pairs or groups.
9 Play can be initiated by a child or an adult, but adults need to bear in mind that every player has his or her own personal play agenda (of which he or she may be unaware) and respect this by not insisting that the adult agenda dominates the play.

10 Children's free-flow play is characterised by deep concentration, and it is difficult to distract them from their learning. Children at play wallow in their learning.

11 In play children try out their recent learning, mastery, competences and skills, and consolidate them. They use their technical prowess and confidently apply their learning.

12 Children at play co-ordinate their ideas and feelings and make sense of relationships with family, friends and culture. Play is an integrating mechanism that allows flexible, adaptive, imaginative, innovative behaviour. Play makes children into whole people, able to keep balancing their lives in a fast-changing world.

1: First-hand experiences that children take into their play

Play feeds on real experience. It would be unethical to deprive children of normal experience on purpose, but there have been some situations (such as in the Romanian orphanages) that demonstrate how lack of real experiences constrains the development of free-flow play with all its features.

A fundamental principle of early childhood education is to give full opportunity to the development of learning. For young children this requires learning directly through the senses, with freedom of movement, both indoors and out of doors.

Helping with everyday life tasks is one of the most powerful ways that children experience the world in which they live. Baking and preparing meals, knowing and visiting where food grows and where it comes from – animals and vegetables, cereals and fruits – are important aspects of being a human. Being out of touch with the basics of nature and how it provides nutrition, shelter and protection through clothing is a problem of urban living. And fewer and fewer children are growing up in more rural settings. Care of pets and younger siblings is another aspect of first-hand experiences, as are visits to the clinic and the shops. Practitioners also report more frequent observations of children involved in knife play, indicating they have some experiences of seeing gang behaviour in urban living.

Play is not always pretend play, and certainly not for babies. Pretend play usually begins to appear as children start to develop language and begin walking, although the glimmerings of it are there at the tipping point from non-verbal communication and crawling and cruising around the furniture. Much of the play that goes on in very early childhood – and to a lesser extent after that – is developed purely from using the senses and movement. Physical play can be with objects and material, or with people.

Figure 4.1 The preparation of meals and the sharing of food is one of the first kinds of pretend play in which children all over the world seem to engage. Many settings now set up mud kitchens so that children can create play scenarios of this kind.

More detail is given in the previous chapter on children from birth to three years. Charlotte Buhler wrote extensively about pleasure and practice play. Piaget called this sensory-motor play, with cause and effect developing and symbolic play emerging from it. Groos saw this kind of play as rehearsal for later life.

2: Keeping control and making up your own rules during play

In their free-flow play children take control, such that they avoid becoming overwhelmed by life. They make sense of what is happening and how people behave; they face situations, cope and deal with their futures with more confidence and better well-being. Having a sense of control is a huge factor in developing a sense of balance in life and becoming a whole person. Children can experiment with rules in their play. They rehearse adult rules, break them and make new ones. There are links here with the work of Catherine Garvey (1977), Lev Vygotsky (1978) and Anna Freud in the work she undertook during and after the Second World War. They all emphasise how children gain control of their lives through their play.

As Pellegrini (1985) reminds us, games have *a priori* rules. Someone else makes the rules. When children play, *they* make up the rules. The Opies (1988), in their groundbreaking observations of street play, found that children often begin by playing an established and familiar game. But once they are 'into' it, they begin to negotiate and change the rules to suit the particular group playing together. The game becomes play. The rules of a game provide a safe structure with boundaries and a sense of a predictable way of being together. Games bring a sense of security. In photographs of parents and children engaging in singing games together in other chapters of this book, the expression on their faces and their body movements demonstrate this sense of security. Play, which develops its own rules as it flows along, develops creativity and gets the brain thinking more deeply, as the children move into unknown and uncharted worlds.

3: Making products and play props

Play has no products, but children at play might make use of products that are made commercially. But more often, the best play props are created out of found objects and materials put together by children and used in their play. This is explored further in Chapter 6, because symbolic representation is interconnected with pretend play.

Play cannot be pinned down. That is the whole point about play: that it cannot be pinned down. It flows. It is on the move. As it begins to fade away, it vanishes into thin air. If it is too fleeting in its duration, it means that it never got underway with any satisfaction for the players. It needs to be sustained if it is to do any good in developing learning. Children need time to play. They need spaces in which to play, and people who are helpful in supporting and extending free-flow play. It will do nothing for their learning if they have only 10 minutes or so to develop their play after finishing their 'work', since 10 minutes is simply not enough (Hakkarainen, 1999, 2006). It takes a bit of time to get into the play and for its rhythms and conditions to come right, so that the play can be sufficiently deep.

If children know that they do not have enough time to get going in their play, the play may become over-excited and unfocused, or desultory. They do not put in the huge effort that play takes because they can see it is pointless. Children need time to play. That is why I gave the title *Time to Play* to the first book I wrote on the subject of play, in 1991. When play is given the support it needs, children begin to make their own props (Bredikyte, 2011: 84). They combine the use of these to enhance the found props that they purloin, and the commercial props are often of secondary importance to them.

Practitioners need to develop with the children clear boundaries about what equipment may and may not be raided to turn into play props in another area. They need to understand that a box of oddment wooden blocks might be raided, but not the expensive set of wooden blocks. Children need to understand the limits to what they can do in order that they can be free to be creative in their free-flow play. There are links here with the theories of Lev Vygotsky and Jean Piaget, who both stress how children develop as symbol users in their play, which involves making something stand for something else.

4: Choosing to play

Children cannot be forced to learn. Learning needs to be mindful (Langer, 1997). It is no good deciding what children ought to know and then trying to make them learn and perform accordingly, because this results in over-teaching.

> … We often sing along after hearing a song only a few times. The learning took place without memorising, without difficulty, and without fear of evaluation; most importantly, it was intrinsically motivating and fun.
>
> (Langer, 1997: 72)

It is a bit like this when children join in with play (Whitebread, 2015). Mixed-age groups benefit children in this respect, because older children tend to lead the play, as experienced players, and they help the younger and newer players with what is involved. In traditional societies this was how children came into play episodes. We see toddlers observing other children and imitating what they do, working things out as they do so. Nowadays children need more help from adults because they are often in mono-age groups (all the same age) in group settings. They do not have leadership in play from more experienced children, especially now that they are being removed from settings and put into school classrooms earlier and earlier. Pretend play typically becomes established between two and four years, and then (providing it is encouraged) burgeons and takes off between four and seven years, with elaborations and depth of characters and complexity of narrative (Nicolopolou and Ilgaz, 2013; Whitebread and Jameson, 2003; Karpov, 2005). But in reality it is almost stamped out of the education system in England by the age of four years, with serious implications for the development of important areas of learning through primary school. Froebel pioneered the educational importance of play in kindergartens, and current research resonates with this view. Play should take its educational place within the education system, and should not be confined and constrained to existence only in 'out of education' situations.

Children whose intrinsic motivation has been damaged from babyhood and toddler times onwards through being channelled into adult-led learning do not play well. Children who are used to following an adult's lead and can follow adult-set tasks do not learn how to think for themselves, to be flexible thinkers with imagination, creativity and problem-solving skills. They come to see adults as people who show you how to do things, rather than as people who open up possibilities (Dweck, 2006, 2012) for you to do your own thinking. In an essay by Greta Fein and Patricia Kinney (in Slade and Wolf, 1994) there is a very helpful observational study of Kirsten (five years). Kirsten is termed by the researchers as a 'master player', who helps Annie (also five years). Annie only plays literally and is out of her depth in pretend play that goes beyond the literal. Kirsten guides Annie, giving leadership signals to the other children, Colleen and Lisa, whose play scenario is about parties. Kirsten's advanced play technical prowess gathers Annie into the play with Colleen and Lisa, such that the play is enriched for all the children as they participate.

Play has a massive contribution to make in the learning process, because it gives children what they need in order to become adults who contribute to society. Friedrich Froebel, who introduced play into the educational context, saw childhood play as providing the cornerstones of what is important in adult work. Play transforms from being part of childhood into work that inspires, is worthwhile and is conscientiously performed (Brehony, 2001). The work of Stuart Brown (2009) points to pretend play being absent from the childhood lives of 26 convicted Texas murderers, and larger studies across the years have confirmed this to be typical of serial killers. Free-flow play helps children to become well-adjusted emotionally with high well-being, but it also develops the skills they need to become socially adept, to cope with stress and to build thinking and organisational skills as well as physical strength. Seeing things from the points of view of other people is a crucial part of this, as different characters and narratives are acted out in play scenarios.

Children are more likely to engage in play if practitioners and those at home create an atmosphere that makes them feel safe about entering into play mode and speaking in their first language. Play helps children to decide what to do when they don't know what to do (Gopnik *et al.*, 1999; Bekoff, 2007; Elkind, 2007), but in a way that makes them feel emotionally safe. Susan Isaacs (1930) suggested they can move into and escape out of play under their own control.

5: Rehearsing and recasting pasts, futures and possibilities

Play lifts children from the here and now. It allows them to create alternatives to the way things are. It opens up possibilities for considering new ways of doing things, visiting the past, outer space, under the sea, or the future, as well as rearranging the present (McKellar, 1957). The educational pioneer Froebel and, later, Vygotsky came to the same view – that play allows children to function at the highest levels of learning of which they are capable.

Play opens up opportunities for children to experiment with life and to imagine, supposing this or that could be true. It brings flexibility of thinking so that ideas, feelings, relationships and physical movement can be explored.

Free-flow play helps children to consider and deal with moral dilemmas. The narratives (stories) that develop involve characters with thoughts and feelings, such that children entering into play begin to reflect on how it feels to be a 'baddy', a victim, or a 'goody'. They are helped in the development of theory of mind (Dunn, 1977; Blakemore, 2001; Bruce, 2004) as they play. Do other people think as I do? What is it like to be someone else? Do they think the same as me? It is little wonder that Froebel, who pioneered learning through play in the nineteenth century, believed it is the most spiritual activity of the child, because it helps children to know themselves in all their relations, with self, others and the universe.

Free-flow play opens up the possibilities for children to pretend. They can pretend that they are other people, and try out the workplace roles of adults whom they live

Figure 4.2 The doll is being fed by her 'mother'. Great care is taken of the baby, with very realistic sequences being followed. This piece of literal, and accurately depicted, pretend play is about what is important in looking after babies in real life.

with or meet. This is usually referred to as role play. It tends to be quite literal at first, but it allows children to act in advance of their present lives. They can drive a car, park a delivery lorry, keep shop, care for babies – 'as if' they were adults. Play allows children to do these things safely, away from the constraints of real life. This kind of play involves fantasy because it is within the realms of possibility.

Children delight in wearing dressing-up clothes. Transformations are at the heart of adult drama, as in the battles between good and evil. Holland (2003) points out that what she terms 'war, weapon and superhero play' is often seen as offering little to children as they crudely oppose good with evil. But this kind of play is often more nuanced that it looks, if adults join the play. The sustained work of Milda Bredikyte and Pentti Hakkarainen (2011) in university laboratory schools in Finland (Oulu), Russia (Moscow) and Lithuania (Vilnius) shows how when adults join the play, the narratives are deeper and the characters more developed.

Figure 4.3 The first dressing-up clothes selected by children are often hats and shoes. It is interesting to reflect on the fact that these mark the beginning and end of the wearer, and this might be linked to the gradually developing sense of identity of children during the first three years. From then, children seem to delight in wearing belts and coverings as they choose dressing-up clothes. Often children in Reception classes become more literal about what they wear, trying to be accurate in the depiction of the character. Adults have an important role in encouraging children to find and make the props they need, rather than relying on commercial clothing without doing their own thinking about the character they wish to be.

Play has many levels. The visible play is not the whole play. External forms of play are only hints of the inner forms, like the tips of an iceberg. Creative, imaginative play is enormously spacious; it can accommodate all possible experiences of the young child and provide the space to explore those experiences and enact them with other children. When we observe children playing we can follow the visible events, the external narrative.

(Bredikyte, 2011: 203)

6: The world of pretend

The Froebel Trust Research Committee sponsored a research project at Canterbury Christ Church University (2013) looking at whether Froebel's Mother Songs (1844) have any relevance in early childhood education today, either for family life or for practitioners working with other people's children. What emerged was that nowadays the parents and practitioners involved in the study place emphasis on the musical rhythms, tunes and rhymes. They did not seem to give much focus to the words. For Froebel the words also need a central place. Singing about meeting a crocodile with babies and toddlers is common practice, despite the fact that this holds little meaning. But a song about greetings and partings in which babies are initiated early, such as 'Hallo', 'Byebye', 'Love you', 'Hooray', or the books with such titles by the Froebelian Opal Dunn (2003), with their poetic rhythms, are a delight for babies. Froebel's songs involved children and families in everyday life. For example, there were visits to the baker and to other people who help us. They were based on the real experiences of children, not on experiences they had not had (such as meeting a crocodile).

The findings of this research are thought provoking because, as the features of play suggest, early pretend play is very literal. Everyday life play scenarios are important. Having a home corner indoors and a mud kitchen in the garden will provide such opportunities. When more abstract themes are offered, such as space travel, children will only be able to engage in a meaningful way if there is the possibility of connecting to their own first-hand experiences. Children are usually not able to take this on until they are about four years of age. And then it will be through driving the spaceship (using what they know about driving cars or operating computers) or what the space crew might eat (using what they know of taking picnics and packaging food so that it doesn't leak and spill). Play that uses what children know is cognitively stretching, and becomes sophisticated. Bredikyte and Hakkarainen (2007) describe this as mature play.

7: Solitary play

In modern urban contexts there is often very little opportunity for personal space, either for children or for adults. Mental health is often affected by this. Everyone needs some personal space each day. Being in nature, among greenery and trees, is also important. Children prefer to learn outdoors, and forest schools and the tradition of the maintained nursery schools in the UK with the garden being an important place of learning are examples that make major contributions in this. Tarmac playgrounds are now often enhanced with allotments and nature, to create wild areas in primary schools.

But children need opportunities for some solitary play, too. This kind of play provides times for reflection, or consolidation, mulling things over, considering things, what is known, and what is puzzling. In Chapter 3 and other chapters of this book, Treasure Baskets and Heuristic Play are put forward as powerful ways to offer children time for themselves in their play. Traditionally, small world and doll's houses give personal space for older children, beyond the toddler period of development. Of course, this does not mean isolating children from others. We are often, as children or adults, happy, and indeed might feel more secure, to be alone in a crowd. Companionship play provides this. Other people might be present (as with the Treasure Basket or the Heuristic Play) as good companions, who do not interfere or meddle in the play.

> It is much easier to disturb creative acts than to support them. If the adult is too active and lacks sensitivity, too much oriented to predefined tasks, he can easily prevent creative acts and even change the character and direction of the child's development (Zuckerman, 2007). The child's active position to do everything themself can be transformed into passivity when the child expects others to do things for them. As we can see from our cases, developmental acts need time, space, care and trust on the part of adults.
>
> (Bredikyte, 2011: 203)

8 & 9: Children and adults play together

There are fashions in the way that play is considered. At times in the history of education in the UK and other countries, possibly even throughout the world, children were left to play and this was not seen to be something in which adults engaged. Older children initiated younger children into the play, teaching them how to participate. Marjatta Kalliala (2004) writes about the problem in an increasingly urbanised world of children being safe to play in the street, or to play unsupervised.

It has therefore become important for adults to join children in their play, to introduce them to what it involves, and to encourage their efforts in developing their play. At times this means the adult will lead, and will initiate ideas. But at other points in the play, the adult will follow and enhance the child's play agenda.

There is an important element here. The adult is there to help the 'free-flow play' (Bruce, 1991) to develop, and not to take it over or invade the play ideas of the children. Every child will have their own play agenda, their own ideas and

Figure 4.4 The teacher places herself in the home corner carefully, so that she has a good overview. She gets down to the children's level. She waits to see if children initiate ideas, and they do, so she doesn't take over. She joins in. Each child has their own play agenda, and she responds in her character accordingly. She talks to one of the children on the phone, as the child initiated this, and while she is doing so, the doorbell rings. None of the children is experienced players, and so no one answers the door, despite her asking someone to help in this. So she does. She adopts a character throughout, and the boys at the door appreciate this.

Figure 4.4 *Continued*

feelings, their own physical body with unique ways of moving. The characters the child creates and represents, and the stories the characters live through, will only be acts of rich creation and imaginative narratives if adults respect the children's play. Two things are important for the adult to keep constantly in mind, and to act upon: that pretend play requires both characters and a story narrative (Nicolopolou and Ilgaz, 2013) for the characters to dwell in.

10: Children at play concentrate deeply. They wallow in their play

One of the most important predictors of later academic success is the ability to concentrate. Children who become good at play have good concentration. They become very focused as their play flows and are not easily distracted.

Play is helped along if children have experience of stories, and have enjoyed listening to adults tell them using books or props, or acting them out. Early theatre experiences, such as the immersive theatre of Licketyspit directed by

Virginia Radcliffe in Scotland (Knight, 2011), help children to participate in stories to which they have some possibility of contributing. For example, two professional actors represent two characters, Shy Margaret and Bold Margaret, and they go on adventures, with the children, who have a say in how things develop. Children are also influenced by television and films they view, and by songs.

Unless children have inside them stories to tell, and characters who have real, direct first-hand experiences to bring to bear, the play will remain literal, and will not mature or become richly nuanced and educationally worthwhile. Play that is rich brings children to cognitive stretch, to the consolidation of thoughts and feelings in useful but also sophisticated ways.

11: In free-flow play children use their technical prowess and confidently apply their learning

Play does involve some new learning, but in the main it is about the application of what has been learnt. In the 1960s it was often seen as a diagnostic tool for practitioners to see what children demonstrated they knew and understood. The two-year-old who takes their doll and changes the nappy, for instance, shows a great deal of knowledge about spatial concepts mathematically, getting the right bits of the nappy in the right place in relation to the doll. The four-year-old who runs a shop and puts on labels with the costs of items, often in emergent mark making but with some conventional numbers appearing, is teasing out how to represent numbers in meaningful ways.

Maulfry Worthington (in Moyles, 2015) suggests that there are three important aspects in developing the mathematical graphics of children of four to six years of age.

> First, a direct relationship exists between the children's cultural knowledge at home and within their pretend play. Second, open opportunities for pretend play (and children's *ownership* of their play) support high quality and sustained pretend play, promoting exploration and elaboration of cultural knowledge. Third, the incidence, sustainability and success of pretend play is dependent on the values, beliefs, knowledge and practices of head teachers and staff members in early childhood educational settings.
> (Worthington, 2015: 247)

In play children try out their recent learning, and demonstrate their mastery, competences and skills. They show us how they are consolidating what they know and understand.

12: Play is an integrating mechanism

Children at play co-ordinate their ideas, thoughts and feelings, as well as their physical bodies. They make sense of the relationships they have with their family, friends and the widening circle they meet as they move beyond their family lives. Play is an integrating mechanism that allows flexible, adaptive, imaginative, innovative behaviour. Play makes children into whole people, able to keep balancing their lives in a fast-changing world so that they are both 'grounded' and 'together'.

> In play a child develops and masters the structures of their own thinking. They lay the foundations of the inner forms of basic human notions. Play provides the channel of expression of the child's emotional experiences and releases their spiritual potential.
>
> (Bredikyte, 2011: 203)

This chimes with the use of the term 'spiritual' in Froebel's description of play as the most spiritual and highest level of learning. This means that through play the child can learn in relation to self, others and the universe. Vygotsky's view of play as a mechanism through which children become a head taller than they really are, lifting them to their highest levels of learning, makes a powerful connection with Froebel's approach to play.

Schemas

Introduction to schemas

Children do not act randomly; they act in ways that are patterned, through the influence of their genetically pre-determined biological development and also through the way in which socio-cultural influences interact with their biological makeup (Bruce, 1991, Chapter 7). Beneath the apparent randomness and chaos (Gleick, 1988) in a child's behaviour there is order, as there is in every aspect of nature.

Schemas are biologically determined patterns, and are socially and culturally influenced in the way that babies and young children behave. Knowing about schemas helps practitioners, parents and carers to understand children better and to be more sensitive to their ideas, thoughts, feelings, relationships, self-embodiment and physical needs. Perhaps most importantly, however, understanding schemas also helps adults to relate to children more easily and to enjoy their company more, as well as helping the children to learn in deep and thorough ways. A schema is:

> A pattern or repeatable behaviour into which experiences are assimilated and gradually co-ordinated. Co-ordinations lead to higher level and more powerful schemas.
>
> (Athey, 1990: 37)

The more we learn about the developing brain, the more the interactions between biological patterns and socio-cultural influences need to be emphasised. Nurture shapes nature (Blakemore, 2001). This means that the people we meet and the experiences we have impact on our biological development, as recent developments in epigenetics show. For example, in adulthood one of a pair of identical twin boys may show a tendency to obesity, but the other not. During childhood one had his tonsils out and ate many pork pies when recovering; the other ate a better diet during that period of childhood. The impact of a different nutrition showed in adulthood, having changed the biological structures of one twin. Similarly, the way schemas are supported or constrained influences which aspects become more strongly or differently developed and which do not.

The pioneering work of Chris Athey

The post-Piagetian work developing schemas was pioneered by Chris Athey, who was Leverhulme/Gulbenkian Research Fellow for the Froebel Nursery Research Project, 1972–77, based at the Froebel Institute. The author was head of the school set up in the grounds of the Froebel Institute College to focus on working with parents in a close partnership, and learning with them about children's schemas within the context of traditional good nursery practice.

Schemas should not be studied in isolation from other aspects of the child's development and learning, but within the context of traditional good nursery practice and a high quality curriculum. The findings of the Froebel Nursery Research Project were published in book form in 1990 in a seminal work by Chris Athey, *Extending Thought in Young Children: A parent–teacher partnership.*

Schemas help practitioners and parents to find words to express what is intuitively known – but they are not a curriculum method

Often when people begin to study schemas they exclaim: 'But I know all of this. I just never used this terminology to describe it.' One of the problems early childhood educators have had during the last hundred years is a difficulty in expressing and articulating in words what good practice is. Those who can

Figure 5.1 Envelopment schema. The girl has chosen to wear a crown. When children have an envelopment schema dominating they often decide they would like a hat. She has also spent time enjoying putting on her apron in preparation for painting. Covering herself with clothes that wrap around her is again typical envelopment schema behaviour. She then gives time to rolling the roller in each colour of paint. She likes the way the roller flattens the whole tray of paint and spreads it entirely over the base of the tray. Her next move is to cover the large expanse of paper with the roller of paint. She concentrates on her painting and refilling the roller from each tray in turn, enveloping the tray and the paper.

speak and write effectively and clearly about their work, as well as put it into practice, are more likely to be listened to. The study of schemas helps early childhood practitioners and parents to develop a vocabulary of observation that in turn informs curriculum planning.

Schemas develop in clusters and are part of networks in the brain

Schemas should not be viewed in isolation from other aspects of observation or good practice. Schemas enhance existing and well tried observation strategies and will only be useful to practitioners if used in an integrated way, alongside what is already known about observation, good early years practice and a high quality curriculum. They provide another lens to enhance our ability to tune in to children in an individual way. They should never replace other observation lenses.

Schema clusters in the brain seem at times to dominate what the child does, and at other times it is as if they have gone into hibernation. At first it was thought that one schema was dominant for a period of time in a child's development. As the Froebel Nursery Research Project developed, and in subsequent years as more practitioners have begun to study schemas in their own early years settings and the New Zealand Council for Educational Research has undertaken research into schemas (Meade with Cubey, 1995; Arnold, 2009; Louis, 2013; Atherton and Nutbrown, 2013), it has become clear that schema clusters dominate for a time, with contextual influences and socio-cultural aspects raising others from periods of quiet.

Schemas are part of being human: the biological and socio-cultural paths of development and learning

There are two paths of a child's development: the biological path and the socio-cultural path. Schemas have both aspects:

○ Biological aspects – a baby is born with a repertoire of schemas that is biologically pre-determined and, as they mature, these co-ordinate, integrate, transform and ripple out into ever more complex and sophisticated forms.
○ Socio-cultural aspects – the socio-cultural aspects of schemas are to do with the way in which experience, as opposed to biological maturation, influences the development of schemas through childhood and also throughout our adult lives. Because the two are in a perpetual state of interaction, each influences the other, causing changes, modifications and transformations in the way we think, feel, move and relate to others.

Schemas are part of human development, from birth to death, but they are not in a constant state. They are always adjusting and changing in the light of experience. This is why they are such a powerful learning mechanism. Children with disabilities and complex needs have schemas. For example the typical rocking of a child with autism or visual impairment is an example of the trajectory schema cluster.

HELEN, seven years old and growing up in a musical family in England, experiences and is taught by her parents several different ways in which a violin bow can produce sounds. The development of some aspects of the trajectory schema will be particularly enriched and strengthened through her developing violin playing. The pleasure and deep satisfaction of music-making with people she deeply loves, and is loved by, is part of Helen's schematic experience.

In the same way DEPEE, two years old, growing up in Sarawak, North Borneo, experiences everyone taking off their shoes on entering people's homes. From the time he can walk, his inside/outside schema (with feet in and out of shoes) is influenced by intermingling this action with the feelings of being welcomed and warmly greeted by friends and relatives and relaxed conversation following. In this setting, feelings of love, pleasure and this relaxed state are linked with putting feet in and out of shoes.

Schemas are an observation tool – but not the only one

Schemas help us to add to our knowledge of child observation (Louis, 2010; Bruce, Louis and McCall, 2014). The importance of practitioners being informed by developing the lenses through which they assess and work with a child's development and learning is stressed throughout this book. The basis of good teaching is informed observation. Once observed and identified, knowing about the schema clusters that children have can help practitioners and parents/carers to plan interesting and appropriate learning experiences.

Schemas function at different levels in early childhood

- ○ **Sensorimotor level** – through the senses, actions and movements. The sensorimotor level emerges first, but is used throughout life.
- ○ **Symbolic level** – making something stand for something else.
- ○ **Cause and effect** – sometimes called functional dependency (if I do this, then that will happen).

The symbolic and cause-and-effect levels of schemas develop alongside each other in an integrated way once the sensorimotor level is established, and these three levels of schematic behaviour continue to be present and to surface, influenced by the context and situations that arise throughout life.

Figure 5.2 Transporting schema. The children have planted pumpkin seeds in the garden, and watched the pumpkins grow. Once they became heavy and fell to the ground, they saw them ripening across time on the window sill. On this day the children helped the staff to scoop out the inside of the pumpkin and to see the seeds, ready for cooking. One boy (aged two years) was fascinated by the pumpkin, and immediately wanted to help the staff carry the heavy pumpkin to the mat. Once transported there, he enjoyed touching it and feeling it above and below, experiencing the weight. He liked scooping the seeds out of the pumpkin, transporting them from there into a bowl with a spoon, or his hand. He then had an urge to transport the bowl of seeds around the garden, showing the bowl to people he met as he went about. He continued to transport the bowl when he came indoors, topping it up at regular intervals with a few more seeds from the inside of the pumpkin, or from the pile that was growing beside the pumpkin.

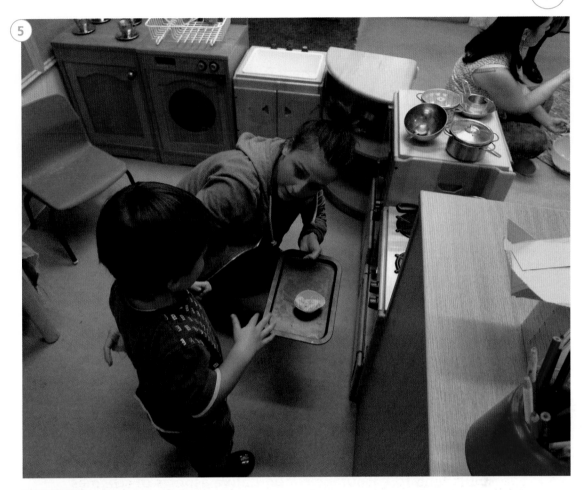

Figure 5.2 *Continued*

○ **The abstract or operational thought level** – manifests itself when there is increasing understanding of reversibility and transformations and a co-ordinated understanding of these. This emerges over time as concepts form, enabling more abstract thinking.

Neither children nor adults stay at one level all the time

Children, like adults, do not function at one level all the time. It depends what they are doing, their mood, who they are with or where they are, how tired they are, if they are hungry or need the lavatory.

Children and adults move in and out of the different schematic levels but cannot go beyond their biological capabilities at any time.

The dynamic aspects of schemas involve movement and actions

The dynamic aspect of a schema is like a video film, linking thoughts together as they flow. When six-year-old Koor spins around and says 'I'm mixing a cake', this is the dynamic side of the schema.

The configurative aspects of schemas are based on perceptions and the senses

The configurative aspect is like a still photograph. When Daniella (four years of age) draws circular scribble, points out a tangled ball of string on the floor and says 'It's the string', this is the configurative aspect of the schema. Chris Athey (1990: 37) suggests that, of the early schemas, when babies are gazing at people or objects or following them with their eyes (tracking), 'gazing leads to knowledge of configuration. Tracking leads to knowledge of the movement aspects of objects, including the self and other persons.' She suggests that babies quickly begin to co-ordinate these two behaviours – gazing (configurative aspects) and tracking (dynamic aspects) – integrating the two into an early network, and realising that the same person or object can be still or can move about. From the beginning, the dynamic and configurative aspects of schemas seem to co-ordinate and integrate with each other.

Adults tend to encourage configurative aspects of schemas

Early childhood settings, schools and parents tend to encourage the configurative aspects of schemas more than the dynamic aspects. Drawings, paintings and models are usually more celebrated than children creating dances or songs. It is more difficult to 'keep' a dance or a song than a model. After all, the configurative often leads to a product, such as a painting of the string. This can be kept as an example of the child's work in the child's folder, or put on the wall or the display, or taken home. It might be carefully labelled with what the child said – 'It's the string'.

Whereas the configurative aspect of the schema can be 'kept', the dynamic aspect of the schema cannot. It is here and gone. Nevertheless, it contains deep thinking and has much greater possibility for transformations.

Chris Athey (1990) and John Matthews (2003), using the theoretical insights that schemas give, demonstrate how children's early mark-making develops in their writing, drawings and paintings. Recently Matthews has also looked at the way that chimpanzees show similar schemas in their development

(Matthews, 2011). There are echoes here, using different theory, of the earlier findings of Rhoda Kellogg in the 1950s or Michaela Strauss in the 1970s.

MORAG (five years old) lives in Scotland. She arrives in school (Primary 1) proudly wearing a kilt of a Gordon tartan. 'This is my new kilt,' she says. In her school she is helped to value her Scottish heritage. She knows it is a Gordon tartan. It is interesting that this aspect of heritage fascinates her at this time. She has a strong concern with grids. She spends time at the water tray, sieving and using the water and fish nets. She also likes the home area windows and peeps through the net curtains frequently. 'I can see you, it's net, so I can see you.' She is enthusiastic about sewing and enjoys simple tapestry work and willingly learns how to use the thread when directly taught by her teacher.

Grid is not her only schema, but it seems to be in particularly active use for a few weeks. There is already good classroom provision in Morag's case. The teacher enhances her interest in the tartan aspect of grid by introducing a display of tartans and helping interested children to see how tartans are constructed. Morag began to paint tartans and people wearing them. She often mixed the colours of paints that she needed in order to make a Gordon tartan. During this time she showed little evidence of schemas such as core and radial. She learned to make charts showing data about the weather, however. In these, although grid was the framework for the chart and gave her enormous pleasure to draw the frame, she used other schemas in the symbols that she chose to represent the sun (core and radial), rain (dab) and clouds (continuous co-ordinated semi-circle).

'Not flitting but fitting'

Chris Athey (1990: 107) gives the example of Randolph, who cuts out a zig-zag pattern. He first said it was 'a bird's wing', then 'a fish tail' and then 'a fan'. As she points out, he was 'fitting' different but appropriate content into his latest 'form' (a zig-zag trajectory schema).

Unless adults observe children carefully, in an informed way, they may mistakenly think a child lacks purpose, or is 'off task' when, in fact, the child is systematically learning. It is important to recognise the difference when working with young children.

Three-year-old KATE at home spread newspaper sheets all over the floor. She said she was making a road. She had a pancake for tea and spread sugar, jam and lemon juice all over it with meticulous care, but then, not surprisingly, did not want to eat it!

The historic background to how schemas came to be studied

When Froebel, Montessori and Steiner were developing their curricula, nothing was known about schemas. Because they were good observers of children, each tuned in to what children naturally do, and so they intuitively facilitated the children's schema clusters in the curricula they developed.

Froebel

Froebel, in developing the Gifts, Occupations and Movement, Mother Songs and Garden in his curriculum, together with his study and increased knowledge of play, intuitively supported and extended the schemas in the curriculum that he developed. He was working before schemas were a known concept. His first Gift was the soft ball (Liebschner, 1991; Bruce *et al.*, 1995; Bruce, Meggitt and Grenier, 2010). The subsequent Gifts were early sets of wooden blocks, ancestors of the modern unit, and hollow blocks that are now regarded as essential in a high quality early childhood curriculum. Froebel's approach encouraged children in the possibilities for both consolidation and extension of schemas. For example, a set of blocks has endless opportunities for rearrangement, new ways of setting out instructions and using schemas in ever-new combinations.

Children love to build towers and knock them down. The more obvious schemas used in block play are vertical and horizontal, lateral trajectories, enclosure, connection, on top, inside/outside, transporting, up/down, dynamic trajectories, dab, clashing trajectories. Both the dynamic (transformations) and the configurative (static) aspects of schemas are encouraged in Froebel's curriculum. Children are naturally drawn to aspects of the environment that allow for opportunities for the consolidation of schemas. As Chris Athey says (1990: 46), 'functioning improves with use'. It is almost as if children actively seek out people and things in the environment that echo their schemas and encourage them in their use. Chris Athey calls this 'recognition' (1990: 69).

Montessori

Montessori's notion of sensitive periods, drawn from the Dutch biologist de Vries, also unwittingly facilitated the development of schemas in a child's development and learning. Unbeknown to her – for she, like Froebel, was working before schemas were known – her Exercises of Practical Life, the Pink Tower and the didactic materials gave highly specific and pre-structured opportunities for children to practise and repeat as they exercised their schemas. Dynamic transformations were not aspects of schemas that were encouraged in her curriculum, but configurative aspects of schemas were (Bruce, 1976). Schemas included were trajectories, vertical, horizontal, connection, on top, inside/outside, envelopment, transporting.

Steiner

Steiner's facilitation of schemas is more akin to the later work of Froebel. Steiner's use of natural materials – drapes with which children can cover themselves, toys with the ability to be imaginatively transformed, wooden blocks or irregular shapes, beeswax to mould, block crayons and seasonal craft materials, the use of stories, circle time, songs and movement games – do not pre-structure or stipulate the way in which a schema is practised or exercised on the environment, but instead invite experimentation, variation and transformations of many kinds. Steiner's curriculum, like Froebel's, encourages transformation as much as configurative aspects of schemas. Examples of facilitation of support and extension of schemas in Steiner's curriculum might be envelopment, enclosure, trajectories of all kinds, push and pull, inside/outside.

Piaget

Piaget developed his work on schemas from the 1920s over a period of fifty years, adjusting his terminology as he did so. In this book, the later terminology is used, as it is in most books referring to schemas (Athey, 1990). By the age of four and a half months, a baby can look at an object, reach out for it, grasp and suck the object. This is a new schema cluster (hand–eye co-ordination). Later, the ability to use and understand the purpose of a pulley, rotation or trajectory becomes linked with these early behaviours in more co-ordinated and sophisticated form. Schemas do not disappear in later life, but they certainly change and transform as they co-ordinate and integrate as networks of behaviour or concepts become ever more complex and sophisticated, and according to the socio-cultural context.

Where do schemas go after childhood and later in life?

Helping a toddler who is transporting, scattering and heaping objects everywhere by providing objects that will not break or be dangerous when thrown, such as baskets and other containers, as well as space to move about unhampered, contributes to the child's journey towards adult life. It is doing so in ways appropriate to childhood for a toddler.

Objects look different when scattered about, or when heaped together. But they are of the same quantity even though their appearance changes. The transporting schema leads towards a concept of quantity. A toddler who has rich transporting experiences is likely to benefit as an adult and develop a sound concept of quantity. There are cross-cultural variations. Some cultures stress transporting food and transferring it from large sacks to small containers rather than buying food in pre-packaged form. Children in these cultures will differ in their early experiences of quantity and transporting in relation to this.

Schemas transform into later concepts

The way children are supported in the early use of their schemas has a deep emotional impact that remains. It is perhaps significant that Seymour Papert, inventor of the Turtle Computer, writes in his book *Mind Storms* (1980) of the way his early love of cogs at about the age of five years was encouraged by his parents. He left a transparent cover on his computer so that children could enjoy seeing the movement of the cogs. Unwittingly his parents were supporting and extending his core and radial cluster of schemas. The outcome of their support during his early childhood for the things that seemed to be fascinating to him was that in adult life he developed pioneer work on computers.

Developing language and schemas

Cathy Nutbrown (2006), building on the work of Chris Athey (1990), stresses the importance of using appropriate descriptive language that links with a child's schemas during conversations. She gives the example of Stuart, looking at a hand-operated sewing machine. He tells the teacher, 'It goes round and round.' The teacher replies, 'Yes, it turns, it rotates,' giving him the language to support his schemas.

Often children do not immediately incorporate new words into their vocabularies, but recognition gives meaning, which leads to deepening understanding and widening vocabulary. As Marian Whitehead (2004) points out, children begin to be able to use language to comment on their world.

Schemas and the whole child

Schemas are about the whole child. They involve the physical development of the child as well as their ideas, feelings and relationships. They adjust and develop differently according to the cultural context, but schemas are a mechanism for co-ordinating and integrating development and learning. Having things that can be predicted helps young children to settle into a group setting.

> AMANDIP (three years old) is new and every day the first thing he does is to go and find two planks in the wooden block area. He holds them upright and seems reassured by this start to his day. It is like his teddy bear. This anchors him and makes him feel secure. Further observations will give clues that he has a strong vertical (up/down) trajectory schema. It turns out to be significant that he holds the planks upright every day. The vertical trajectory schema co-ordinates and helps him to make sense of what he finds in the nursery. It helps his feelings to be anchored and helps him find calm as he settles into a new environment.

Schemas and friendships

> JOSH wanted to make a row out of the wooden blocks (horizontal trajectory). WANDA came and took the end block and put it on to the tower she was building. She wanted to build upwards (vertical trajectory). Josh strongly objected and snatched back his block, accidentally knocking down Wanda's tower. A quarrel broke out, with adults needing to intervene swiftly.

It would not be helpful to emphasise the importance of sharing and working together at this moment. These children are trying to do different things. Gradually it might be possible to suggest that Josh makes a row of blocks that end at the base of Wanda's tower. This might encourage the children to co-ordinate vertical and horizontal trajectory schemas, but not today. Instead, each child's schema needs protection from an adult in order that each has freedom to learn.

Schemas and everyday life

Every day we wake up, get up, do things, go to bed and sleep. For toddlers and young children, teenagers and even for adults, getting dressed is a whole schematic experience. Putting on a T-shirt or pants involves going through, inside/outside, over and under, enveloping, enclosing, to name only some of the schemas.

Meal times are very emotional for children. It is a serious sadness for a child when an adult pours custard *on* their treacle sponge when they had wanted it *beside* the sponge cake. The schema is on top or enclosure. Putting curry on rice, rather than beside it, is a similarly emotional experience for adults. If a toddler, who has just begun to take note of enclosures, is given a broken round-shaped biscuit, there is likely to be a strong reaction.

There is often a fashion for wearing ponytails and plaits and an interest in Afro-Caribbean hairstyles when children are developing a core and radial schema cluster. Nancy would not go to her nursery until her hair was done as she wanted it. For several months her mother had to allow extra time to plait her hair each morning.

Bedtime rituals involve schemas. It matters whether Teddy is under the bed covers or on top of the pillow when the on top and underneath cluster of schemas is strong.

Children helping with everyday chores are demonstrating their schemas

The following few examples show how important children helping with everyday chores can be, providing they are not cajoled and nagged into helping. A positive approach is more likely to encourage children to want positively to help. Children 'recognise' what is involved in helping before they can 'perform' competently.

○ **Infilling** – put the blocks in the box in patterned order.
○ **Trajectory and containment** – children can sweep up sand with the dustpan and brush.
○ **Trajectory** – sweep the floor or the playground. Remember that the child may not be aware of the beginning and ending of the handle (trajectory) and might concentrate only on the end with the brush on it. This is an important safety factor.
○ **Envelopment** – wipe over the table tops to clean them.
○ **Vertical trajectory** – (inside and outside) stack the saucers and the plates in the home area and put them away in the cupboards.
○ **Inside/outside containment**– (divided space grid) sort and put the cutlery away in a divided cutlery box in the home area.
○ **Envelopment, inside/outside, containment, transporting** – put away the dolls in their beds in the home area.
○ **Snacks and washing up. Rotation of the taps in order to fill the jug and pour water into the washing up bowl** – this involves containment and rotation and transporting. The soap bubbles are spheres. The dish mop might be a core and radial type. Wiping up with a tea-towel involves a child in envelopment of crockery and cutlery.

Schemas and the child's sense of identity and embodiment

Children use and explore schemas first of all in relation to themselves. Babies spend time putting their hand into the mouth of those to whom they are close. Where do I end and where do I begin? Toddlers put the whole of their body into a cardboard box and love to climb in and out, over and over again. The first dressing-up clothes that children enjoy putting on and wearing in an early years setting tend to be hats, shoes and belts. These involve very basic schemas (in, out, containment and enclosure) in great evidence when observing toddlers. Soon they enjoy wearing capes or surrounding themselves with drapes. This is envelopment.

GEORGE (three years old) was Spiderman for several weeks. He was almost completely covered by his clothes.

Schemas are not just to do with ideas that children are developing (e.g. pretending to be Spiderman). They are also to do with feelings, relationships and physical development. It is an emotional experience to pretend to be someone else.

Children love to be in dens (envelopment). A willow den or drapes making a den under the climbing frame in the garden results in children wanting to be learning outside in all weathers.

Dens and dressing-up clothes are popular, when children use their whole bodies to exercise the inside schema cluster, but gradually they use objects as well as self. Going inside a den is about feelings and physical behaviour as much as it is about relationships, ideas and thoughts. Cosiness, completeness, safeness and feeling anchored are feelings, but intellectual ideas are also integrated within the schema clusters of envelopment, inside and outside. Recent studies of the brain emphasise that the chemistry of the brain brings feelings as well as thoughts (Damasio, 2004). For example, anger, frustration and joy are all associated with chemical changes in the brain.

Schemas and feelings

Recent work on brain studies (epigenetics) suggests that the electrical activity of brain cells actually brings about changes in the brain's physical structure. The schema clusters are modified and changed by experiences the child has. Experience, good or damaging, brings refinement or atrophying of thinking, feelings, relationships and physical developments. Children who do not play are not exercising their schema clusters. They therefore are not firing and wiring their brains optimally. This means that they learn less.

In his foreword 'The gears of my childhood', Papert (1980: vi) traces the way he developed a positive affective tone towards mathematics to the early enjoyable experiences he had playing with cogs, cars and gears. Cogs are resonant of the core and radial schema, usually very strong in four-year-olds, the age he was. Emotionally and intellectually rich childhoods that allow involvement and play in natural biological schemas quite literally lead to richer brains.

Relationships, feelings and interactions between adults and children (Arnold, 2010), as well as the material provisions offered, contribute effectively to the child's learning.

Schemas are integrated, co-ordinated networks of behaviour through which children can gain access to knowledge and understanding, and sort out their ideas, feelings and relationships. They are part of the way the child's brain is wired.

The work of Elinor Goldschmied and schemas – babies and toddlers

Although not explicitly designed to empower children's schema clusters, the Treasure Baskets developed by Elinor Goldschmied (Forbes, 2004; Froebel Trust Elinor Goldschmied Project, 2013; Goldschmied, Jackson and

Forbes, 2014; Hughes, 2015) for sitting babies, and her bags full of objects for Heuristic (exploratory) Play for toddlers, do in fact lend themselves to the rich development of children's schemas.

Tuning in to children's schemas

A teacher helped the children to extend their mathematical learning. She rigged up a pulley with a bucket and hung it above the paddling pool. Four-year-old NAYAM and three-year-old SHAZIA worked with this most of the morning. Nayam was concerned with filling the bucket before it was released. He focused on fullness, sometimes with water, sometimes with toys he had collected. Shazia, on the other hand, was concerned with holding the rope right until the bucket reached the top and then releasing it. Her interest lay in the splash, which she enjoyed enormously. She and Nayam tended to argue, as their concerns were different.

Adults can support schemas with appropriate language. With the help of the teacher, they reached a compromise by which Nayam filled the bucket and Shazia hoisted and released it. The role of the adult here was, as Bruner would assert, to diagnose the incipient intention of each child in order that the mathematics in the situation could be developed. The teacher used the mathematical language of 'full' and 'empty', 'half full', 'nearly full', and so on for Nayam.

One of the important functions of language in mathematics is that it should help children to comment on the world (Whitehead, 2007). There is a need for adults to extend learning through appropriate language in genuine conversation. Genuine conversation seems to arise more often when adults have an understanding of schemas and so tune in to what the child says (Meade with Cubey, 1995: 70; EPPE, 2003; Bruce, Meggitt and Grenier, 2010).

SHAZIA had also shown great interest in the paper aeroplanes introduced by the teacher, and the balloons that were blown up but not tied, so that when released they darted across the room making a squeaky noise. These were other experiences of hold and release that added to Shazia's knowledge of trajectories. She would repeat the trajectory action with her finger, using words such as 'up' and making squeaky noises in imitation of the balloon. This was a mathematical experience, but it was also non-verbal communication, spoken language related to the schemas ('up') and co-operation with friends.

Three-year-old **PERRY**'s teacher introduced paper aeroplanes and noted that he was fascinated by the vapour trails left in the sky by the real aeroplanes that passed over the school. She brought in some streamers and Perry ran, with the streamers unravelling behind him. She was helping him to make tangible a trajectory path rather like the aeroplane's vapour trail. By tuning in to his interests, the teacher informed her planning.

Topological schemas

Shazia and Perry were both using a repertoire of topological concepts to explore trajectories (Athey, 1990: 83–85): on top, under, over, near and far. The relationship between the bucket and the top of the pulley, the throwing of the paper aeroplane, the starting-point of running with the streamer, the bucket in the water in the paddling pool, the aeroplanes landing on the floor – all are an exploration of beginning and end points, and the relationship between them, or of order (Athey, 1990: 85). The topological aspects involved are proximity, separation, connection and relationships between them, or order.

Schemas inform curriculum planning

Knowing that a child is exploring schemas such as trajectories is not enough. The adult can extend this exploration using different areas of knowledge, and introducing materials and engaging in appropriate language or conversations. Knowing the schema informs the adult's curriculum plans, and helps them to plan with appropriate selection and flexibility.

Mathematics and dance

Although it is certainly true that mathematical knowledge is being introduced here that matches the child's developing schemas, these schemas could also be developed in ways that are not purely mathematical. Schemas also contain the 'stuff of dance' (Davies, 2003). The child's schemas are a resource, an access mechanism, which can be used to tackle any area of knowledge. Observing and identifying schemas informs curriculum planning. The adult needs to be aware of the child's schemas, and then to consider different curriculum possibilities and next steps in learning for the child at that stage. The adult needs to bring the two together, as Perry's teacher did in introducing the streamers, or Shazia's in introducing the pulley.

Figure 5.3 Trajectory schema. At a first glance this sequence might look as if there are a few children playing on the slide in the garden, supported in their play by an adult. That is true, but something fascinating is also happening. The children are demonstrating the trajectory schema, and exploring beginnings and ends of trajectories. This is an emergent aspect of the concept of length and measurement. The boy (1) is walking up the slide. Another boy (2) is siding down sitting. Another boy (3) is coming down the slide too. (1) walks up while (2) comes down, and the adult gently and with great sensitivity moves across to ensure that no-one crashes and gets hurt. (1) gets off, avoiding this possibility and there are smiles all round. There is an interest in the top and bottom ends of the slide, which continues in the way they stand at the bottom of the ladders, and move to the top. The boy who walked up the slide moves from one end of the ladder to the other, and is imitated by the boy and the girl on the opposite ladder. Ladders and slides are a great joy to children. They offer many ways of learning. In this instance, the beginnings and endings of the trajectory made by the slide and then the ladder give opportunities for learning.

Figure 5.3 *Continued*

Four-year-old **KUANG** was using a remote-controlled computer toy. He wanted to push it. The adult showed him that he needed to instruct it to move forward, backwards and sideways by pressing the appropriate key (marked with a direction arrow) and another key (marked with a number) telling it how many paces to move. He quickly understood this, and made it go forward to the end of the room. Then he wanted it to go to the other end. He picked it up and turned it round, ready to go back. The adult showed him how to use the backwards arrow to reverse the direction, but he found this intervention annoying. Kuang could deal with trajectories going in one direction, but not with reversing the direction. Reversing is a more complex level of thinking.

He was taken to see trains at Waterloo Station in London. Since this is a terminal, when trains reach the end of the line they have to retrace their direction out of the station. After seeing the trains he enjoyed action songs about trains reversing

▷

their paths – for example, 'Puffer Train' – and stories by Rev. W. Awdry such as *Thomas the Tank Engine*, with shunting and so on.

He was also encouraged to play games such as 'What's the time, Mr Wolf?', in which children reverse in their tracks when the 'wolf' comes. It was six months before he began to retrace his steps in games. Once he did this, he used the reverse button on the computer toy. He was using a horizontal trajectory schema in developing these understandings.

Computer work

Computer work does not teach children concepts that they do not yet possess. It is simply another experience through which to broaden what they can already do. It was a useful tool for the adult in identifying Kuang's schema level, and a worthwhile additional experience once the structures of reversing a trajectory were emerging.

Music

In a Reception class, the children had a huge magnetic board with magnetised musical notes in a box that could be put on the board. They would sing a tune and put it on the board without inhibition. Sonya, four years, made a flat line of notes, and sang it 'da, da, da, da', pointing as she went. Her sounds were the dynamic aspect of the horizontal schema and the notation on the board was the configurative aspect of the schema.

The teacher played an arpeggio on the piano, pointing out that it went up and then down. Sonya asked her to put it on the board. Sonya saw an open semi-circle. She was just beginning to use these in her drawings and paintings. This was why her teacher thought she might enjoy the arpeggio. The teacher's observations and identification of the open semi-circle schema informed her curriculum planning so that she directly taught Sonya about arpeggios. She learnt to start practising singing arpeggios going up and down the scale, again and again. Her teacher began to wonder whether it had been such a good idea to introduce arpeggios since she sang them non-stop for several days!

She also learnt to play her flat 'da, da, da, da' tune on the drums, the piano, the xylophone, the shakers and the African talking box, as well as the descant recorder. This was a trajectory schema – horizontal in this instance.

Drawing and painting

John Matthews (2003) in his study of his three children as they grew up, followed their development in painting and drawing as well as their model making. He writes about his son Joel (13 months) who liked to carry his cup of milk around with him, frequently spilling it. He was fascinated by the resulting milk on the floor, and used both hands to mark-make with it. Over the next few weeks Joel was introduced by his father to paint. Joel kept repeating vertical and horizontal arcing movements.

Each child is unique

Joel, in his own unique way, is using basic schemas in his early mark-making. The way he uses his schema network links with this statement by Judith Jamison, an American contemporary dancer (in Davies, 2003: 160): 'There is only one of me. There is only one of anybody. That is why steps look different on different people.'

Everyone has schemas

Pat Gura (1996: 55) also emphasises the universal aspects of schema clusters:

> Schemas have remained the same since the dawn of humankind and this is why we can detect similarities between things like megalithic structures and children's block play. Points, lines, boundaries, connection, enclosure, envelopment are all examples of schemas. All occur in block play and all occur in the early dry stone building of our ancestors.

> … If we are looking for connections between our human past and the world we live in today, schemas may be a promising way to go.

Schemas connect us with our past, with humans on a trans-global scale, and help us to reflect on who we are as unique individuals.

Children with disabilities and complex needs

The work of Lillie Nielsen, awarded for her work in Denmark, is interesting. She designs Little Houses for children with disabilities, based on her observations of the child's needs and the observations of the parents, which also both support and extend schema clusters. The child is observed over a period of time, and when the team of parents and staff feel that they have some idea of what captures the child's awareness or interest, a 'Little House' is built around the child. This links with the time-honoured tradition of den building, participated in by children all over the world.

BARRY, a child with cerebral palsy, liked to feel enclosed and to reach out and touch the walls, and to reach up and touch the ceiling in his Little House. He did this lying on his back. He tried to catch hold of circular objects that were hanging, especially those of the bracelet or ring type. Envelopment, enclosure and rotation were strong interests. He selected objects with these properties as they hung from his ceiling. He cooed to himself contentedly as he reached out for them.

▷

> The dominant schema cluster (envelopment, enclosure and rotation) helped the less-dominant action schemas of reach, grasp, hold and release, and also encouraged their co-ordination. By working with Barry's strengths and interests, the aspects of his development that needed attention were also developed. It is best to access the weaker aspects of a child's development through their strengths.

The work of Lillie Nielsen has been developed in the UK, particularly through the influence of Robert Orr (2003), working with children with complex needs. Whereas Lillie Nielsen's work can be linked implicitly with schema clusters, Orr has made direct links with schema clusters.

Adam Ockelford has developed work with music for children with profound disabilities, with an emphasis on visual impairment but also suitable for all children in the spirit of inclusivity. The music implicitly uses schema clusters such as rotation, enclosure and trajectory.

Developing self-discipline and self-management

> MARK, three years of age, began spitting at people. He could target someone's eye with unerring accuracy. The schema was a targeting trajectory with dab (the spit was the dab schema). His mother bought a pea shooter and suggested he could target cereal boxes on the kitchen table. He played happily for hours. He had a straw and newspaper pellets as objects. He willingly picked them up when he had finished and helped throw them in a rubbish bin (targeting the rubbish bin by throwing things into it). In the bath he blew water at floating objects. The pleasure of these pursuits and his enjoyment of the company of his mother and other friends far outweighed the frustration of people's reaction when he spat in their eye. This was a better use of his targeting trajectories, and he stopped spitting in people's eyes. The learning possibilities of targeting trajectories gave him autonomy of learning about forces in physics, but he needed an adult's help to do so in an acceptable and worthwhile way.

> KEVIN, at three years old, loved to climb. He climbed on furniture and was reprimanded constantly for doing so, but he had no access to climbing frames or gymnastic equipment, except 20 minutes a week in school from the age of five years. By the age of nine years he was scaling walls and stealing from houses and flats. He loved the danger and the thrill of heights. By the age of 13 years he was sent to an experimental unit where he was closely observed, assessed and given appropriate therapy and education. It was decided, amongst a variety of measures, that he should be taught to rock climb. He

loved it, quickly learning the techniques. From age of 13 to 16 he slowly began to change from delinquent to ordinary citizen, and remained so in adult life. He spoke of the importance of being set clear boundaries in the unit, of not stealing other people's property. He was taught to think about the cause and effect of this and the implications of his actions. To steal was not acceptable. Later, as an adult, he spoke of his experiences in the unit, of being able to find an acceptable way to fulfil his joy of climbing heights, of being valued in his own right and having his needs specially thought about, being nurtured and feeling that he mattered. His vertical trajectory schema and the thrill of the danger of climbing remained important from childhood, through adolescence and into adulthood. It became an important access tool or mechanism that took him from childhood 'naughtiness' (climbing furniture) to adolescence (delinquency) into ordinary adult life (with a passionate hobby of rock climbing).

Chris Athey (1990) points out that it is not necessary to love a schema when it is identified. The schema itself is morally neutral, it is simply a biological pattern of behaviour. The way that it is used socio-culturally, however, is not morally neutral. Its use can annoy others or be morally unacceptable. It is very important that adults do not feel they must support unacceptable behaviour just because it is a schema cluster. Allowing a child to be unacceptable does not help the child. It makes children unlikeable and often they are emotionally rejected or shunned by other children and adults alike. Finding acceptable ways in which a child can use a schema cluster, however, enhances a child's self-esteem, as it did for Mark and Kevin. When children feel disliked or disapproved of, their behaviour usually seems to deteriorate and their self-esteem plummets (Roberts, 2012). When they feel valued and approved of, their behaviour improves. Rejecting unacceptable behaviour is different from rejecting the child. Children need to be unconditionally accepted by adults who work with them professionally. Some adults have problems in managing to achieve this with some children, but children are deeply aware when this happens and are sensitive to it.

REBECCA's mother became ill. Rebecca carried paper tissues to her whenever requested, and sometimes spontaneously. Her behaviour was, fortuitously, appropriate for the occasion. She felt that it had been a success, and after some flowers were delivered for her mother she regularly took these to different points in the room. Her mother and her friend praised her for looking after her mother so well. She used her ability to transport objects to care for her mother

▷

(for example transporting tissues, flowers, drinks and slippers). In this way she experienced being kind, caring and responsible. Not only were her efforts praised, but they were recognised and genuinely appreciated. Since her mother had not been ill in this way before, Rebecca was also gaining a new experience – caring for the sick.

Judy Dunn (1988) suggests that children learn self-discipline if they are helped to see the results of hurting and helping people, and showing them that you care. The concern children have for themselves develops and becomes concern for others, too. Helping children into the appropriate use of schemas helps in this.

PAUL, three years old, is observed to be often involved in a schema cluster of rotation, enclosure and connection with trajectories. He does not yet draw using the core and radial schema. He loves to unlock doors with keys and turn door knobs, which annoys adults. He spends ages at the sink turning taps off and on. He is removed from the bathroom when the floor constantly becomes flooded. He does spiral-shaped scribbles when he draws and paints.

He is interested when an older child brings a conker into the nursery on a string. He swings it dangerously and has to be stopped.

He likes the windscreen wipers on the car, and wants to put the umbrella up and down and up and down, but he is very rough with it so it is taken from him to save it from being broken. He is frustrated. It seems that he is stopped each time he tries to exercise his partial rotation schema. In light of these observations, the staff decide to introduce a pulley into the outside area. Indoors, a tea urn is introduced and he spends long periods turning the tap off and on and making the water spray out as he puts his hand over the tap (a dynamic core and radial effect). The classroom provision and experience offered helps his schema cluster to be exercised in ways that are more acceptable to adults than before. When using the pulley he is concerned with the cause-and-effect aspect. When he rotates the handle, the bucket goes up. When he rotates the handle the other way, it comes down.

He does not yet understand how the pulley or the tea urn work at an abstract or operational level of the schema. He can, however, see the cause-and-effect relationship of turning and twisting the handle one way or the other on either the pulley or the tea urn.

By supporting what he knows of partial rotation in educationally worthwhile ways, Paul is less frustrated (and so are the adults!) and he learns more effectively.

The cluster of schemas in evidence is:

- ○ rotation
- ○ connection of trajectory to enclosure
- ○ emergent core and radial.

The level of schema in the example of Paul is cause and effect.

- ○ Both his emotional well-being and his involvement (Laevers, 1994) in experiences are good.
- ○ The learning is mostly in relation to the 'knowledge and understanding of the world' area of learning in the English Early Years Foundation Stage.

It is important to note that Paul does not yet draw or paint using the core and radial schema, but he does seem to have some embryonic understanding of it. Children use schemas embryonically and are attracted to the way their schemas are echoed in the socio-cultural and material world long before they can 'perform' them at will. In other words, recognition of a schema and some early awareness of it come before the ability to perform.

TOM, three years old, spent an afternoon throwing a stick into a bush in the garden. His mother could not understand what he was doing but left him to it, staying near because of the potential dangers of stick throwing. It was months later that he began to draw core and radials, and yet sticks in a bush made the same prickly effect. Prior to this he had picked out pictures of beetles and ladybirds in books. Recognition of the core and radial schema comes before performance of it.

Tom is safe playing alone, throwing sticks in the garden with his mother nearby, but this would not be acceptable in a group situation. He could be offered other choices over and above the basic provision, of clay and large numbers of wooden twigs at the clay table or a dartboard with suckers on the darts, splash painting, dish mops, buckets of water and a wall to bash, or a hose on a hot summer day, and fountain-making in the water tray.

Children are born wanting to learn

Children are born wanting to learn. We need only to help them. We do not always know exactly what is needed. If we observe and support a child's schema clusters and see what the child is serious about, we find this informs us over time, but we can begin to extend the learning because we know the general direction that the child is taking.

Schemas help adults to support and extend what children naturally can do, but in socially worthwhile directions. In a traditional early years setting, children make relationships with adults and other children and are given materials, equipment and experiences that emphasise 'can do' rather than 'cannot do'. The traditional toddler group or nursery/infant classroom has always implicitly made good provision for the 'can do' aspects of schemas and given children access to learning. The traditional equipment and provision, and the garden, which is an important part of the curriculum, offer children opportunities to 'recognise' and reflect their emergent schemas, to practise and consolidate their repertoire of schemas and so gain access to higher order ideas and deepened feelings and relationships that they can actively use in their lives.

In offering a 'can do' quality curriculum that integrates within it an active understanding of schemas, early childhood workers need to be aware of three things. These involve being able to:

1 observe and identify the child's schemas
2 support the child's schemas through effective use of the material provision and interactions with the people in the environment
3 extend the child's learning from the starting point of what the child can do by enhancing and adding to material provision, environment and interaction with people.

As we saw at the beginning of the chapter, schemas have different levels of complexity within them. A child may function at an earlier or later level of the schema by moving in and out of levels according to the newness of the materials and experience, or the intimacy and relaxed nature of the relationships with other children and the family worker, enjoying being spoken to in a small group.

Observing the schema cluster and how this informs planning (Sue Rice, 1996, 72–76)

When **JOANNE** (3 years, 11 months) is at home, her mother reports she likes to overfill containers and cover surfaces, and to be wrapped in a large towel and to wrap toys in towels or blankets.

She also likes to dress up in flowing clothes and veils, and to collect toys in her arms until they overflow. When she is swimming, she loves to feel waves of water breaking over her head.

Schema: envelopment cluster.

Supporting and extending the schema cluster

JOANNE was offered containers to fill and objects to cover, and fitted them inside boxes in the workshop area. She used a selection of boxes, with cones, acorns, conkers, leaves, etc., to put in the boxes. She had a particular interest (along with EDWARD, a fellow enveloper) in a ring box, a box with a sliding lid and a pencil box.

She was drawn to a bowl of cornflour and water and smothered her arms and hands in the green slime with great energy and enthusiasm. Her envelopment cluster was also evident in the increasing amounts of time she spent in the home area wearing layers of dressing-up clothes. At home she used more veils for dressing up and covered her hands in chocolate when making crispy cakes. She was interested in the number of mattresses on which the Princess slept in the story of 'The Princess and the Pea'.

Joanne's mother, during conversations with staff about envelopment and how she and Joanne were enjoying their time together, expressed her pleasure in what she had observed and how Joanne's activities seemed to have taken on a new meaning.

The cluster was supported when the teacher initiated Kim's Game (with an adult and two other children), involving covering a selection of objects then guessing which one had been removed. The teacher also encouraged Joanne (with a small group and an adult) to wrap potatoes in foil to bake at a barbecue to celebrate Divali. She enjoyed a bowl of papier-mâché (small group and an adult). In water play, the teacher provided her with small polythene bags filled with water of different colours. She pummelled them until they burst.

Further support came by way of parcels buried by the teacher in the sand tray: when Joanne approached, the sand looked smooth and she looked disappointed. As she pressed her hands in, she discovered a parcel and her face gleamed with a smile. She opened the parcel carefully to avoid tearing the paper, and then gathered all the objects revealed, scooping and pushing the sand with her other hand to make sure nothing was missed. She found a box with a lid in which to collect the treasures until they could be shared.

Chris Athey (1990: 63) states:

> … most adults know when they have struck a chord in a child. The child's closely focused attention usually signifies that a good match has been made between an adult stimulus and some particular or general concern in the child.

NATASHA, two years old, made constructions with wooden blocks. Each time she did this she seemed concerned that her construction should look symmetrical at each end.

She was videoed in the nursery making these constructions while her family worker sat alongside her, gently protecting her block play by his presence. Other children came and appeared interested in her construction.

As soon as the video was shown to Natasha's mother, she recognised her concern for symmetry and linked it with the mathematical concept of quotity (the kind of twoness that has symmetry). She loved to hold two identical objects, one in each hand, and to set them down opposite each other. Wooden block play lends itself to experimentation with mathematical concept of quotity. This means that she loved to hold two identical objects, one in each hand, and to set them down again opposite each other. Quotity is a kind of symmetry that is linked to holding objects in the hands, and so it appears during the toddler years.

Because the practitioner and parents shared what they knew of Natasha's interest in symmetry, they were able to be more sensitive to her, both at home and in the early years setting.

Natasha's mother felt justly proud of her daughter's mathematical achievements, and this warmth was felt by Natasha. The family worker felt that his work with Natasha was being valued by her family.

Children thrive when the adults around them work well together and respect and value the contributions that each makes to the child's schema clusters as they develop and learn.

> Nothing gets under a parent's skin more quickly or permanently than the illumination of his or her own child's behaviour.
>
> (Athey, 1990: 66)

Elizabeth Whalley (1994) introduced schemas to parents and staff. Parents willingly kept observations of their children at home, and shared them with staff.

ASHLEY (four years old) made lines of cars on top of the sofa, used hoopla to drop rings on hooks on a board, connected pegs together in a line, helped wash up and enjoyed seeing water run down the plate as he squeezed the sponge. He tied things up with string and rope, and on finding his toy handcuffs, handcuffed anyone willing (such as the milk lady!), made traps out of rope for Daddy and enjoyed the film *Home Alone* at a friend's house. He painted handcuffs at nursery.

His schema cluster is trajectory, connection and enclosure.

When adults spending time with children enjoy their company and can understand more about what they do and why, both the children and adults relax. The result is more quality in every respect.

Schemas make an important contribution to a child's development and learning

Although schemas are very complex to study and need plenty of time to observe and come to understand, over time they help adults working with children, and children and their families, to enjoy their time together more easily. It is worthwhile making the effort to study them.

○ Schemas make an important contribution to a child's development and learning through the socio-cultural context in which they develop.
○ Schemas support children in what they know.
○ Schemas extend children into what they do not yet know about – ideas, feelings, relationships and physical development.
○ Schemas are biological brain patterns through which children are helped to think, feel, move and relate to other people and environments.
○ Schemas influence and enhance a child's uniqueness.
○ Schemas modify, change, transform and become more sophisticated as they develop.
○ Schemas challenge those who argue that there is only fragmentation of humanity across cultures and no common ground across child development trans-globally.
○ Schemas help us to tune in to children and families and so help development and learning.
○ Schemas help us to make progress as we develop in an evolutionary (not revolutionary) way towards best practice, building on the early childhood traditions.
○ Schemas help us to link and find shared ground, but not to become standardised and uniform in our practice.
○ Schemas help us to celebrate human and cultural diversity.

Representation: children as symbol users

6

Representation – something stands for something else

When we represent, we find a way of bringing back something or someone from a previous situation. The process of 'representation' is the means by which we manage to keep hold of our past experiences in an orderly way. The more we learn about how humans develop, the more it seems that everything links and interacts in a web or a network. When we represent something, we:

- remember back and have an image in our mind of something or someone from a prior experience, and replay it in our mind
- make something stand for something that is not present, by using a symbol to represent it.

Bruner (1990) says that this process of representation works in three interrelated ways:

1 Through the enactive mode.
2 Through the iconic mode.
3 Through the symbolic mode.

The enactive mode is the way that we represent experiences through the doing. We learn through the senses, and the brain co-ordinates these sensual experiences so that they are integrated. Neuropsychologists such as Colwyn Trevarthen at the University of Edinburgh see this brain co-ordination as a bio-cultural experience. The brain remembers sensory experiences. Our movements (the sixth sense) co-ordinate with the olfactory (smell), gustatory (taste), visual, auditory and tactile senses, and all come together as a whole experience. For example, after a while we have only to get on a bike and we can ride it. Balancing movements and the body's relationship with the ground (Greenland, 2010) work together with what we see as we ride along, and the sounds that rush past, how the handles and pedals feel, the smell of the air, and the taste of it, too. Early childhood educators have long believed in the importance of 'learning by doing' for young children, as this quotation from a nursery school prospectus shows:

> The children are learning through the doing, at this stage of development. This means that they will experiment with materials and get messy, very messy. Please do not send your children in good clothes that cannot take glue, paint, cooking mixture, pet food and the many activities that we provide.

Figure 6.1 The toddlers with their mothers and childminders at the 'Play and Stay' session are exploring different materials and how they work. For example, in 5 and 6 the glue stick behaves in a different way to the piece of chalk. The adult gently takes the glue stick from the child, which would spoil the slate and ensures the toddler experiences success with the chalk and slate. The child is given the right help at the right time in the right way. The adult doesn't take over, but the child isn't left to damage the equipment.

Figure 6.1 *Continued*

The iconic mode is the way we represent a person, event or object with an image. Take, for example, a photograph. Traditional early years practice has always encouraged children to make images in their minds, as well as using books, pictures, photographs and interest tables, to keep fresh in the mind experiences that the children have had. For example, after a visit to a pond to collect frog spawn, the interest table might be set up complete with photographs of events in sequence and displaying the equipment used (for example, nets and jars). As children interact with the interest table, they keep their experiences alive and learn from them. The emphasis that Bruner places on doing ('active learning') – imaging and making things stand for other things symbolically – demonstrates the importance of real and powerful experiences, which children can reflect on and learn through.

Learning outdoors is equally as important as learning indoors. Young children do their best learning outdoors because the enactive mode can be used to the full. Every aspect of learning interacts with every other aspect in a network or interwoven web. It is important to remember that children will find drawing and early attempts to write easier if they also use the 'doing' and 'imaging' modes to the full.

The symbolic mode, in Bruner's theory, means that we can represent something in a code that is used as a shared convention. Language is a code of this kind. We can say the word 'cat' to stand for a cat. The word is not the real thing. It is a symbol of a cat; it stands for a cat.

Children are encouraged to develop symbolic codes through, for example, drawing and painting (Matthews, 2003), dancing (Davies, 2003), imaginative play (Gura, 1996), making models and creations (Bruce, 2004a), language and literacy, writing and reading (Whitehead, 2004), arithmetic, algebra, geometry (Worthington and Carruthers, 2003), and so on. Malguzzi was an Italian educator who was part of a post-war community movement in Reggio Emilia to reduce the power of the Roman Catholic Church in relation to education.

Figure 6.2 This group of girls spent more than half an hour at the drawing table. They were joined for part of the time by interested adults, but one adult was an anchor throughout. Each drawing is different because each child has a different idea. There is some discussion about drawings within this group, but along the way the conversation is about other things, too. The best creative thinking often emerges in this way. When there is a relaxed atmosphere without pressure to perform, with intellectually stimulating discussions, both children and adults feel comfortable and try out ideas as they draw. This inclusive approach also makes it possible for any child to be near or alongside. The children are not put out when the little boy sits on the table, and they carry on with their drawings, knowing that his Key Person will support him and encourage him to use the chair. He likes to be near other children and to play with them sometimes.

He spoke of the 'Hundred Languages' of the child. Some of these are referred to in this paragraph. Some are verbal and some are not. The ability to create ideas that are symbolic is a deeply important part of human life, and it begins to emerge in early childhood.

Children need experiences that give opportunities for all three of Bruner's modes of representation:

- O doing
- O imaging
- O making things stand for something in a symbolic way.

Traditionally, early childhood practice has done this.

Figure 6.3 'Formula' drawings, simple and complex

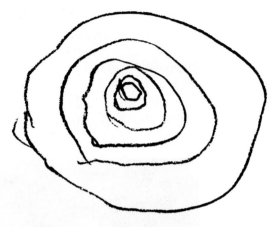

Figure 6.5 Girl, 3 years 3 months

Figure 6.4 Boy, 1 year 9 months

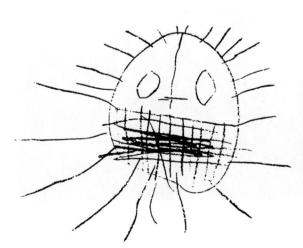

Figure 6.6 Boy, 4 years 5 months

Figure 6.7 Boy, 4 years 4 months

The beginnings of representation: becoming a symbol user

Some children need a teddy or some other favourite object with which to sleep. It helps them to feel safe and secure as they sleep. It links the child with other people, especially parents and close family, when they are separated from them, perhaps by going to sleep, when going to the childminder or early childhood setting, or

Figure 6.8 Stevie reaches out to kiss and hug her teddy. One of her favourite books is from the series by Opal Dunn, which includes *Hallo*, *Goodbye* and *Love You*. There is repetition of the phrase 'Big hug', which she enjoys in the book. Hugs in her family, in literature and representations of these with the toy teddy are the beginnings of representation.

when spending an afternoon with friends or neighbours. Winnicott (1974) said objects such as these are 'transitional objects'. Some children use their transitional objects (for example, the teddy bear) as a substitute for important people in their lives whilst they are away from them. Other children need important people to be present if they are to fully enjoy their teddy bear or transitional object.

I spent a weekend with a two-year-old girl called **ELLEN** and her transitional object, 'Baby Lion'. I had not met Baby Lion before. He became a new friend. Baby Lion was taken up by Ellen when her mother started leaving her with a friend one afternoon a week. Baby Lion is truly transitional, standing for the mother who returns at the end of the afternoon, acting as the link across the separation between them. Also, Baby Lion can stand for Ellen, who goes to a friend's house and has adventures without her mother. Baby Lion is also Ellen's companion while she is there. He is both Ellen's possession and her creation. The transitional object belongs only to the child. No one else can presume to alter it in any way. This situation has strong links with children's early attempts at writing, which we shall explore later (in Chapter 7 on communication, language and literacy).

At the weekend, Baby Lion had a pony ride. Ellen did not. Baby Lion ate lunch and slept. Baby Lion is quite a character, having moods and ideas that have to be accommodated.

Something significant is happening here. Imaginative, representational play is developing around Baby Lion. Other children and adults are willing to have him watch while they play with Ellen. He is sometimes on the edge of games with the children. Sometimes he is part of them. He was taken up a mountain (the stairs) and had adventures. He helped Ellen to find her way into group play with other children. There was a great deal of 'drama' that weekend.

Another enjoyable time was spent during a week with six-year-old **RAYMOND**, for whom the selection of a transitional object varied, its attractiveness lasting for a day or two. One day it might be a camera, then two days later a whistle. Within a few weeks of joining his foster parents, he began to require a transitional object. It always took him into group play and helped him to find a 'role' for himself.

Perhaps Bruner would say the transitional object helped Raymond to explore different modes of representation, but in Winnicott's terms it allowed him to do so with safety. Raymond acted as a defender from wasps on the beach – he believed that they would go if he blew his treasured whistle. He lined everyone up and 'took photos' of them, legitimately controlling a group of people. He experimented with leadership, power and kindness in different contexts and in an acceptable way. Within two days, for the first time, he was 'in the game' with four- to seven-year-olds, helping them to make a museum with their holiday treasures. Although we are primarily concerned with the first five years, it is as well to bear in mind that for some children, like Raymond, the roots of representation come later, but nonetheless healthily.

Winnicott believes that these early imaginative representational plays develop into group relationships and that they are natural and healthy. Educators of young children need to recognise the importance of transitional objects for the child and to treat them sensitively. Not all children have transitional objects, but they will use favourite toys, or special voices, or imaginary friends, depending on the socio–cultural setting in which they grow up. By observation and empathy the adult may be allowed into the world of the child's representation play.

Transitional objects and other similar behaviours are not leftovers from babyhood, but an exciting development from it. They are the essence of play, which is heavily bound up in representation and being part of a group, as well as being important in literacy and other individual representational work.

Early childhood educators need to consider how to welcome transitional objects in their settings. Perhaps they should not be put away out of sight or access. It is worth considering a special small chair, where the objects can sit when not needed, where they are safe from other children. This allows them to be cuddled or carried round, rather than put away in a cupboard until home time. Winnicott would argue that to put the object away denies the child both possession and the chance to develop play and creative ideas. Ellen would not have had her adventures without Baby Lion working alongside her. Transitional objects are a rich resource of children's representational development.

The development of representation and symbol use in children

Being able to represent (keep hold of prior experience) by making images or symbols that stand for people, events and objects in their absence – or in their presence – is an important part of human behaviour. But two similar people who have the same experiences will, in fact, experience them quite differently. This is because, to some extent – without realising we are doing it – we can select on what we focus. This is not a conscious process and when it happens, which it does all the time, we call it having interests, or hobbies, or favourite places and activities.

Piaget says that we have a network, a repertoire of behaviours (which he calls schemas – see Chapter 5) that influences what we are interested in at the time, and that alters and modifies in light of feedback from real socio–cultural experience. This means that the biological aspects of our development interact with the socio–cultural side of development, making each of us a unique person. This is confirmed by recent evidence from the neurosciences (see Bruce, 2004a).

Piaget thought that the process of representation developed rapidly from toddler times until after the start of statutory schooling, which in most countries is at six or seven years of age. This is the period when the process of representation really begins to flourish. For Piaget, as for Bruner, there is an important network of processes developing in the child, each of which interacts with the others in a web-like way.

It is a network or web that involves a child in:

- ○ active learning
- ○ imitation
- ○ memory
- ○ making images, which might be auditory (sound) or visual, or based on touch, smell or taste
- ○ making symbols, where something stands for something else.

Imitation

When Piaget says that imitation is important as part of representing experience, he does not mean copying. Imitation differs from copying in that the child makes use of and reconstructs an event after the event.

Figure 6.9 Maya in the bottom of the photo makes the fish wiggle. The wiggling echoes the sign for a fish, which she has seen used since six months when regularly attending the baby sign and sing group with her mother.

> Three-year-old **WILLIAM** sees a friend, two-year-old Charlotte, eat cheese on toast cut into small squares in a grid pattern. He usually has toast fingers. The next day he asks for his honey toast to be made like Charlotte's. He is reconstructing in light of a new situation and context. He is adapting an idea he wants to use.

Through imitation of this sort, children experiment with different behaviours, roles, ways of painting, swimming and much more. This is a strong argument for not separating educational provision for three- and four-year-olds, since the younger children benefit from imitating the older, who in turn benefit from the leadership and sense of responsibility involved. Although Piaget's notion of imitation gives strong justification for the mixing of ages, the practice of mixing three- and four-year-olds is currently being eroded.

Children making images

The images that children form are difficult for adults to study, because they are inside the child's mind. Piaget calls the period from two to five years the 'dark ages' in our knowledge of child development. Later on, children can often describe the images that they have and put them into words, although even as adults some of the most important images we have remain unspoken, and so they should. Words are only one way of making symbols and should not be overemphasised in human development.

Adults can encourage imagery. For example, when finger painting with children, a practitioner might comment that their handprints resemble a peacock's tail seen by them previously on a visit to the zoo. Also that it looks like a horse-chestnut leaf or a fan. In this way adults are giving the opportunity of at least three images – the tail, the leaf, the fan – without imposing any of them on the child. Adults can help children to construct images and should value those that children create that are based on experiences.

> Four-year-old **DOMINIC** brings home a butterfly picture made by dropping paint on the paper and then folding it, still wet, in half. He says to his mother, 'This is like a bird with its wings out. This is like a bull's head. This is like a butterfly. This is like a cloud.' This is a series of images of his own. This is different from the adult saying, 'Today we are going to make a butterfly painting. What colours will your butterfly be?'

In the latter approach, the adult is in control of the images, not the child. If encouraged to do so, children will use real experiences they have lived through as the basis of imagery that they are increasingly prepared to articulate and share.

Two-year-old **WILLIAM** finds some pieces of wood on a beach. One reminds him of a fish. One reminds him of an aeroplane. Similarly, in their paintings and drawings children will often label their efforts because they are reminded of something – for example, a drawing that represents a maze for William at three years of age might represent a honeycomb a few hours later, if he had recently visited Hampton Court and eaten honey from a comb.

It is also important that adults do not offer narrow experiences to children and so restrict the processes of imitation and forming images.

A student on teaching practice in a nursery school one day took in a model windmill for a group of three- and four-year-olds to make. The children were eager, but needed almost constant help and the student found herself, in effect, making a dozen windmills. She tried a new strategy the next day, which was still to encourage the children to make a toy as a present for a baby about to visit the nursery. This time, however, she made half a dozen or so different toys, including a windmill. Again, the children were eager, but this time her offering to them seemed to trigger a range of images. They chatted about their ideas, and made a wide range of windmill-type toys, although they certainly used (imitated) some of the ideas presented in her model.

MARY made a tube and fringed the ends of it, cutting with scissors. **GARETH** tore off strips of paper from a sheet and stuck them onto a box he found in the scrap material. **SHANAZ** stood the cylinder she made upright, stuck a stick on it and another across to intersect it.

These children were imitating, taking ideas from other people, and forming images. Both are of great importance in Piaget's theory.

Symbolic representation

Piaget values the personal, highly individual symbols that children develop to make something stand for something else. He also values the shared conventions that are developed by groups, cultures and societies in different places and parts of the world:

- O personal, individual ways of making symbols (which is when something is made to stand for something else).
- O the shared conventions used to symbolise (stand for) something, agreed by a group, culture or society.
- O making links between the personal idiosyncratic symbols children make and the arbitrary agreed signs that groups make, can lead to a good balance between creativity and conformity.

Symbolic representation – making something stand for something else

- Idiosyncratic, highly personal symbols that are special to the person who devises them.
- Shared conventions, arbitrary signs agreed by a group of people and the norms of the culture.
- Creativity and imaginative representations.
- Using the cultural conventions and conformity in the way experiences are given symbolic representation.

AMANDA (four years old) went on an underground train. Later that day she made her legs wide apart, and then close together. She explained it was the Tube doors opening and shutting. This is an idiosyncratic, personal, symbolic representation. It is very creative.

DAVID is two years old. He goes to his grandad and makes a thumbs-up sign. His grandad replies, using the same sign. This is an agreed convention for 'okay' or 'all's well' in the culture in which David is growing up. He is conforming to the socio-cultural context in this example of symbolic representation.

Learning a verbal language or sign language, learning to use agreed mathematical symbols or musical and dance notation, or learning to write, are all examples of different kinds of symbolic representation that involve shared conventions of the culture. In most countries in the world children are encouraged to use their own personal symbols until six or seven years of age, while at the same time actively exploring the shared conventions of their culture (Ferreiro and Teberosky, 1983; Ferreiro, 1997).

In some countries, children are expected to learn symbolic conventions from the age of two, three or four years of age and to abandon their personal symbols and experimentation. The emphasis is on using the conventional symbols of their culture. This is likely to lead to conformity and performance in prescribed tasks and crafts rather than creativity in adults. The younger the child, the more emphasis there needs to be on the child's own personal symbols, and active exploration and problem solving in relation to conventional symbols. This is discussed in more detail in Chapter 7, when the development of 'writing' is considered.

Adults need to offer children examples of dance and music, and children need to be encouraged to develop these in their own way.

A question of balance

- Developing personal, idiosyncratic symbols – creative: thinking for yourself and being unique.
- Learning the conventions of symbol use in a particular culture – conforming to cultural expectations.

Piaget and Bruner agree that active learning (learning by doing) is important. Copying is not useful, but reconstructing an experience in your own way (by imitation) *is* useful. Images, although often hidden inside you, are important. Children need to master symbolic codes.

Piaget: representation is a whole network

Piaget values the child's own personal, idiosyncratic symbols as much as the conventional codes of the socio-cultural context in which the child grows up. Children who use both personal and conventional symbols become increasingly imaginative and creative.

Figure 6.10 The adult discusses the drawing with the child, moving to the child's height and eye level. If adults are to understand a child's representational ideas, they need to show interest and take time to tune in to the child's way of thinking.

For Piaget, representation is a whole network.

○ Imitation – not copying someone else, but reconstructing (imitating) in your own way.
○ Images – from memories of experiences that are visual, etc.
○ Symbols – idiosyncratic and personal, as well as shared and arbitrary cultural conventions.

Bruner

○ Enactive: learning by doing.
○ Iconic images.
○ Symbols: mastering cultural codes such as numbers, music and dance notation.

Vygotsky

Vygotsky's work is useful in pointing out the value of play props as a means by which children represent things, events and people.

○ Children use play props such as cups or plates. They also represent these and make their own. Sadiq, at three years old, uses a beech leaf as a play prop. He pretends it is a plate. He uses a daisy as a play prop to stand for a fried egg.
○ Children move into role play and dress up, pretending to be someone else. A paper plate might become a driving wheel, a long skirt might be a prop that symbolises the 'lady from old fashioned times'. Dressing up helps children to move into role play. In their pretend play children develop stories.

Vygotsky says that the child, such as Sadiq above, sees one thing (the daisy) but acts differently towards it (treating the daisy as if it were an egg). He gives the daisy a different meaning. That is what children do when they make something into a play prop.

The theories we have looked at in this section, of Bruner, Winnicott, Piaget and Vygotsky, lead us to some practical strategies. We have established that children need direct, powerful, emotional experiences, and a consistent environment that offers diverse, enriching opportunities. Young children require a supportive setting in which imaginative play is encouraged, through which there is frequent opportunity to reflect.

Some practical strategies for encouraging the development of representation

Recent research emphasises the importance of context, both in social relationships and the influences of the culture.

Throughout this book, the advantages of younger and older children playing together are emphasised. Vygotsky's and Piaget's work shows how important it is for younger children to see older children handling materials with confidence and pleasure, and to see moments of struggle and recognise how the adults in the environment are supportive and enabling at such times. The motivation to learn and move forward is closely linked with security, self-confidence and self-esteem. Adults can help children in these areas.

Observing children

Careful child observation comes first, as illuminated by Matthews (2003), or using a very different Steinerian perspective (Strauss, 1978), so that the emphasis is on looking at and identifying what the child can do, before leaping into action. Adults working with children will also need to act on their observations of children (see Chapter 2).

The adult first observes the child's themes of play, drawing, models, conversation and so on, then attempts to help children individually, or as a group, to elaborate on these themes. This might be through conversation or through suggestion, or by providing relevant and appropriate materials and experiences in a sensitive way. There is a world of difference between intervening sensitively and appropriately, and interfering when adults move into teaching without first tuning in to the child.

Working with young children, providing appropriate materials and experiences, might also mean that adults need to allow themselves to be used as an extension of the child – for example, holding the sticky tape while children cut it, to stop them from giving up at a difficult moment, or helping to keep a theme going in the home corner when the play is breaking down.

Two three-year-olds, **BARBARA** and **CLARE**, wanted to play nurses, but a quarrel broke out over who should give out the medicine. The adult intervened, saying, 'I am the sister. Nurse Barbara, would you take the patient's temperature? Nurse Clare, please would you wash the patient?' Both are given attractive nurse-like tasks. The adult has kept the theme and the roles going and has also extended the children's play in adding to the range of nurse-like activities.

Materials that can be used for representation

Material provision involves the people, events and objects with which the children interact. Materials can be set out in many ways to excite curiosity and surprise, and yet there must be security for the children. Different kinds of provision make different demands. Children need to experience the challenge of many different experiences, and of wide-ranging provision.

> At three years old **HANNAH** danced a rosebud unfurling. This was her idea. She was very frustrated when she tried to draw this event.

It is important to bear in mind Bruner's three modes of representation, and the conflicts the child must resolve between them. This implicitly argues for a rich, wide range of media for young children to experience and work with.

Children need to become proficient in the representational possibilities of different clays, doughs and woodwork, as well as plasticine, mud and wet sand.

They need different papers, brushes and paints, from oil to poster to powder paint, thick, thin and medium. They need to draw with pastels, charcoal, pencils, felt pens, chalk, ink and so on.

A broad material environment becomes very exciting to provide. Children need to experience and tell stories, hear and see, make music, and dance in different styles – dramatic, comforting, romantic, folk – from different cultures. Endless possibilities emerge.

The ways in which materials are set out, the range and variety of materials offered (Gura, 1992; Bruce, 2004a; Bruce, 2011), and the way adults help children to learn how to use materials, are all important in encouraging children to represent.

> ○ It is necessary to have some anchor areas always in the same places and forms, for example, the book and home areas. Other areas might change regularly to link with recent experiences that the children have had as a group, for example, a visit to the park.
> ○ Different kinds of materials make different demands. Children need to experience the challenge of many experiences and a wide range of materials. Depending on the material, the representational experience and degree of symbol use will be entirely different each time.

Figure 6.11 The adult encourages the toddler by talking about how he is loading the lorry with sand. There are the glimmerings of two important elements here. The narrative of loading a lorry is one, and the development of the characters (lorry driver and lorry loader) is another.

GEORGIO (four years) wants to make a representation of his bathroom pipe freezing and bursting (a dramatic experience for him and his family) in clay, woodwork, sand, dance or drama, but he manages to do it at the water tray.

It is important for children to try out what it is like to represent in different ways with different materials. A broad material range becomes exciting and interesting for adults to provide and watch, and to help children to use when representing. Some children will show more strength in one area and less in another; others will be all-rounders.

WILLIAM, at three years old, almost never paints, although the opportunity is constantly available. He rarely draws, either. He rejects dough and clay. But he models a blackbird out of Plasticine, with a black body, head and wings, a yellow beak, two yellow eyes, and yellow legs and feet. He is angry when it will not stand up, and only grudgingly accepts the suggestion that it could sit on a nest made by a helpful adult. He wants it to hop. The representation of movement is what he really wants. He knows that blackbirds have a springy hop. He represents this with his body, briefly, before a rough-and-tumble game develops with his sister. William prefers to represent using three dimensions, and through dance-like movements.

KATE, at three and a half years, rarely drew or painted, but made marvellous models. She made a model of her school classroom one day with a cardboard box and bricks to represent furniture, accurately placed spatially.

Interestingly, at five years old, both these children were doing meticulous and beautiful drawings and two-dimensional work, but both were easily frustrated if their efforts did not work out. Kate went on to study art at 'A' Level and William studied physics.

It is easier to change clay or bricks and re-organise them than it is to change a drawing that has not gone according to plan. On the other hand, it is easier to fall into a stereotyped and narrow formula in drawings, and to let dance-like musical and three-dimensional work atrophy as the imagination increasingly fails. Kate and William were encouraged in the early years (birth to eight years) to experiment, explore and value their own personal idiosyncratic representations. They were not 'forced' to adopt cultural conventions or to draw in formulas. In this way they made use of conventional symbols and ways of representing, while developing their own personal symbols with imagination and creativity.

Representation in all its forms is important. Dance, music, sculpture, construction toys, drawing, painting, mathematics, making scientific theories, literature and drama all offer different possibilities. Each offers something special, something worthwhile and unique. We can keep hold of past experiences of people, situations and objects by representing them.

Offering children performances, stories, music and dance so that they are introduced to other people's ideas and representations

Much of the theatre, dance and music offered to children is, at best, patronising and, at worst, undervalues their possibilities for sophisticated understanding and appreciation as developing symbol users, who are attuned to their cultural and social contexts and communities. Children deserve the best in theatre, dance and music. Good children's theatre, dance, music and literature has layers of meaning, which fascinate adults as much as children, such that everyone takes from the piece that which holds meaning for them.

Conclusion

- ○ Representation is a process in human development.
- ○ It gives children and adults ways of keeping hold of important experiences through images and symbols.
- ○ Images can be to do with what we hear, see, smell, taste and touch, or what we do in terms of movement.
- ○ We use symbols to make one thing stand for another, usually in the absence of the person, object, place or event. Some symbols are very personal and idiosyncratic. These are understood only by the person using them and perhaps by those close to them. Some symbols are shared conventions, arbitrary by nature, such as words, writing, music and dance notation, or algebra.
- ○ The early childhood curriculum encourages children to:
  - be active learners
  - make images
  - develop symbols, both personal and using shared conventions.
- ○ Special objects or toys might become what Winnicott calls 'transitional objects', easing children in and out of situations involving separation from those to whom they are close, and at the same time encouraging the representational process to develop.
- ○ The process of representation leads towards children (and adults) developing interests and hobbies in life. The biological path of development (our genetic programme) is constantly in touch with, part of and influenced by the socio-cultural path of our development. Consequently, even identical twins might develop different interests.
- ○ The process of representation develops as a web or network involving:
  - the senses
  - movement
  - imitation
  - making images – making symbols.
- ○ The process of representation involves a sense of ownership by the child: young children are representing their own experiences, their own ideas, feelings and relationships, and not those of others who are not part of their experience.

7 Communicating with and without words: the foundations of literacy

Non-verbal communication

Communication is central to being a human. Non-verbal communication never stops. Even when we are asleep we communicate to others whether we are restful, physically comfortable or dreaming. Non-verbal communication is the main way in which we communicate, through our facial expressions, body language (movements and gestures), tone of voice, pauses, and much else too. Non-verbal communication is a background to living. Some estimates suggest that it forms 85 per cent of our communicating; others suggest 75 per cent.

Non-verbal communication in babies

Work over many years by Colwyn Trevarthen (1993a, 1998; Mulloch and Trevarthen, 2010) shows how babies communicate and 'speak' to those close to them in non-verbal ways. They move in synchrony with the voice of the parent or sibling in a dance-like fashion. They 'reply' when spoken to, providing the person pauses long enough for them to make the reply and does not constantly 'talk at' the baby.

Children communicate non-verbally with much-loved family pets

Animals, especially mammals, also communicate non-verbally. It is not a feature only of human living. Researchers working with the American Academy of Child and Adolescent Psychiatry suggest that:

> The strong emotional bond that develops between a pet and a child can also have a positive impact on the way a child is able to communicate. Children who have pets are more able to understand non-verbal communication, as they derive signs of an animal's happiness from a wagging tail or stiff posture. Children apply these skills to their interactions with people and become better at working out what people's postures and facial expressions mean.
>
> (Crown, 2004: 16)

The example is given of Ben, aged seven years, who notices of his collie-cross dog that, 'When Tarka is confused, he does not meet my eyes, and he slouches. People do this too sometimes' (Crown, 2004: 16).

It is important to note that children need intimate, sustained, warm, affectionate relationships with people (and perhaps with much loved family pets) if they are to learn to read their own feelings, ideas and movements and those of others with sensitivity. Having animals in a group setting may, however, have the opposite impact to the one intended. Often, animals kept in early childhood settings lead miserable lives, with children handling them too roughly and without any bond or real relationship.

Spoken or signed language

Spoken language is also about communication, communication with self and communication with others

- O Spoken language helps people to move from the here and now to the past, into the future and into alternative worlds.
- O It uses agreed signs that evolve to fit the times and the setting in which the language is used.
- O It enables people to think and feel at an abstract level about ideas that are hypothetical and imaginary, in effective, efficient, deep and moving ways.
- O It involves talking and listening.

In Western culture all four of these elements are important areas of language in the school setting and in life generally. To be unable to talk or listen cuts people off and brings loneliness and frustration, along with the lack of opportunity to communicate with others. Language does not have to be oral. It can be 'talked' or 'listened to' in different ways. Some deaf and blind people talk and listen through touch. The language of the deaf has gained recognition as an official language, British Sign Language (BSL). This is not an oral language. It combines gestures (agreed and shared signs) with finger spelling.

The earlier work of researchers such as Mary Brennan (1978) and Judy Kegl (1997) has helped those who use oral language to appreciate that sign language has a syntax and has evolved just like any living language; it has regional dialects and enables abstract thinking. It contains features shared by verbal languages – it facilitates thinking, feeling and communication. It allows those who understand it to construct shared meanings together. Like some other languages in the world, it has no written form and so cannot be read. Current work at the University of Amsterdam led by Professor Anne Baker working with Professor Beppie van den Bogaerde suggests that the deaf children and hearing children between birth and eight years in the sample become bilingual if introduced to Dutch and NGT (sign language of the Nertherlands). But they use different modalities in doing this. Deaf children use sign language more in making language choice, and in their development of syntax, morphology, lexicon and turn taking.

Listening and talking

Creole languages

After the Sandinista Revolution of 1979 in Nicaragua, a group of deaf children came together for the first time when a school for deaf children was founded in Managua, joined by the researcher Judy Kegl (1997). When the children met in this special school they had only a few idiosyncratic and personal signs, as they had grown up isolated as one deaf person living amongst a hearing community.

As they continued to meet, a natural development occurred. They began to develop a 'pidgin language', which was a basic language that gave them the means, for the first time in their lives, to share ideas and feelings and to communicate with each other. The older children (teenagers) continued to use this language, but the younger children continued to develop it until what linguists call a 'creole language' emerged out of the pidgin language. This was a fully-fledged, sophisticated sign language, which was quite unique in the world, using grammar and a rich vocabulary.

Judy Kegl argues that humans are genetically and biologically predisposed to develop grammatical language systems. These children did it – out of nothing! But, and this is important in looking at the way language develops, there are two socio-cultural aspects to her findings:

1 Both the basic pidgin language and the sophisticated creole language had taken in elements of gestures used in the Nicaraguan culture and transformed these in a more developed form into the vocabulary of the language.
2 When Judy Kegl visited deaf children in rural areas, living at home without contact with other deaf children, they used only primitive gestures and signs without any grammatical element. When she introduced the children to each other, and taught them the full creole form of the sign language, the younger children quickly took it up and became fluent.

In other words, biology alone is not enough. A Language Acquisition Device (as proposed by Chomsky in the 1960s) needs the company of other people to be triggered to the full. We need other people because we are social animals. We need, literally, to participate with other people in our culture and language. It is not as simple as teaching children to talk. In this case, the younger children were teaching the teenagers and adults the creole, the more sophisticated form of the language.

Most of the time adults and children, through participating with each other in the language and the culture, will be teaching each other different things. It seems that Froebel's statement that we 'need to live with our children' still holds true today.

Bilingual children listening and talking using spoken languages

Marian Whitehead (2007: 15, 2009, 2010) points out that in many countries of the world, including Wales, Quebec, Belgium and South Africa, more than one language is spoken officially. Where this is the case, there is a more positive attitude in society towards children who are multilingual. The result is that it is easier for children to learn several languages. She identifies four aspects of the complexity and achievements of children who are multilingual.

1 Competence changes according to the language being spoken. If the child switches from their first language to the second, their vocabulary may be reduced, and they may not be able to read or write with the confidence they show in their first language. Very few children grow up as balanced bilinguals.

2 She suggests that children use different languages with different people and when they are in different situations. They might mix two languages, but this could be by choice to enable them to express and find the words for what they want to say, rather than due to any confusion. Marian Whitehead (2007: 20) suggests that these so-called 'mistakes' are in fact very successful strategies for language learning.

3 Children often speak but do not read or write in a language. Some languages are oral and do not have a written form.

4 When situations change, languages can be lost. A child might move to another community, for instance, or a Key Person who spoke to them in a language might leave or die. Some linguists take the view that when this happens the language becomes dormant and can be activated at a later time, rather than it becoming lost.

Children who are bilingual grow up more easily able to appreciate and value differences between people and cultures. This helps them to make sense of social situations. It is important that early childhood educators make every child feel that their language and culture are welcomed, valued, respected, acknowledged and visibly supported.

Children who speak three languages that have entirely different roots have a range of sounds and understandings that are, in every sense, mind expanding. Examples would be to be able to speak Arabic, French and English, or Swahili, German and Italian, or Finnish, Danish and Xhosa. This, Marian Whitehead (2007: 20) points out, gives children the advantage of thinking about the system behind a language, so that they are well equipped for literacy learning.

Encouraging language

We learn to talk through talking. Children need to spend time with people who are sensitive to their needs and who encourage them. Often one child will 'translate' to an adult what another child means. Parents are also able to signal to early years workers about events and situations that will help the communication between them and the child. Similarly, early childhood practitioners can promote the parent–child relationship by telling parents what was done in school and inviting them in to show them.

> Three-year-old **RICHARD** was met each day from nursery class by his mother. The early years worker made a point of suggesting that, if parents were not in a rush, their child could show them round. In this way parents had an idea of the activities, models, paintings and so on in which their child was involved. When, in school, Richard talked about 'my yellow one', the teacher knew that he meant a new teddy bear because his mother had mentioned it. His mother knew what he meant by having had 'butterflies' for lunch because she had seen on the classroom wall that the menu for the day was pasta with tomato sauce.

Figure 7.1 The welcoming atmosphere encourages parents to settle their children happily, and to exchange thoughts and information with staff.

As children grow up they can be helped to become aware of the need to explain and fill in necessary information in order to bring meaning to those who were not present. Listening to stories, reading and writing facilitate this process. There are strong links here with the ability to develop a sense of 'audience'.

A group of seven-year-olds was going round a stately home. The guide wanted to talk about the ceramics. The teacher sensed that this held no interest for the class. She did know about some of the paintings and asked the children to look at a painting of a lady. She asked what **ZOE**, **MARK** and the picture had in common. The situation changed, from a monologue by the guide to suggestions from the children with the teacher acting as chairperson. Eventually, it was established that Zoe and Mark had both recently acquired baby sisters. The children wondered if that was the link. Had the lady just had a baby? In fact, the fine lady in the painting had founded a maternity hospital for the poor. The children asked about her, why she did this, who she was.

This teacher had taken the children into history and helped them to glimpse the social order of a different time from their own. The language introduced

Figure 7.2 Conversations need a context or they become very false. Here the children are enjoying looking at shells and sharing a book about where shells are found.

Figure 7.3 Babies and toddlers benefit from one-to-one stories, so that conversations can take place around the pictures and storyline. Sharing a book requires the adult to be very sensitive to the baby's interests, at the same time as guiding the baby through the story.

was rich but welcomed. The teacher had helped to establish a partnership by starting from something that the class found interesting and relevant. Her share of the partnership was achieved – it was to link up with a project on Victorian Britain, including the contrast between wealth and poverty, and the social order of the times.

Children need to have opportunities to initiate conversations in early childhood settings during activities and during group times. They also need individual and small–group times – for example, when involved in music, dance or story. In these settings they can interject and the adult can use these interjections to make the story meaningful at a deeper level.

'I've got one of these' may seem an egocentric response by four-year-old **JASON** to the story of *Titch* by Pat Hutchins. It tells the early childhood practitioner, however, that Jason knows about a pinwheel. He explains how it goes round if you blow on it. He wants to abandon the story at this point and talk about his pinwheel instead. The practitioner can let him talk with her because it is a small group of three children. The other children bring in information about how the pinwheel works. When the early years worker has listened to each child's contributions about the subject, she takes them back to the text. Jason often returns to this story, provided it is in the book corner. Old favourites are an important part of leading towards reading.

When adults are involved in discussions with small groups (of two to four children) the advantages are that children are less likely to lose the focus of the conversation when it is not their turn to speak. They do not have to wait too long if they are bursting with a thought on the subject. It is also easier for the adult to draw children into the discussion, and to make use of the contextual back-drop of what children say. Even so, there are frequently times when adults need the help of other children to 'translate' or give the contextual clues needed for the conversation to flow and make sense to everyone participating.

Iram Siraj and colleagues (EPPE, 2003) stress the importance of 'shared sustained conversations' with children around rich experiences.

Three-year-old **LUCKDEEP** sat down for story time when the teacher told the story of 'Mrs Wishy Washy', and kept saying 'in there'. The teacher wanted to respond but did not understand. **SANDEEP** explained that Luckdeep wanted the teacher to put the scrubbing brush in the bowl to make soap bubbles. The shared socio-cultural context was not enough. It was necessary to negotiate a shared meaning, too. The practitioner then built the bubbles into the story.

Children are active in their learning and need to be encouraged in this. Their active feelings affect their active thinking. One deep, powerful experience is better than many pedestrian ones.

Six-year-old **TOM**'s mouse died and he was very upset. A story about a mouse and his experiences in a cage, and how he runs away leaving his owner sad, contained in it some of Tom's grief. He loved the story. It evoked the memory of the feelings he had in ways that were comforting for him. Tom did not choose the story; his mother did, as she recognised the importance of the death of his mouse.

Adults need to choose books for children that help them to meet and extend both powerful and everyday experiences. Sometimes these will arise spontaneously, as with Jason and the pinwheel. Sometimes they need to be planned by the adult, as with Tom. Children relate their own experiences to those of others through books, shared activities and outings, provided that adults allow them to be active in the process. Sometimes the child initiates, sometimes the adult, but the child always needs to be active.

The importance of feelings

Margaret Meek (1985: 43) stresses the need to 'foreground the emotive' in this process. She sees emotion as an integrating force in children's experiences. As well as listening to stories and being helped to interact with the text, children produce nonsense rhymes and jokes that are a very important aspect of their being active in their language development.

Chukovsky (1963), and more recently Marian Whitehead (2007, 2009, 2010), Goswami and Bryant (1990), Palmer and Bayley (2004) and Bruce and Spratt (2011), all note the value of rhyming sounds as a central element in learning to read. Jeni Riley (1996: 28) emphasises the importance of adults capitalising on the way children naturally enjoy songs and rhythm.

Piaget sees playing with ideas and making jokes as the highest level of understanding. Helping children to develop a sense of humour was one of the central aims of Chris Athey's work (in Chapman and Foot, 1977). Having fun with language, or with any area of knowledge, implies good understanding and can be used as a means of assessing what children know well.

Rearranging ideas and words is the basis of the creative process. Talking and listening, partnerships and being active in language development, all lead into literature. Peter McKellar (1957) defines the imagination as the rearrangement of past experience in new and fascinating ways.

The importance of making language errors free from criticism – experimenting

In talking, children are attempting actively to formulate the rules of language. They hypothesise, for example, 'I hitted the ball.' If adults reply by extending, 'Oh, you hit the ball, did you?', they give the correct form without rejecting what the child said. This helps children to adjust their 'rules' for themselves. Direct correction of children's speech is ineffective and may create stress – for adults as well as children. Self-correction is an important strategy as children check for meaning. It also tells adults where children are in their development.

> ... the value of errors, to learners [is] as elicitors of helpful feedback and for teachers [is] as a source of insight into the meanings that their pupils are making.
>
> (Wells, 1987: 18)

Writing

Writing is an aspect of language, which itself is an aspect of representation. The previous chapter explored the importance of the transitional object in the early development of representation (Winnicott, 1971). Baby Lion (page 109) stood for the link between the mother and the child, as well as the space between them when they were apart. Baby Lion was Ellen's first possession and creation.

Vygotsky, in agreement with Winnicott, goes further. He is quite clear that early representation leads directly to written language. He points out that gesture is of paramount importance: playthings and drawings initially acquire meaning supported by gesture. The work of Trevarthen (in Lock, 1978; Eckerdal and Merker, 2009) on early communication and the establishment of gestures in the first year through communicative actions between mothers and their babies resonates with this. Gradually, as the toddler period develops, objects acquire a meaning independent of gesture. Make believe, says Vygotsky (1978), is a major contributor to the development of written language. So is drawing: a pencil becomes a person. A book cannot become a person, but its dark green cover could allow it to be turned into a forest.

Representation is one of the keys to writing. Vygotsky's thinking is very much in tune with that of Dame Marie Clay (1975, 1982, 1986, 1993, 1998), whose work has been a sustained, rigorous and important influence on research and thinking about early writing. She suggests that children need to construct their own writing system, a theory of their own that they can operate. They need to be allowed to experiment and develop their own theories.

Early writing must be unhindered by external demands for neat letter forms, proper spacing, writing on the line and conventional spelling

Ferreiro (1997; Ferreiro and Teberosky, 1983), building on the work of Vygotsky, and Dame Marie Clay argue that thinking about early writing has overemphasised the graphic shapes (the transcriptive aspects) and underemphasised composition. Handwriting, letter formation, legibility and speed have tended to be adults' main focus in helping young children learn to write.

Like Vygotsky, Ferreiro and Teberosky believe that children first try to 'find the frontier that differentiates drawing from writing'. Initially, children begin to put letters into their pictures, but they suggest that the letters do not 'say' anything by themselves. There is only a vague relationship between letters and drawing.

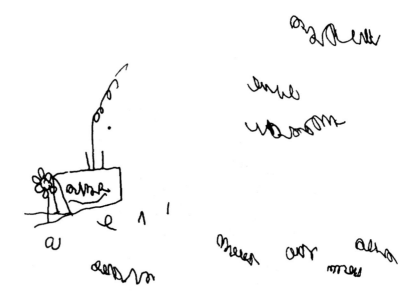

Figure 7.4 The zig-zag lines represent writing but they are not yet separated from the drawing.

Adults have the key role of acknowledging and responding to a child's first attempts at writing and of knowing at what stage to intervene sensitively in order to develop writing skills. This is vital if a child is to develop the confidence to become a writer. It is therefore important that all staff are enabled to develop the skills of observing children and of analysing these observations with an understanding of both the curriculum content and a thorough knowledge of how children learn and develop.

(Bunting, 2003)

Six-year-old **RAYMOND** uses the letter R to represent himself, the D to represent his foster mother, Daphne, and the H for his foster father, Hywel. Some letters are easier to write than others. Prospective parents choosing names, please note! Curves, such as those in C and in J with an open semi-circle, are more difficult.

Capital letters are easier for children to write – so children usually select them for their first attempts at writing

Vygotsky, and the later work of Ferreiro and Teberosky, add support to Marie Clay. Children do not seem to be 'taught' capital letters by ignorant, tiresome

Figure 7.5 The first letters children write are full of feelings: the people they love often feature, as in this example.

parents, although practitioners often accuse innocent parents of this! Children probably use them, if Piaget is right, because they very sensibly select patterns that they can easily draw. They use complete enclosures and trajectories, separate and in combination. This means that, broadly speaking, they tend to use capitals first, and the more difficult lower case letters later.

Children are active problem solvers as they try to encode their marks into writing

The alphabetic symbols used by children could well be the stepping stones towards conventional writing. I remember using a nail file to carve my name in capitals with painstaking care on the wooden mantelpiece. My mother tells me I was four years old.

Figure 7.6 Enclosure, trajectory and core and radial schemas.

Nigel Hall (in Hall and Martello, 1996: 98) writes:

> Just as they create non-conventional versions of spelling patterns, so they generate non-conventional rules for punctuation. Although their rules may be non-conventional … it is reasoning not guessing that is involved.

An inclusive approach to writing that embraces diversity

It is important to create learning environments indoors and outdoors that encourage writing. Putting notepads into the home area next to the telephone, for example, encourages children to write (Christie, 1991). It is also important to embrace the diversity of the socio-cultural contexts of home literacy. Charmian Kenner (2000: 23) emphasises the importance of making literacy links between home and the early childhood setting that embrace principles of equality, inclusion and diversity. In the UK today many children have varied experiences of literacy that do not necessarily mirror the way it is approached in schools.

As young children begin to experiment with writing in their play, for example, using shopping lists, seeing the writing of other children and adults, and seeing print in school, Ferreiro (1997) suggests they experience a conflict. Ferreiro, giving resonance to the findings of Judy Kegl on language development, suggests that learning to write is not entirely dependent on the external socio-cultural environment, but that there are also internal organisational mechanisms at work. She argues that children, as they learn to write, are learning about the nature of the link between oral and written representations. Jeni Riley (2006) reiterates the importance of this connection.

As children observe and write, there are conflicts to be resolved and experiments to be made in writing. For example, Ferreiro's research demonstrates how children find monosyllabic words a challenge, because they like to have between three and five characters in a cluster in order to feel that they have written a word. AMA stands for Amanda, and matches the number of syllables in her name. BO+ stands for Ben, but does not match the number of syllables in his name (children tend to put in a 'dummy' – extra – mark because of their minimum rule; they like to have three 'letters' to make a 'word'). For this reason, according to Ferreiro, children find longer words, with more syllables, such as 'dinosaur' with three syllables or 'refrigerator' with five syllables, easier to tackle than 'boat', with only one syllable. There are links here with the work of Rebecca Trieman and Brett Kessler (in Snowling and Hulme, 2007). Whereas Ferreiro and Teberoski begin by observing what children do, across several different languages, Trieman and Kessler begin with what is involved in writing from a more theoretical standpoint.

The importance of your own name

Again, the child's own name cannot be given too much emphasis. It may be the first 'fixed string', as Ferreiro and Teberosky (1983: 207) call it, that the child meaningfully encounters. It serves a useful purpose in causing internal conflict in the child between the alphabetic and syllabic codes (between the number of letters and the number of sounds). Striving to resolve this conflict between letters and sounds takes the child into a new level of understanding of what is involved in writing. As children resolve the conflicts inherent in this, they gradually crack the writing code. Ferreiro and Teberosky (1983: 277) say:

> Let children write, even in a writing system different from the alphabetic one. We must let them write, not so [that] they invent their own idiosyncratic system, but so [that] they discover that their system is not the conventional one, and in this way find valid reasons to substitute their own hypotheses with our conventional ones.

It is a serious matter when children enter school at five years old, thinking that they do not know how to write their own name and believing that only by tracing and copying will they come to know this.

> The distance between copy writing and children's spontaneous writing is as great as the distance between copy drawing and children's spontaneous drawing.
>
> (Ferreiro and Teberosky, 1983: 278)

If children entering school are seen as deficient in knowledge of the alphabetic code, and in dire need of swift initiation into it, the teaching of writing will be tackled by asking them to trace letters, copy sentences, correctly form their letters and, as soon as possible, by introducing punctuation, spelling and grammar.

The importance of adults who support and extend literacy learning

Ferreiro is not arguing that children should be left to themselves in learning to write. Like Weinburger (1996), Riley (2006) and Whitehead (2010), she suggests that children need support and help as they move into the role of writers. Riley stresses the importance of children working out letter–sound relationships as part of this. Donald Graves (1983) works on the principle that the adult's role is to help children to 'find their own voice' in writing. It is very important to encourage children to write with confidence and enjoyment. The writer and playwright Michael Frayn says:

> I start with an idea I want to explore; then, as I write, I just have to decide what format it will take. It's the same with characters – you might think you know what you want a character to do or say, but as you write you find you have to make compromises based on what the character wants. It's quite disconcerting!

Ferreiro (1997), Clay (1975, 1992), Miller (1997) and Whitehead (2010) suggest that at an early age, in the first five years, children can be truly educated in the writing process. There is a desire in this approach to build on what the child already knows and, with adult and peer group help, progress from there. The two-year-old who draws and makes believe is perhaps already sharing creations with the significant people in his or her life, and this is the basis of writing.

Family literacy

Colin Harrison (1996: 25) gives a three-part definition of family literacy:

1 The spontaneous family literacy activities.
2 Inter-generational projects to improve literacy levels of both parents and children.
3 Support or intervention programmes encouraging children's literacy development within the family.

Denny Taylor (1983: 87) sees the family as the base of literacy: 'Literacy is part of the very fabric of family life' (we ought perhaps to add 'in some cultures'). Denny Taylor also believes that 'literacy can be a barrier between home and school, and a contrivance of familial dissent' (1983: 87).

> ANDREW would not do word and picture matching with his mother. Instead, he made the cards intended for this purpose into an eagle, which he cherished. His mother sensibly gave up!

The damaging impact of a narrow skills approach to early literacy

Kathy Goouch (in Goouch and Lambirth, 2007) interviewed a group of highly educated parents whose children were about to begin Reception class in English primary schools. She found parents anxious that their children should continue to enjoy books and the writing efforts they made in their families. They did not want this to be spoilt through pressure. They were unaware of recent developments towards a phonics-first approach, and were nervous about the possible harmful effects of an over-emphasis on skills work in the early years of education.

The way that the family's approach meets the school's approach to literacy is a very important consideration in working with young children, but the way that the child interacts with his or her own family in relation to literacy is also important. Personalities are involved, as well as the education style of the parents, and they influence the literacy experiences of the children within the home. From the beginning, the child is both active and reactive to his or her own family's literacy experiences and presentations of them.

> Parents find that each of their children differs in their responses to 'writing'. At three years HANNAH would 'write', in zig-zagging cursive, a shopping list whenever her mother did so. She loved to sign greetings cards with a capital H. She loved stories, often demanding them during the day, as well as expecting as many as possible at bedtime.
>
> At three years, WILLIAM, from the same family, the second child, would just about concentrate for a bedtime story. Mother had to work hard to keep his concentration, whether he chose the stories or whether she did. He loved to lie in bed and listen to his five-and-a-half-year-old sister read to him until he fell asleep, however. This also helped her reading to develop, of course! At four years, William began to enjoy his bedtime story with Mother, often choosing the same one several nights in a row, for example, *The Tale of Mr Jeremy Fisher* by Beatrix

▷

Potter. He would not tolerate any deviation from the text, which he knew inside out. He showed no interest in writing, except for the W of his name, with which he would sign the occasional drawing.

At four and a half years, Hannah was reading a few words, such as 'Hannah' and 'Mummy', and writing all the time. By five years, she had 'cracked' the alphabetic code. At four and a half years, William began writing his name frequently, and then cutting it out and sticking it on to models he had made. By five and a half years, he had cracked the alphabetic code, and was always asking his mother for just one more episode of a story. He showed no desire to write, except his name, but constantly wanted his mother to write notes as reminders to do things.

Practitioners need to tune in to the child's family literacy

Shirley Brice Heath (1983), amongst others such as Goouch and Lambirth (2007), has stressed the importance of the teacher tuning in to the child's family. What is the family's understanding of and approach to literacy? To bedtime stories?

Denny Taylor (1983: 54) shows us how families 'salute and hurt' each other through print. Seven-year-old Hannah writes her mother a note: 'I'm terribly sorry about the nail varnish remover.' Mother writes to Father, 'You are late. Supper burnt. Serves you right.'

Functional literacy at home

More often than not children are introduced to functional literacy in the home. Gains children make through family literacy programmes are difficult if not impossible to measure reliably until children reach the age of nine or ten years (Hall and Robinson, 2003). Hall and Robinson emphasise the importance of home visits, and how parents appreciate help to support their child's reading at home. It emerges that parents do not naturally or automatically know, simply because they are parents, how children are helped towards literacy (Goouch and Lambirth, 2007). Children learn about the multiplicity of literacy activities as they participate in different actions (for example, birthday cards, shopping lists, bills). In fact, children often engage in writing activities of which the parent is unaware. Scraps of paper that are purposeful and functional might exist all over the house, with phone messages, reminders, stories and so on written on them. The home is where children are introduced to functional literacy. Its importance cannot be over-emphasised. This is supported by the EPPE research (DfES, 2003).

There is a potential problem if those working with young children from outside the family setting, whether in the school setting, the day nursery or during home visits, attempt to tell parents what they should do. This is a partnership on professional terms; an equal partnership demands a reciprocal approach to the relationship (Athey, 1990; Bruce, 2004a).

Children need to see adults 'writing for real'

It is important to give children experiences that build on those of their home life. For instance, a child might have been to the corner shop, the market or the supermarket. Any of these experiences can be added to or taken further. Another consideration is the need for children to imitate. Seeing adults involved in functional writing, for example, at the bank, when making shopping lists with the children or writing notes for the milkman, is important in this respect. Writing needs to be demonstrated in a functional and purposeful way, so that children can select about what they will represent or write. There is an issue developing of children more frequently seeing their family using technology when writing than using a pencil and paper.

Figure 7.7 Technology is now an embedded part of family life and gatherings. Adults often catch up on emails as they chat with their children. These children, however, normally eat a meal with their parents where no technical equipment is used during the meal. This is so that parents and children can communicate with each other during the meal.

Peta, a student, took in plenty of found materials for the three- and four-year-olds in the nursery school. She set the materials out attractively, made herself very available by sitting at the table, and the children flocked to make models. JOHN experimented with glue, covering the box! SEGUN had a plan to make a can; he wanted to 'do writing' on the can of food he made. No two models were the same, and not all were representational. Peta was not imposing her theme of 'shape' on this group of children, although there was plenty of skilful 'shape' talk popped in at appropriate moments, in sensitive ways. Donald Graves might say that Peta was helping the children to find their own voice, rather than to echo the thoughts of the adult, which would be a narrow and passive response, and would soon become boring.

If children are to find their own voice, however, they need a great deal of support and encouragement from adults, since to do this is much harder than copying. If they are to reach satisfaction and a sense of fulfilment, they need to be helped through the inevitable struggles involved in any worthwhile activity. Being there at the right moment to hold the glue pot still, to stretch out the sticky tape for it to be cut by the child, to hear the story the child has woven around the model, to support them in their writing on the model – all these actions by adults are part of encouraging representation and all have implications for early writing. In early writing work, representation is a key factor.

Children need a wealth of first-hand experiences to make learning to write meaningful, and to set it in a functional and purposeful context.

The importance of play scenarios

Representation through writing during play is important in all its facets: in stories, dance, songs, home corners, dolls houses, construction toys, paints, models and drawings. Amongst all this, children can be encouraged to 'write', in the classroom post office, restaurant, hairdresser, bank and so on. 'Real writing' is only the culmination of a long process towards it.

Early pretend play helps children to explore roles and themes, beginnings, endings, transitions – all of which are vital to the writing process. A significant body of research is building practitioner understanding of how to develop pretend play such that it also supports early literacy development. Schrader (1991) emphasises the role of the adult in encouraging and supporting dramatic play. Mandel Morrow and Rand (1991) focus on the necessity of preparing the classroom environment to promote literacy during play. Pellegrini and Galda (1991) demonstrate the longitudinal advantages of play for emergent literacy, as does Rathnarsdottir (2006).

Figure 7.8 The boys are in the outdoor café with the adult. They look at the menu, and they draw on the blackboard, mark making with enthusiasm. They give the practitioner tea, and she gently, without dominating, suggests that she would like to see the menu to make an order. One boy writes the order. The other boy looks at the menu, which the practitioner reads to him. She also helps the boy to write the order. She points at the words on the menu. This brings the act of writing with meaning (functional literacy) to the attention of both boys.

Figure 7.8 *Continued*

She found in a longitudinal Nordic study that many children in the sample appeared to be developing literacy competently until the age of about eight or nine years. They then hit difficulties in their creative writing. Children who had participated actively in pretend play from three years fared better than those who had not. For example, they could move forward and backward in time when writing a story, with appropriate grammar and clause formations to signal the reader about the characters and their narratives. The Helicopter Project by Make Believe, which developed the work of Vivian Gussin Paley, improved the communication and literacy engagement of children, but demonstrated the need for adult support in this process (Cremin, Swann, Flewitt, Faulkner and Kucirkova, 2012). The work of Licketyspit in Scotland directed by Virginia Radcliffe (Knight, 2011) also resonates with this.

The importance of drawings

When a child does four apparently identical drawings, they may be the equivalent of attempts to revise and redraft in the writing process.

Two children, **WILLIAM** and **TOM**, discuss a drawing. Both are four years old. 'Why is its mouth there?' 'It's hungry, silly. That's its tongue, going like that.' Tom sticks out his tongue. They break into laughter.

Frank Smith (1983) believes that, at first, representational work is the child's creation, to be admired but not submitted like a manuscript to be scrutinised and criticised. He is in agreement with Winnicott in this, in believing that the creation belongs to the child. No one else can presume to alter it in any way. Vygotsky says that the willingness to take criticism, to submit a manuscript for the scrutiny of others, emerges from the social relationship formed with the 'interested person', who is invited by the child to share in and work on the creation.

Just as there needs to be a truly reciprocal relationship between parents and professionals, so there needs to be a reciprocal relationship between a child and the adults who will manage to extend development in an educative way. Joan Tamburrini (1982) sees this informal teaching as the strength of early childhood education. Teaching does not have to be direct and formal; indirect teaching is just as powerful, and often more powerful, when working with young children and their families.

Reading

The importance of being read to cannot be over-emphasised

Shirley Brice Heath (1983), Henrietta Dombey (1983), Caroline Fox (1983), Marian Whitehead (2010), to name a few, are in complete agreement about the importance of reading *to* and not *at* young children. Older brothers and sisters also make an important contribution when they do this, as do the partnerships when children in Year 6 read to younger children.

The bedtime story is one important way in which, in a one-to-one situation, an adult can give meaning to a text. Dorothy Butler (1980) stresses that babies appreciate books. This has been taken up with the SureStart 'Books for Babies' initiatives in England. By looking at books in this intimate and individually sensitive way, adults can take up children's initiatives, giving and extending the meaning in them. In this way children begin to meet different worlds, with the adult as translator (Geekie and Raban, 1993; Whitehead, 2010).

Figure 7.9 The children are enjoying a story with the Key Person. This has many of the characteristics of the 'bedtime story' but children also need one-to-one story times.

The importance of song, dance and story in interpreting texts

Children from four to seven years of age watched a puppet show of the story *Handa's Surprise*. This shared experience was important in enabling the children to grasp what is involved in formal book and story language. Pictures, dancers, puppets and songs help children relate to formal book language. It is of central importance that children experience stories of their culture and its roots.

Knowing a story well – the old favourites – helps children to predict when they read. Reading is largely prediction. Children need to understand about syntax semantics and grapho-phonic aspects of texts in order to read. Their own knowledge of language, the way they have 'cracked the language code', will enable them to tackle syntax in a text. Children who are bilingual develop understanding of the way language works because teasing out differences across languages is part of their lived experience. Being aware in this way is called having 'metalinguistic knowledge' (Pafford, 2011, personal communication). Having core texts selected by the staff, and favourite texts that emerge from the children responding to literature from home and other settings, supports prediction through familiar texts.

Listening to stories with a rich variety of texts helps children to learn about words and sentence structures in book language. The interpretations children have about meanings, the way they bring their own experiences to bear, enables this process. The more help they have had in using language with others in a meaningful way, and in understanding book language and its ability to create imaginative ideas in what Margaret Meek calls 'possible worlds', the better.

Phonological awareness

When children learn to read and write, they are on a journey that requires many things to be in place before they learn how to map sounds on to letters. Phonological awareness is about becoming aware of the sounds of the language and being able to hear and manipulate the way that these fall into syllables and rhyming chunks (Bruce and Spratt, 2011).

There are three phonological grain sizes according to Goswami (2007). These are syllables, rhyming chunks and phonemes. The word 'breakfast', for example, has two syllables. An example of a rhyming chunk is 'money' and 'honey'. These can be learnt quite naturally by children across the world, it seems. The third grain is phonemic awareness, and it is about the smallest sounds in the word, e.g. 't-ea'. Research suggests that children develop these three phonological grain sizes in that order. Children do not seem to develop phonemic awareness without direct teaching (Goswami, in Goouch and Lambirth, 2007).

Some languages are phonologically consistent, such as Welsh, Finnish and Italian. Some languages are consistent in the written form; Italian is an example of this. It is therefore no surprise that Maria Montessori chose to teach children to read using synthetic phonics as the central part of her method. This makes sense for Italian-speaking children, as in Italian there is almost a 1:1 correspondence when mapping sounds on to letters.

Syllables

Children enjoy finding the syllables in their own names. Jack has one syllable, but Sarah has two. Clapping hands helps.

Rhyming chunks and families of words

Children find it easier to understand print when there are rhyming chunks. This links with introducing children to families of words.

○ *Going, knowing, sewing, blowing, doing* are all 'ing' words.
○ *Hat, bat, cat, sat* are all 'at' words.

Children vary in the order in which they establish these connections and understandings. This is why it is important to build observations and to assess each child individually. Tuning in to each child's needs is the joy of being an early years practitioner.

Phonemes

These are the smallest sounds in the language. 'C–a–t' has three. Children seem to explore and learn about syllables and rhyming chunks quite naturally, if they are in a supportive environment with people who help them.

They need to be directly taught to understand phonemes, however, but as Bruce and Spratt (2011) emphasise, this does not mean sitting them in large groups to be taught by rote. Singing and dancing traditional rhymes, chants and stories with discussion of the phonemes in context works well. A 14 per cent improvement (compared with a national improvement of 8 per cent) was found in the Communication, Language and Literacy scores at the end of the Reception class (Bruce and Spratt, 2011) following use of a carefully thought-through sequence of finger rhymes, action songs, nursery rhymes and poetry cards.

Mapping sounds on to letters – the alphabetic principle

Poetry cards (Bruce and Spratt, 2011) are invaluable in helping children to move from phonemic awareness to mapping those sounds on to letters. When children sing traditional nursery rhymes and other songs, they begin to hear the differences in the sounds. Adults can support them in this. But 'red' and 'bread' don't look the same when written down in English. It helps children if the first chunks of text have some consistency, and carefully chosen poetry cards can provide this. Marian Whitehead sees these as manageable chunks of text. Bruce and Spratt (2011) have developed a sequence of synthetic phonics learning. This is based on the biological sequence of speech sounds (as advised by speech and language therapists), phonemic awareness through song and traditional rhymes, and poetry cards giving children the support they need in mapping sounds on to letters and a growing understanding of the alphabetic principle. They support alliteration and rhyme, as well as blending and segmenting of sounds.

English is one of the most irregular languages in the world. It is not consistent in the way it sounds or how it is written down. Seeing the word 'read' in isolation is a good example. According to the context, it will sound different, 'Would you like me to read you a story?' or 'Have I already read this to you?' This is why asking children to read English words out of context is of doubtful use. There is no sense in making learning to read more difficult than it needs to be (Bruce and Spratt, 2011), especially with an irregular language like English (Goswami, in Goouch and Lambirth, 2007).

Connecting the text and how it sounds when read out loud – listening posts

Reading stories and then encouraging children to listen to them through headsets while following in the book gives further variety and helps the auditory aspect of reading. These are some of the ways in which children can be helped to move from picture books to reading the text, both at home and in early childhood settings, and later in school. The diverse cultural aspects are, as for learning to write, crucial in learning to read. Children need to connect with texts, and there is now recognition of this in developing simple stories and texts that engage children. Many of these are translated into different languages, so that they are accessible core texts for a diverse range of children, and yet offer a shared narrative. Having shared stories is part of being in a community and feeling that you belong.

Effective reading teachers help beginners to draw on what they know about reading, and to use this in a wide range of strategies. These include semantic, syntactic, grapho-phonic, phonological awareness and bibliographic conventions, such as 'Where on the page do I start?' Taking all this into account, it is no surprise that by the time children reach the stage of 'real' reading and 'real' writing, they are already a considerable way along the route to literacy.

The best early start to literacy

- ○ We need to nurture non-verbal communication with sensitivity, in alignment with spoken or signed language or, even better, languages.
- ○ Children need dance, music, rhythm, rhyme and song, together with poetry and stories with which they can feel connection, become involved, feel included and participate.
- ○ They need to be read to, sung, danced and storied with.
- ○ They need to see their families and those with whom they spend time writing for reasons and purpose. They need to understand the functions of reading and writing in daily life, for information and for pleasure.
- ○ They need to share texts in the intimacy of the bedtime story traditions, very individually and sensitively. They need to discuss stories and what moves them, stirs them, scares them, makes them feel comfortable.
- ○ They need to discuss and explore how texts work, and their mechanics and components in embedded contexts. What is a letter? How does it sound in this context? How does this word work in this sentence? Where do I begin to decode this (break it down)? Where do I begin to encode it (build it up)?
- ○ Communication, spoken and unspoken, must help children to become attuned to self, others, situations and stories, with plenty of talk around issues, otherwise reading and writing will not develop richly. They will develop dutifully, which is not the same. Print-rich environments energise and give children freedom to explore print in ways that turn them into bookworms and keen writers – for life.

Learning how you and other people feel and think

| Thinking about other people

Catching feelings and showing sympathy to someone are important developments. Colwyn Trevarthen (personal communication, 2008) prefers the word 'sympathy' to 'empathy'. Recognising how someone else feels and thinks, and understanding that this may be different from how you feel is the key to developing theory of mind. Sarah-Jane Blakemore (2000: 6) suggests that this recognition does not develop until about the age of four years. Children make the journey from wanting to feeling as they develop pretend play as toddlers. They begin to tease out what is and is not real as they pretend. Three year olds, for example, are beginning have beliefs about whether or not the sweets are in the cupboard. Being able to read how other people feel and think develops out of the ability to know yourself, however, and to recognise and identify how you feel and think (Damasio, 2004; Gerhardt, 2004).

At a few months of age a baby will cry in sympathy with another child, as if recognising that someone is crying. By about 15 months, toddlers will often comfort a brother or sister, friend or a loved adult in the way they would like to be comforted themselves, perhaps with a kiss or by bringing a special toy (Dunn, 1991). This ability to separate from self, at first caring for others as you would like to be cared for (sympathy) and gradually caring for others by recognising that they may have different feelings and thoughts and needs, is crucial for the development of spiritual, social and moral behaviour and well-being. In this chapter these important aspects of human development are given high focus.

Thoughtful feelings

Feelings, Damasio (2004: 28) suggests, are our most private property. Emotions are more public, showing in our body reactions. They are the bedrock of our minds, but they are 'preludes to our feelings'. Both the emotions and our feelings are basic mechanisms of life regulation, but feelings operate at a higher level. Damasio's 'nesting principle' suggests that raw emotions are simpler structures nesting within more complex and thoughtful feelings:

> Emotions are built from simple reactions that easily promote the survival of an organism and this could easily prevail in evolution.
>
> (Damasio, 2004: 30)

Figure 8.1 The clay is hard to roll for a beginner and although the toddler can't yet put this into words, she points to indicate the problem. The practitioner comes to help her. As a result, the little girl stays and focuses on the clay. We concentrate better in life if we feel supported. Well-being helps our thinking to develop and gives the energy to puzzle things out and develop our skills.

Figure 8.2 The toddler has been playing outdoors. He is too hot now that he is indoors. This is noticed by his Key Person, who encourages him to take off his coat. He does as much as he can, trusting and secure that she will help him. He is then comfortable physically and can turn his attention to playing with the train.

Key elements in learning how others feel and think

- Judy Dunn (1988, 1991) and Sue Gerhardt (2004) place great emphasis on the importance of helping children to recognise how they feel and think. Knowing yourself and reading yourself as you go through different experiences and relationships is of central importance.
- Children are helped when they are encouraged to discuss and reflect on situations and events and to identify how they felt or thought, what went wrong and what they might do in a similar situation next time. Interestingly, this approach was central to Froebel's philosophy. The current emphasis in the literature is on supporting children in awareness of their feelings, and encouraging them to express these in relation to others. In the 1980s, however, the emphasis was on metacognition and being aware of your own thinking, an approach that built on Piaget's work on intellectual egocentricity.
- Judy Dunn stresses the importance of learning through and with brothers, sisters and close friends in small groups in home settings. The quarrels and shared good times all contribute to the way children begin to learn how others feel and think. Children need to spend sustained time with the same children, ideally in mixed-age family groups, so that they learn to 'read' each other and tune in to how the others might react, feel and think. Seeing how others react to what people do is a crucial element.
- Children find it easier to recognise the feelings of others than to recognise the way those people think, but only if they are supported in reflecting on and analysing events and situations (see Bruce, 2004a).
- Sue Gerhardt stresses the role of the adult in helping children to identify and name their feelings, tuning in to first the baby and then the young child's constantly changing emotional states. Babies and toddlers need enormous support in moving back to their 'comfort zone' once it has been wobbled or disturbed. This can be done:

> By entering a baby's state with him, engaging him with a loud mirroring voice, gradually leading the way towards calm by toning her voice down and taking him with her to a calmer state.
>
> (Gerhardt, 2004: 23)

- Well-attached babies with parents who are well attuned to them (Stern, 2002) develop empathy for others more easily, having experienced sustained loving care, and developed a strong, embodied sense of self.
- Goleman points out, however, that empathy is not all. Some children can empathise but because they have endured sustained emotional abuse, they 'become hyper-alert to the emotions of those around them, in what amounts

> to a post-traumatic vigilance to cues that have signalled threat' (Goleman, 1996: 103). These children tend to become adults who are emotionally mercurial.
> ○ Good relationships are about constantly seeking balance between tuning in to your own feelings and thoughts, and reading and tuning in to the feelings and thoughts of others. The co-ordination of the two – self and others – is the key.

The girl watches her friend build with the blocks, and is sensitive to her anxiety, keeping a good distance from her construction so as not to crowd her. The boy also respects her space, empathising with her situation.

Thinking of other people often slips when a child is tired, with strangers, hungry, in a bad mood, in the company of those who are uncaring or unkind, or herded in large groups. According to Celia Kitzinger (1997), this is probably the case for adults as well as children.

These issues have significance everywhere in the world, although in some countries the rights of and respect for the individual may assume greater importance than those of the group as a whole, or vice versa. This has led to a debate at international gatherings on the issues surrounding human rights, the problems of market forces and individual greed, or the neglect of the needs of individuals in the cause of the state's needs.

Until recently, it was thought that young children were unable to put themselves into the position of someone else to any great extent. The influence of Jean Piaget's work (1968) led early childhood practitioners to see children younger than five years as 'intellectually egocentric'. In fact what he said resonates with Sarah-Jane Blakemore's developmental sequence, such that children only establish beliefs and theory of mind at around four years of age. This does not mean that younger children are selfish. Practitioners are often trained to become skilled in diverting children, rather than attempting what was considered to be impossible – that is, trying to get the child to look at a situation from another child's point of view. As we saw in the previous section, new research evidence shows things are more complex than Piaget suggested.

Four-year-old **WALLY** had himself been unhappy when settling into school. When he saw that three-year-old Peter was about to cry on his first day, he took Peter by the hand and cuddled him. He knew what it was like to be 'new' and so he could sympathise.

Six-year-old **VICKY** and three-year-old **MARK** were eating ice cream. Vicky dropped hers and cried. Mark offered her some of his. He recognised the 'tragedy', as it seemed to him, of dropping an ice cream, as it had happened to him previously.

Learning from everyday situations

Margaret Donaldson (1978) reminds us that children are able to perform at a higher level in a meaningful context. Piaget's tests presented children with formal tasks that were not in such a context. Margaret Donaldson distinguishes between two types of task:

- Disembedded tasks: abstract tasks not performed in a realistic situation.
- Embedded tasks: those that confront children in everyday, spontaneous events and situations.

The examples of Wally, Mark and Vicky, quoted above, are embedded in meaning and so the children could relate to the situations.

The current practice is to show children sets of disembedded photographs of facial expressions and to ask them about feelings gleaned from the expressions in the photographs. This is the equivalent of using disembedded flashcards with words in isolation from literary texts in order to teach reading. Children respond readily to literature through the meaning and context of words. Words or feelings in isolation from where they belong, in situations and stories and real life, are of little use in helping children to become bookworms or empathetic people in any real and lasting way.

Figure 8.3 Mealtimes create excellent opportunities to encourage children to think of others in meaningful contexts. The Key Person asks one of the boys to fetch more water as none is left in the jug. He does this, and is given warm appreciation for doing so. It is pointed out to him that doing this means that other children can enjoy a drink of water. It helps him to recognise in a practical context the value of communities caring for each other.

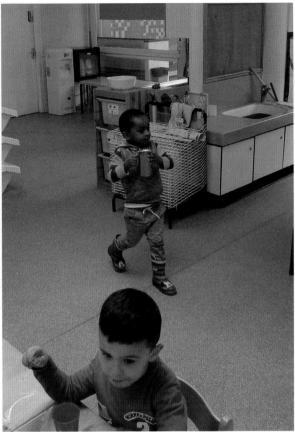

Figure 8.3 *Continued*

Well-being

Moral development, which involves respecting and valuing others, emerges out of situations where children have sufficient sense of their own well-being to feel they can give as well as take what they need in a relationship (Laevers, 1994). Children, or adults, who feel bad about themselves are less likely to be highly developed morally, as they will not so easily be able to move beyond their own needs to respect and value those of other people. Research has shown that giving and contributing to others and the community brings higher well-being than does addressing only self needs and desires (Haidht, 2006).

Children need variety in the ways in which they mix with other children. Children need to work with children both older and younger, and more and less advanced, as well as those operating at the same level. This applies to both partnership and group situations. Partnerships can involve older and younger children, those who are more and less advanced, or children of the same age or stage. The following example shows partnership between two children at different points in their learning.

> Five-year-old **HANNAH** reads each night to three-year-old **WILLIAM**. The books he enjoys are at the level she can read 'approximately', from her knowledge of the story and the picture clues. She is thinking of stories that he enjoys, but she is gaining satisfaction from the giving by using her latest learning in a meaningful setting.

In batting a ball to a partner, or skipping together, each child has to think of the other and get into the right positions, or the game will not be possible.

Figure 8.4 Children give up when they find materials difficult to explore and use. It is important that they are helped by adults in ways that give them the confidence and desire to persevere and succeed, without removing the sense of agency, control and ownership.

What did I do? Why did you react like that?

Judy Dunn shows how children, young though they are, begin sorting out what they are allowed to do. They begin to predict what people would disapprove of. Adults might well disapprove of kicking when you do not get what you want, for example, or a brother or sister might react strongly if you take a toy away. Young children need to explore and to discover what happens when they hurt other people, help other people or show care for other people. Judy Dunn's research suggests that families where quarrels are followed by discussions of what went wrong and how to make things go better next time, help children to tease out moral issues. Even before children can talk she found that they benefit from learning about situations that make them angry, excited or joyous. The cause-and-effect relationship seems to be crucial. Before children can speak they know what makes people angry, and how people might react. It is initially through their relationships within the family that children learn to be caring of those they love.

Identifying different emotions

Knowing about anger, love, jealousy, disgust, pride, humiliation and shame, disappointment, etc., and how to deal with each, is an important contribution to moral development. Goleman (1996) and Gerhardt (2004) suggest that it is also fundamental for emotional health. Once there can be more discussion, this helps reflection and analysis around issues where children are not allowed to do something, share sadness and joy together, or play with other children.

> Six-year-old **JENNY** asked for another pancake but there were none left. She was angry. Her mother reminded her that she had already had two and that there were no more eggs. She said she understood that Jenny felt disappointed, acknowledging her feelings rather than suppressing them. Goleman (1996) and Gerhardt (2004) stress the importance of allowing children to feel how they feel but helping them to deal with their feelings appropriately.

Negotiating with (not manipulating) people

Children in intimate settings, such as the family, learn to negotiate with other people rather than to manipulate them. Negotiation is part of moral development in that it respects other people. The process of manipulation of other people means grabbing for oneself, and indicates low self-esteem and lack of well-being in the child. It is, of course, normal to experience moments like this, but when adults help children to move on from these, moral development grows.

Four-year-olds **ALISTAIR** and **STUART** made a tune out of circles stuck on stave lines on a board. It was a monotone. The teacher sang it for them, and moved away. Stuart changed it so that it went up at the end, but Alistair did not want to change it. He tried to put the note down again, but Stuart grabbed it and ran off. Alistair gave chase; he was furious. Stuart's mother, who was helping in the classroom, said, 'Give him back his tune, Stuart.'

It was suggested by the teacher that Stuart should start another row underneath Alistair's, going up at the end. She then played this on the xylophone, Alistair played his row and Stuart played his. Here the negotiation broke down and the partnership required adult help. Neither child could decentre without help. The adult could have made Stuart apologise to Alistair, but instead she preferred to give the message that it is more satisfying and produces better results to co-operate rather than fight.

Six-year-olds **TOM** and **WILLIAM** were in the garden together. Both were particularly interested in natural science and this had been the basis of their friendship since the age of three. They found a crusader spider and made an assault course for it. They were delighted when it climbed up a pole and along a string they had rigged up. William tried to help it to realise there was another pole for it to climb down. He gently touched it, but the spider bit him. He was interested in this, as there had been discussion in his family for years about whether spiders did bite people. Both boys chatted constantly. 'Let's put a dead fly out for him to eat, then he'll come.' 'No it's got to be in a web.' 'Does he have a web or is he a pouncer?' 'What's a pouncer?' 'He hides and then pounces.' 'Oh!' There was a lot of negotiating.

The knowing–doing gap

It is very unusual for someone to give their life's work over to fighting a cause involving a moral principle. In the main, from adolescence to adulthood, people take on the socially expected conventions of their culture. It is only outstanding people, such as Nelson Mandela, who go beyond convention to take a moral stand. In other words, most people are more influenced by what other people do than they are by their conscience. It is no good therefore to expect children to know right from wrong if they consistently see adults doing wrong. There needs to be a strong link between inner moral values and outer moral conduct. The expression 'Do as I say, not as I do' is important where moral development (or in this case, lack of it) is concerned.

MATTHEW (three and a half years) and his baby sister went with their parents to supper at the house of some friends. He was used to sleeping at other houses and happily went to bed upstairs. His father asked him to call out if the newly born baby started to cry. He agreed. A few minutes later he appeared downstairs crying and saying, 'I don't want to.' His parents did not know what he meant, but it emerged that he did not want to tell the adults if the baby cried. He was happy to sleep upstairs, but did not want to think about the baby.

The parents reassured him and he was asleep in five minutes. His mother said that at home he took pride in telling her when the baby had woken up in order to help her. In this case he was tired and in a different setting, but the adults were sensitive to him.

Four-year-old PETER had a friend to tea and his mother joined them. There were soon only two scones left and Peter assumed that he and his friend would have them. His mother made no comment. Peter was not being helped to think about the problem of three people and only two scones. In a sense, his mother was holding back his social, spiritual and moral development by not raising this.

Good intentions and how others respond to them

Piaget found that children in middle childhood (approximately 8 to 12 years of age) were very concerned with what someone's intention was. If a child broke a cup by mistake when trying to clear the table, a younger child, for example, a five-year-old, would say the helper was 'naughty' because the cup was broken, whereas an older child would understand that the intention had been to help and that breaking the cup was an accident.

In the early childhood years, it is therefore important that adults help children to tease out the importance of 'intention' as well as 'outcome'. This erodes the expression 'the end justifies the means'.

HAYLEY (six years old) went to fetch the pudding from the fridge to help her mother. She spilt custard in the fridge and left a trail of custard across the floor, and spilt it on her shoes and clothes. Stacey (three and a half years) said, 'You're naughty. You made a mess.' Stacey does not yet see that intention matters as much as outcome. Their mother said, 'Hayley was trying to help. She didn't mean to spill the custard.' Motive is as important as results, and motives involve feelings as much as ideas. Hayley's mother tried to keep alive her feeling of helpfulness by emphasising it, rather than the mess. Undermining a desire to help damages a child's long-term moral and social development.

Never call a child naughty – it widens the knowing–doing gap

It is probably best for adults never to call a child 'naughty'. Almost every juvenile delinquent has very low self-esteem. Feeling bad about yourself holds back social, emotional, spiritual and moral development, which are all closely interwoven.

> Seven-year-old **ANTHONY** purposefully scratched a mark on a wooden table. The practitioner told him that he must not spoil the table in that way. He was crestfallen. So that he did not feel that she had rejected him, but only what he had done, she praised him when he picked a toy up that might have got crushed on the floor. She was firmly operating on the principle that there should be respect for property in the classroom in a meaningful context for Anthony. The practitioner pointed out that she had cared about the table being spoilt and she was glad that he cared about the toy being crushed. In this way she linked the two events.

Erikson (1963), through his eight stages of development, emphasised that through a basic sense of trust in the first year, self-esteem emerges in the second. If toddlers are constantly told that they are naughty, this soon withers.

The quality of early relationships is important.

> ○ Intention needs plenty of discussion. Words such as 'meant to' and 'accidentally', 'on purpose' and 'mistake', would be part of the discussion.
> ○ Being sorry about what has happened involves looking at a situation from another point of view, someone else's point of view. A child who can do this can be helped to try and make the situation better.

By helping to clear up the spilt custard (page 157) some four-year-olds can think in the empathetic way that leads to this kind of respect and sensitivity towards others. Hayley is not being blamed or made to feel guilt-ridden or ashamed. She feels sorry this happened, can see why it is upsetting to others but knows that her mother realises that it was unintentional and is doing what she can to make it better. Hayley's sense of well-being is not undermined. When a child intends 'wrong', for example, by spilling custard on purpose, there can be discussion about it. 'I am sorry you did that. I don't like it when you make a mess on purpose.' In other words the adult is not rejecting the child, but only what he or she did. The message is not:

> ○ You are bad.
> ○ I don't like you anymore.
> ○ You are naughty.

The message instead is:

- ○ I don't like what you did.
- ○ But you did try to clear it up.
- ○ I still love you, unconditionally, whatever you do.

Resonances between toddlers and teenagers

There are strong links between the early childhood years and the teenage years. Parents and adults with teenagers often reap the results of how they tackled moral development in the early years. Children brought up in the early years to explore the following areas are not so likely to become delinquent teenagers:

- ○ Intention when things go wrong.
- ○ Empathising with how it feels to someone else when you do something that makes things go wrong.
- ○ Seeing the consequences of your actions.
- ○ Understanding cause-and-effect relationships of events and actions.
- ○ How systems develop that are just and fair and that can be enforced – this means discussing rules, whether or not there is any flexibility in the rules.
- ○ How to make sure those in authority are just and fair in the spirit in which they operate the system of justice.

Young children are dependent on parents, carers, teachers, friends of the family and older children to be fair in the way with which they are dealt. Adolescents and adults participate in the whole social justice system in their society and how it relates to their culture, for example, to issues such as the importance of policing by consent.

Judge Tumin (*Sunday Times* Lecture Series, 1994) said that one of the features of young offenders in his then role as Chief Inspector of Prisons was that they had little understanding of the difference between formal and informal situations and formal and informal behaviour. They tended to tell him personal details when he was a complete stranger to them and not a friend in whom to confide. Roberts (2002) reports the importance of children learning to recognise the difference between informal behaviour at home and going out, and more formal behaviour in their family lives.

At three years of age, **HANNAH**'s mother explained the family was going to meet someone from Daddy's work, and it would be important to be on best behaviour. Hannah's response was, 'No one say bloody.'

Figure 8.5 Stevie, in her Treasure Basket session, selects the cheese box and places her favourite metal ball inside it. She watches intently as it rolls round in the box. She rips it out and puts the round raffia mat into the box, with concentration. She consistently chooses round flat objects or spheres from the Treasure Basket. She likes the Maori pawpaw ball on the string, Froebel's first Gift (the soft sphere on a string), the check-patterned metal jam jar lid, the brown plastic coffee jar lid. She concentrates for 45 minutes, exploring these selections she has made, and sometimes putting them back in the Treasure Basket, sometimes not.

Adults who focus on positive role modelling, set clear boundaries, engage in positive negotiation and conflict resolution with plenty of discussion, and demonstrate listening, talking and warm concern, are more likely to encourage moral and social behaviour in young children. This will also have a forward influence into adolescence and adulthood.

Knowing who you are and who you want to be

From an early age, children begin to tease out that what is appropriate behaviour in one cultural setting is not in another. For some children, the difference between school culture and home culture is slight, for others it is huge. This is important because the 'fitting in' is part of social and moral development. It partly involves being able to be sensitive to those you are with, but it also involves remaining who you are in different situations. Being swayed away from what you normally do shows a weak sense of self-embodiment. Below, Nikolai is being helped to develop a strong sense of who he wants to be.

> Six-year-old **NIKOLAI**'s mother thanked him for thinking of her by offering her one of his sweets. She praised his kindness but did not take one, thereby encouraging him to take such a risk again!

The damage done through herding children in large groups

Some adults demand too much from young children in this respect, for example, making them sit for long periods in school assembly at three and four years of age. This is inappropriate, and likely in the long run to put children off trying to fit in with the system, and so ironically to damage their moral development. Young children are often accused of naughtiness during assemblies. In this case naughtiness is simply not doing what an adult wants. Young children are unlikely to be clear about the difference between naughtiness that inconveniences the system and the naughtiness of hitting someone or stealing. For the young child in assembly, naughtiness becomes that which adults do not like. The crucial dialogue, central to moral development and good behaviour in the long term, is missing. Without adult help, children cannot sort out the interplay between intention, motive, outcome and consequence.

When adults and atmospheres in settings are insensitive to children, children are insensitive to others

If the system is utterly insensitive to the child, we cannot expect the child to be sensitive to the system. The system is not, in this case, making appropriate demands on the child. It is also important to bear in mind that a child who can ask such questions as 'Why must we sit so long, it is boring' is actually thinking about the social conventions of life (in this case the inappropriateness of putting Nursery and Reception children into assembly).

In the days of Nazi Germany, or during apartheid in South Africa, it took great courage to question the social conventions of these regimes. The 'fitting in' aspect of moral development must be seen side by side with the development of the child's conscience. It was the voices of individual conscience that led to the abolition of slavery and of apartheid, not the voices of those who 'fitted in'. The four year old who questions being made to sit still for long periods of time, such as in assembly, does not yet realise the enormity of the challenge he or she is making to social convention, but that does not mean the child is wrong to challenge what many early childhood educators regard as a form of child abuse. Sally Goddard Blythe's work (2004) has led her to the view that sitting still is one of the most challenging things we can ask of a young brain. It requires enormous co-ordination physically. There needs to be a balance between encouraging children to question, explore and develop a conscience, over and above conforming to the socio-cultural conventions in which they live. It is important that adults do not let young children down by ignoring the questions they ask about these things, which help them to think about what is socially appropriate and morally right (Lancaster, 2003).

> Three-year-old **AMANDIP** is beginning to use English in school. He is enjoying the fact that he can express himself in Punjabi and English. He chatters throughout group time and requests songs and sings them solo, because he cannot wait for the group. He wants to answer all the questions the teacher puts to the group of children. He is irrepressible. His teacher does not stop him – she encourages him, bringing in other children's contributions around his. She recognises his 'explosion' in English, but she does gently insist that the group finishes one song before he suggests another.

Research (Kitzinger, 1997: 16) indicates that, in a group, most people become passive and the 'bystander effect' operates. This means that if, for example, someone is attacked in front of a group, often no one does anything. It takes leadership to step out of being in a group and to call the police. This has serious implications for young children.

If children are herded about in large groups for large parts of their day (as they often are in large Reception classes), the 'bystander effect' is encouraged and moral behaviour discouraged. Children in smaller, intimate, quality early childhood settings are more likely to respond to situations as individuals and to learn to empathise and show care.

Helping social, emotional, spiritual and moral development

- ○ Social, emotional, spiritual and moral development is helped when children are treated sensitively by adults.
- ○ It is also helped when there is plenty of discussion and negotiation in the family and in early years settings.
- ○ Children need to feel closeness, trust and understanding with adults, who explain things to them and help them to express their thoughts and feelings about issues and events.
- ○ Children help each other through the quarrels they have and the negotiating and discussing they do.
- ○ Free-flow play (Bruce, 1991) encourages children to see things from other people's points of view as they move into and out of different roles and imaginary situations.
- ○ Giving rewards for good behaviour undermines long-term moral and social development (Kohn, 1993).

How adults can help social, emotional, spiritual and moral development in the young child

Parents and practitioners working together in partnership

In the children's centre, the practitioner was doing a project on flowers. She had an interest table full of them, with some that children could take apart and look at under magnifying glasses. Three-year-old **MELISSA** enjoyed putting things inside others (a topological, spatial schema in Piaget's theory). She homed in on this interest table, and began putting flowers into vases with gusto. At home time the early years worker explained this interest to her mother and asked her if she would like to take the pot of flowers home to follow up the school work. Melissa's mother had problems in getting her to come to the table at meal times because she always wanted to bring her toys with her. She found that by asking Melissa to put some flowers (even weeds from the garden) in a vase on the table she could overcome this problem. Delighted, she told the practitioner about this the next day. This marked a turning point for Melissa, who began to help her mother prepare the table for meals at home and then sat down readily.

The difference between social and moral rules

Turiel and Weston (1983) demonstrated that by the age of five years children can distinguish between different types of rules. Moral rules (e.g. 'it is wrong to hit') were regarded as unchangeable. Social rules (e.g. 'you must tidy the room before going out') could be changed.

The importance of play with other children

Group situations with peers, whether more and less advanced or at the same stage, are important during early childhood. Group play involves children in giving up their immediate wishes in order that the play can continue successfully. Vygotsky (1978) sees this as an important attribute.

A shoe shop had been set up in the classroom. The family of four-year-old **NEELAN** owns a shop. She wanted the early years worker to pretend to be the shopkeeper; the practitioner quickly assumed that role. She took younger children, three-year-olds **SHAZIA** and **TOTO**, as customers. Certainly she dominated the play, but she was inducting them into what imaginative play is about. They willingly stayed, but could have left at any time. Toto and Shazia needed Neelan to show them how to play 'pretend games', how to take roles and become other people, how to decentre and see other viewpoints.

ANNA MARIA is another typical three-year-old. The practitioner was working with a group of children on the large wooden blocks. Two girls and two boys were sitting on them as a table and chairs. Four-year-old **TRACY** brought a small wooden block and said, 'Would you like a tin of beans?' and laughed. The teacher said, 'I'd love some – but I need to open the tin.' She pretended to do this to a rapt audience. Then she asked for a saucepan in which to heat the beans. **SADE** found a flatter cylinder (a thoroughly appropriate representation of a saucepan). The teacher pretended to pour in the beans and stir. Then she asked for some plates. The children found more blocks and the teacher made toast using rectangular shapes. At this point Anna Maria came in and watched the activity. She came up to the teacher and said triumphantly, 'You're only pretending, you know.' She did not want to join in; she only wanted to watch the game.

Young children need to see high level imaginative play before being helped into it. This has implications for later work in school. Getting on the inside of roles and themes in imaginative play requires the child to go beyond 'self' and to 'become' other people in other situations in a meaningful context. Becoming someone else, acting out a role and a theme, requires considerable tuning in to self and others, reading situations and co-ordinating different points of view and feelings. The spontaneous scripts that develop during imaginative play are the stuff of later story-writing. This form of play encourages the embryonic sense of audience that will flower later on.

Seven-year-old **HANNAH**, three-year-old **KIT** and five-year-olds **MATTHEW** and **WILLIAM** decided to play King Arthur. Only Hannah and William knew the story and the game quickly disintegrated. All the children knew the story of Robin Hood.

Hannah suggested that they play this instead and she co-ordinated the story. There was a lot of discussion: 'You say "I am hurt" and I say "Get up",' and so on. The script was agreed and carried out in action. All dressed up in clothes from the dressing-up box, with swords. Kit (the youngest) followed. He made mistakes, went to the wrong place, killed the 'wrong' person and the other children (mainly Hannah) alerted him to what was needed. Interestingly, in games of mixed ages or large groups of children, there often seems to be a great deal of rushing about and follow-my-leader activity. Younger children need the stimulation and leadership of more advanced children. Older children need to lead and organise complicated games, with younger children as willing participants.

Hannah, if the game is to succeed, needs to help Kit by trying to see his difficulties. She needs to keep William and Matthew happy about Kit's 'errors', and to negotiate, smooth situations over and make acceptable suggestions. Maid Marion, she pointed out, when Matthew made a bid to become leader of the game, is as good at shooting arrows as Robin Hood. Matthew was Robin Hood. He insisted that he was a better archer. William supported Hannah. 'It's in the book,' he declared. Hannah got around this by suggesting that they all surround the Sheriff of Nottingham (a bush in the garden), but do not kill him. Group play, like partnership play, is important in helping children to develop the ability to empathise and develop theory of mind. In these ways children begin to put themselves into other people's feelings and thoughts, whilst remaining themselves.

The long-term undermining effect of extrinsic rewards

Extrinsic rewards for good behaviour are only effective in the short term, and according to Kohn (1993) may well inflict long-term damage to moral and social behaviour. He suggests that:

- ○ Rewards punish because they control us. Feeling controlled by others damages autonomous learning (principles 4 and 5, see page 20).
- ○ Rewards damage a sense of collaboration and teamwork, or community. They are divisive because they set children against each other as rivals.
- ○ Rewards mask problems and ignore the reasons why children or adults behave as they do.
- ○ Rewards discourage risk taking because they assume children are naturally lazy rather than naturally adventurous and creative.
- ○ Rewards damage genuine interest by implying that it is not worth being good for its own sake. Rewards undermine intrinsic motivation.

Being controlled by extrinsic rewards does not lead to fulfilment and well-being. Being controlled by the rewards others in positions of power give for hard work is not empowering. It creates dependency on and the need to please those who hold power. It means competing with peers in order to gain prizes, so that a ruthlessness towards others easily develops.

It is sometimes argued that we need to reward ourselves with treats when a task is completed in order to motivate ourselves. But completion of the task is in itself the reward. Nelson Mandela did not develop the groundbreaking Council of Reconciliation because he was told he would be rewarded with a prize if he did so. He did not give himself a prize, either. He did the work because he believed it is better to encourage those who have committed atrocities to reflect on what they have done and to truly see the consequence of their actions, and for those who have suffered to see that punishment as an attempt to reform wrongdoers is a better way forward than using punishment as revenge. The Nobel Prize for Peace that was awarded to Mandela was entirely different from a reward used to goad someone into a required action. This was an acknowledgement of the deep contribution his influence has had in developing a peace-making process that is ethically framed.

Perhaps the last word should go to six-year-old Maisie. The head teacher came into the classroom and said to a group of children engaged in a mathematical calculation, 'If you can give the right answer, I will give you a star.' Maisie said, 'I will give you the answer, but I don't need the star.' The reward, as Maisie knows, is getting the right answer. That is satisfying, inwardly. Maisie is intrinsically motivated. She works hard for her own feeling of fulfilment. She is not extrinsically motivated, always doing things to please others or to have proof of her success in a reward form. She has no need for a star chart for herself, or for her class. It is concerning that extrinsic motivation seems to be widespread in its application in current practice. It prevents the development of intrinsic motivation where it is not in place, and undermines it where it exists.

Moral development is helped when children's self-esteem is not undermined by being told they are naughty or bad. Rejecting what they have done, but valuing, respecting and loving them unconditionally helps children to discuss the results of their actions and how these make other people feel (Dunn, 1988).

Moral development is concerned with:

○ moral values
○ moral behaviour.

Children who are supported and helped to reflect on their feelings, ideas and relationships develop a strong sense of embodied self and well-being. This developing self-awareness takes place as they relate to others, especially those with whom they develop close and intimate relationships. Being helped to read and tune in to the feelings and thoughts of others leads to empathy and theory of mind, and the understanding that others feel and think differently because they are individuals who are unique. The spiritual development of children is about the way they relate to self, others and the universe.

Summary – learning how you and others feel and think

Even babies and toddlers recognise and imitate the feelings of other people. Real empathy and being able to put yourself in someone else's shoes comes from toddler times onwards, so that children:

○ develop a conscience (moral values that are not just about obeying what adults and authority Figures say is right and good)
○ learn how to make and change rules (laws), and to see why they are needed
○ behave thoughtfully, influenced by their inner values more than by external rewards.

Knowing right from wrong means:

○ judging someone's intention
○ recognising how much children know and understand
○ seeing the consequences of actions and words.

People who matter to children

9

Bronfenbrenner developed what is now known as a bio-ecological systems theory (Ryan, 2010), which proposes that a child's development occurs within a system of relationships. Its emphasis is on the context of the complex network of relationships of people and institutions in which the child grows up (Conkbayir and Pascal, 2014). The significant others in a child's life are their immediate family/carers and friends, and the professional workers in statutory and voluntary agencies with whom the family/carer has contact. Relationships with peers are explored in this chapter, because they are of central importance for children as they grow up. Children relating to other children is a theme that pervades this book. It is at the heart of the Froebelian approach to education.

Other children

In Chapter 8, the importance of the relationships that children develop with siblings and close friends was emphasised. In Chapter 3 the role of the Key Person, and the triangle of trust between the practitioner, the parent and the child, was highlighted. Throughout the book there have been examples of children relating to each other, and this is further explored in this chapter.

Groups

Zick Rubin (1983) suggests that there are four skills that children need to develop in getting on with other children. These are:

1 To be able to gain entry into a group.
2 To be approving and supportive of one's peers.
3 To manage conflicts appropriately.
4 To exercise sensitivity and tact.

The examples that follow show Rubin's four strategies in action.

Figure 9.1 Young children often need help in playing as a group, or gaining access to a group playing together. One boy wants to play in the sand with the dinosaurs and the teacher supports him in this, with a typical theme of two dinosaurs fighting. Other children arrive, and the teacher helps the boy with the dinosaurs into the larger group. The children find their focus and play alongside each other most of the time, but with moments of co-operation, often as pairs.

In a nursery school, a group of children was playing pirates. The pirate ship was a scrambling net on a prism-shaped climbing frame. The game involved climbing the 'rigging' and, when another ship was spotted from afar, rushing out and capturing treasure from it, and returning with the booty. The enemy ship would be an agreed place where there was a pile of leaves. The leaves were then brought back as booty.

The children were predominately four years of age. Four-year-old **JAMES** was the pirate leader. Three-year-old **ALICE** wanted to join in. She watched from a distance, walking round the edge of the playground.

She approached and stood hopefully at the foot of the climbing frame/pirate ship. She was ignored. She began to climb the net with the others, smiling at her success. As James shouted, 'Ahoy there – a ship. Let's go!' and scrambled down, hotly pursued by the others shouting 'Let's go!', Alice imitated them. She had been watching for long enough to know that she needed to pick up leaves from the pile. She had successfully joined the game.

William Corsaro's sustained and important ethnographic work (1997) suggests that Alice's tactics were typical of successful 'access strategies' for entering into the game. She encircled the game, made careful 'verbal overtures', joined in with the other children's 'Let's go!', did similar things to them, and so was not rejected.

Four-year-old **MATHILDE** wanted to join a group of children in the home corner. She tried to walk in through the door, saying, 'Can I play?' 'No,' shouted the other children in chorus, and shut the door on her. She had not had the opportunity to encircle, and her opening conversation invited rejection.

Corsaro's (1979) work suggests that children need to use 'similar behaviour' in order to be accepted. Mathilde could not see what was behind the door, so she was not in a position to engage in similar behaviour in her actions, or to back this up with remarks such as, 'We're moving the furniture, aren't we?' William Corsaro calls this kind of remark 'reference to affiliation'.

Group play offers children the opportunity to see things from other people's points of view. It also offers the child possibilities to experiment with relating to others in a safe way. When children first begin to attend early childhood settings, however, they appreciate small group times with their Key Person, perhaps sharing a story together and using props so that each child participates. This also provides experiences of rehearsal for free-flow group play (see Chapter 4).

Further examples of group play were given in Chapter 6. Adults often find it difficult to justify large groups as educationally worthwhile. Some children

Figure 9.2 Being in a small group with the Key Person and sharing a story is a helpful precursor to the challenges of group play scenarios together. The skills identified as necessary by Rubin are present here as well as in the group play. Each helps the other along (Nicopoulos, 2007).

tend to be involved in this sort of activity almost to the exclusion of any other if given the choice. In the examples in this chapter, and in other chapters of this book, it emerges that group play is an important but undervalued aspect of what early childhood practice can offer. Adults need to develop skills in encouraging and promoting this.

Four-year-old **GAVIN** started to put large wooden bricks round the edge of the room. Other children copied. Adults intervened when quarrels broke out, or if equipment that other children were using needed to be moved. Soon there was an enclosure of bricks round the whole room. Children began to move around on them as if they were stepping stones. About 15 children had become involved in this joint activity. Adults had taken a supportive role, letting children watch until they were 'ready' to join in and altering the physical environment in discussion with the children.

Group times, when children come together for stories, music, singing, dancing or physical education, are naturally more adult-led than child-initiated. These can be difficult times for a considerable proportion of children, particularly in the earliest

Figure 9.3 One of the first ways in which children join groups beyond their family circle is when they, with their family or childminder, widen the circle by attending something like a 'Play and Stay' session or a 'Drop In' group. Here children begin to meet other children, but their parent or childminder stays near them or with them so that they feel secure.

years. So far as this chapter is concerned, it is sufficient to say that sitting with a friend often helps children to settle in to a group time more easily. The comfort of sitting with a friend – or family member or childminder – is a powerful support.

Partnerships

LINDSEY and BARBARA, two three-year-olds, are playing horses together. Lindsey puts a long belt around Barbara's waist and 'leads' her. She rehearses what she is going to say so that Barbara is in on the script.

'I say, "Whoa there!", don't I, and you go, "Neigh", don't you, and then I pat you and I give you some hay, don't I, and you bend down like this, and you eat it, don't you?'

Then they act out the scene. This helps the children to plan their story in advance, to be clear about the theme and their roles in it. It is interesting to note that at this time, both Lindsey and Barbara were showing interest in things that could be made to encircle. The belt surrounds Barbara's waist. Early friendships are said to be fleeting; one possibility is that they may be based on shared interests and that when these change, the friendship loses its base. After all, the basis of any friendship lies in having shared interests.

It is also interesting that this play scenario was based on a shared experience. The group had been taken to see the police stables, and had been shown the harnesses. The play centred primarily around harnessing and unharnessing a horse. Shared interests and experiences are fundamental aspects of early partnerships.

Six-year-olds Dominic and Michael had both seen a fight on the television. They were acting out a shared secondary experience with a lot of 'stop–go' in this game: careful play punching, holding at gun-point, kicking to the ground. No one gets hurt. This is the sort of play that adults find difficult to allow (Holland, 2010). This kind of play, when indulged in by girls, tends to be firmly squashed. In fact, the skill that lies in not hurting each other, the refinement and variety of movement, the planning together, rehearsing and carrying out of the plan, is not unlike the processes of draft, revise, redraft, refine involved in story-writing. It is important to recognise the sophistication that may have developed. The kind of play that Michael and Dominic were involved in was not simply rumbustious. It was helping the children to develop on a variety of levels.

There is a range of people who are significant in one way or another to the development of a young child. In particular, family members, professional workers and other children the child meets regularly all become important for that child in a direct way. In this chapter, the impact of the family, professional workers and other children is discussed in turn, with particular reference to the role of the early childhood practitioner.

Figure 9.4 Cecilia and Stevie are playing together. Cecilia rolls over, while Stevie watches and explores a beaker. Once Cecilia has completed her roll, Stevie raises her arms in celebration, and Cecilia raises her arms in response. They move in synchrony, crawling together, tuning in to each other's movements with obvious satisfaction. Stevie affectionately touches Cecilia's head before they set off together.

Family and carers

Gillian Pugh and Erica De'Ath (1984: 169) state:

> The great majority of parents are concerned to do their best for their children, even if they are not always sure what this might be.

More recent research suggests that parents/carers are not clear about what quality provision involves (Bennett, 2004), and that they rely on the recommendations of friends or the view of official experts in making choices (Ofsted). Every family is different, and has different needs. The key to partnership with parents lies in having a network of strategies that can be employed so that different approaches are used with different families, approaches that support and build on the families rather than undermining what the parents/carers do. Some families do not wish to or cannot come into school often. Some families enjoy being in school, or an early years setting, but in the parents' room. Others prefer to be visited at home. Others want workshops, meetings, films, talks in the evenings or at weekends, after school, often provided that there is a crèche. Others will make equipment, raise funds, come to social functions but do not want further contact. Some parents actively seek help in child-rearing and in the education of their children, others do not.

The early years worker's role is to build a partnership with every parent. Clearly, it is easier to do this with some parents than with others. Situations involving suspected child abuse, whether physical, mental or sexual, are the most difficult and, where these exist, the staff need to work with other professionals as much as with the parents.

The tendency of professionals to undermine any parent's self-confidence with their 'expertise', and the isolation felt by many while bringing up young children, however, contribute to the difficulties experienced by many parents/carers.

Most parents are not interested in children in general. Their main concern is with their own child and the child's friends. They are not teachers, nor do they wish to be. Practitioners and parents do not bring the same qualities to the partnership. Their roles are complementary, and should not be seen as threatening to each other.

The parent/carer is highly emotionally linked to the child, and prepared to go to 'unreasonable lengths' for the child, as shown by Elizabeth Newson's study (1972; cited in Kellmer Pringle, 1980: 37).

Parents want their children to be happy in school or in any kind of early childhood group care setting, or with a childminder in a home learning environment. So do early childhood practitioners. The Key Person is a crucial role, and has an official place in the different early childhood education framework curriculum documents of each of the UK countries.

Figure 9.5 The mothers are enjoying a chat together. Their children are well settled in the nursery school, and enjoy finding their pegs, and then self-registering. When their children need them, the mothers are available and give full attention. Parents know they are welcome in the school, and they respond positively to the atmosphere created by the staff in making them feel comfortable.

The Key Person

For a more detailed understanding of the role of the Key Person it is important to read Chapter 3. The Key Person is an important part of the staff of any group setting, and the younger the child, the more this is so. The aims and concerns of parents and practitioners in fact coincide in important areas. Practitioners who look below the surface of what parents/carers are saying can find a shared basis for work on which trust can be built. But they need to share what they know about child development and curriculum provision, rather than guarding their knowledge. When parents/carers and practitioners build their observations of children together, and use them to inform the next steps in planning for the child's learning, the impact is deep.

The Froebel Nursery Research Project emphasised parent–staff partnership (Athey, 1990) and found that different parents liked to work with staff in different ways, with different parenting styles. It was important therefore that the teacher tuned in to the particular needs of individual families. There is no one way to work with parents.

The following examples show how staff can work with a wide variety of parents, as described below.

○ Parents who recognise or try to extend the learning of their child.
○ Parents who are eager to work with staff in early childhood settings in ways that do not fit in with the teacher's methods.
○ Parents who are bodily in the early childhood setting, but not active in the classroom.
○ Parents whose main contact with the setting is bringing and fetching children, and perhaps attending parents' evenings.
○ Parents who do not bring children to the early childhood setting, nor seek contact with the staff.

Parents who recognise or try to extend the learning of their child

Three-year-old **SHANAZ**'s father was a bus driver. He wanted to be with his children as much as possible, and managed to arrange his shift work accordingly. He brought Shanaz to the early childhood setting whenever he could and normally stayed for half an hour. (He brought his younger child, a toddler, with him, too.) He wanted to know the purpose of each activity. He took great pleasure in watching Shanaz in the nursery once he realised that water play and other messy activities could be used to teach her mathematical language (for example, 'out of the water', 'in the water', 'high', 'low', 'long way', and so on). He used these terms with relish as she played. He was 'teaching' his daughter mathematics. His enthusiasm was invigorating for the staff, who found him a positive adult to welcome into the school. His basic trust of the teacher's knowledge made it easier for the school staff to work with him.

Parents who are eager to work with staff in early childhood settings in ways that do not fit in with the teacher's methods

It is not for practitioners to tell families how to bring up their children, nor to insist that learning must be approached in one way. Just as staff need to establish a child's intentions and build on them in worthwhile ways, so they need to find out what parents think quality learning is, before they can begin a successful partnership with parents/carers.

All too often the parents/carers are asked to listen to the staff's view, but not the reverse. Parents/carers need to know what staff are trying to do, but staff need to know what parents/carers consider to be important. This is the basis of mutual respect – respect for each other's expertise, respect for each other's commitment to a particular child, respect for the different skills and strengths each brings to a complementary partnership. Two examples follow that show how the practitioner can use his or her skills to encourage appropriate parental involvement.

Five-year-old **BETTY**'s mother liked to work in the early childhood setting. She was eager to 'teach' an activity. The practitioner suggested that she help the children to make dough and use it. She wanted Betty's mother to see her do this activity with the children before she had a group on her own. Betty's mother could not resist joining in while the practitioner worked with the group. The practitioner asked an open-ended question: 'I wonder what we do first?' Betty's mother instantly swooped in: 'We need a bowl, spoon, flour.' She began transmitting the knowledge. This was how she saw the role of the 'teacher', not asking obtuse questions that did not get to the point. The practitioner suggested that Betty's mother should all the time check what children learned by asking them questions about what they were doing. Betty's mother accepted this and acted on it, as it was part of her view of learning – teach the knowledge, then test the knowledge. Over a period of a year Betty's mother and the practitioner began to discuss the importance of getting children to anticipate what will happen, to plan what will happen, to organise equipment they will need. Initially, the practitioner built on the parent's view of a teacher's role and so did not undermine her confidence and did not reject her views.

Some parents experience difficulty in leaving their child in school. They are sometimes unfairly referred to as clinging or over-protective. They are often parents who enjoy a very close relationship with their children, and are very sensitive to their child's feelings and deeply concerned about their child's education.

When four-year-old **STEPHANIE** made a preliminary visit to the Reception class, prior to beginning school, her mother instantly settled down to work with her and the group of children at the construction toy table. She talked to each child about what he or she was doing, and skilfully involved Stephanie in contributing, and in talking to the child next to her. So far, so good. When Stephanie began to attend regularly at school, her mother wanted to stay until she was 'settled'. The

▷

teacher suggested, on the second day, that her mother should take a short coffee break in the staff room. Stephanie cried; Mother would not leave her.

The next day, Stephanie began to cling to her mother all the time, anticipating that she would try to leave to have coffee. Mother reassured her, insisting that she would not leave her at all. Stephanie wanted to keep her mother very close to her, and stopped attempting to relate to the other children. By the end of the week, the pattern was set. Stephanie would not become involved in activities. Neither could her mother become involved, because Stephanie thwarted any attempt she made to work with groups of children. Stephanie's mother was upset. She felt that she had done all the 'right things', and yet her child would not let her go at all. Her 'good' mothering was being punished instead of rewarded. She needed the teacher to help her, as someone who was not involved in this 'eyeball-to-eyeball' situation.

The teacher could not discuss anything with the mother since Stephanie clung to her, so she asked her to phone from home. The teacher then discussed strategies, telling her that this was a not uncommon experience for very good, sensitive, devoted parents. Of course, Stephanie did not want such a treasured person to leave. She suggested that Stephanie's mother and the school take a united approach, and insist that she left for 15 minutes immediately on school arrival, warning Stephanie that this would happen. In this way, Stephanie did not have the worry of anticipating her mother's going until coffee time. They would gradually increase the time out, agreeing its length in discussion together. Once Stephanie was settled, her mother would be able to come into school and work with the children, say once a week, since she wanted to be involved in the classroom. At this stage, it would be too complicated for Stephanie to grasp that pattern. They needed to wait until she was established. In this way, the teacher reassured the mother that she could be trusted with her child, and would be sensitive towards her. She made it clear that she thought highly of her parenting, understood her child's behaviour and wanted to welcome her to the classroom in principle, but the timing of this had to revolve around what would be appropriate for Stephanie. Stephanie's mother relaxed. So did Stephanie, who settled into school happily during that term. The next term, her mother came regularly to school to help with cooking, reading, model-making and so on.

Parents who are bodily in the early childhood setting, but not active in the classroom

Some parents, if encouraged, will linger after bringing their child to the setting but will resist greater involvement. The early childhood practitioner needs to develop strategies for encouraging the parents' interest in their children to develop into active expression.

Three-year-old **KHALIQ**'s mother regularly brought him to the early years setting, and went immediately to the book corner, where she was friendly, but did not seek contact with the practitioner while her child settled into the group. Khaliq's mother was in the setting regularly, but as yet there was no partnership with the practitioner. Each week there was cookery, and the practitioner asked her if she would make chapattis with the children. She said her English was not good enough, but the teacher encouraged her to speak in Urdu. She enjoyed the cookery session, and stayed on for the end-of-the-morning singing, sitting with the practitioner and children. She liked the songs, which included 'Humpty Dumpty'. The practitioner explained that the song was to help the children use mathematical language ('up' and 'down'), and that the next day she would do 'The Grand Old Duke of York'. She invited the mother to join the session. Mother was delighted, and was heard saying 'up' and 'down' to Khaliq as they went out.

The next step was to encourage the mother to watch her child with the practitioner. Khaliq was observed putting a pile of bricks into the classroom 'telephone kiosk' one by one, and then, once a pile had formed, picking each one up and throwing it into a large cardboard box outside the kiosk. He did this for some time. He was transporting, and placing objects in containers. The member of staff asked if he did anything like this at home. He had put a pile of dried chick peas into a saucepan from a colander, but his mother could not explain this in English. She demonstrated with equipment in the home corner, and the following day brought in chick peas and demonstrated again. Meanwhile, the staff had organised a paint-mixing activity with Khaliq in mind. This involved putting powder paint into pots and adding water. Khaliq did this for half an hour.

His mother was beginning to see how reporting his home activities to the practitioner was important, as the staff used this information in their lesson planning. She began to see that activities were planned, and that mess was necessary and could lead to science. The 'mixtures' were an early chemistry lesson, the teacher explained. So was the cookery lesson, making chapattis. These were both examples of changing a substance: from powder (paint) to sludgy liquid (paint and water), and from powdery flour to a solid chapatti. This activity is a precursor to understanding chemical equations. Khaliq's mother could also see that the staff wanted him to learn mathematics (up and down songs). She gradually became more relaxed about messy activities because she could see that they led on to science and maths. She was pleased that he could engage in these at school, where it is easier to manage messy experiences than in the home, where it is often too challenging to undertake.

Staff need to share the importance of these different areas of learning with parents. Valuing messy home activities (cookery) and giving them high status in school is one starting point. Khaliq's mother also liked gardening and grew vegetables at the school, as she lived in a flat with no garden.

Outdoor activities were then given high value. This is another area that is often not understood to be important by parents/carers. Studying worms, snails, slugs and the different properties of soils (clay, sand and gravel) is messy, but leads to natural science. By beginning with what the parent valued – cooking and gardening – the practitioner was able to share the importance of messy and outdoor activities with this parent, over a period of time. Khaliq's mother also began, very gradually, to see the need to observe the child before planning lessons, so that the lesson was effective and appropriate, and to see that her observations mattered as well as the teacher's. She became active in the classroom, cooking, gardening, helping with paintings and so on, using her strengths. She was a home garment-maker, and a sewing machine was set up for her in the classroom where she made clothes for the dressing-up corner, or for her child, out of a big box of materials that was always available – and she let the children have turns, too.

She did not see herself as a teacher. Her presence enriched the activities, introduced Urdu alongside English, and helped the staff through her developing skill in observing her own child. Her interest was in her child. In doing the activities she enjoyed, in which the children participated, she enhanced rather than threatened the teacher's role.

Khaliq's father visited the school to 'inspect it' when Khaliq first came. The practitioner talked about his learning, mainly the beginning of the three 'R's. Khaliq's father came when dolls' wash day was in progress. He was about to leave this 'women's activity' and take his son to something else. The practitioner explained to him that this was a mathematics lesson. She told him that she and his wife had noted Khaliq transporting objects and putting them into containers. This washing activity had been designed to help Khaliq to do both. It helped his ability to make a series (of largest to smallest clothes to peg out), and it helped him to classify (soapy water, rinsing water, and so on). She explained that Khaliq needed to both seriate and classify in order to be ready for number work later on. She demonstrated this difficult theory in a practical context. Father and son stayed at the activity. Khaliq's father did not visit again, but gave his approval for his wife to continue bringing Khaliq.

The developing partnership in Khaliq's family took a year to become established, and a further year to flourish. Most teachers work with a group of children for only one year, and so emphasis is required on the importance of working with colleagues as a team and of having a whole-setting policy in relation to working with parents. The importance of five terms in the nursery where the partnership pattern is established also requires consideration.

This example also demonstrates the indirect approach to structuring learning in the interactionist style. One of the central aims of this approach is to respect and include the parent's/carer's views.

Parents whose main contact with the setting is bringing and fetching children, and perhaps attending parents' evenings

Five-year-old **KIM**'s mother brought and fetched her from school each day; she would have a quick chat with the teacher, but showed no sign of wishing to become involved in the classroom. She was anxious for Kim to learn to read and write. As is quite common, she saw teaching Kim to do this as the main function of school. She had taught Kim to write her name before she came to school.

There was a problem here in that the mother was also encouraging Kim to copy words. This differed from the school's approach, which advocated children constructing their own letters when writing and where children are introduced to conventional spelling as involving problem-solving. Here was a clash between home and school. Kim's mother was not going to be convinced that the way she herself had learned to write 'was wrong', because she had successfully learned to write that way.

The teacher organised an exhibition of written work from Reception to top infants, asking her colleagues to help her. As parents brought their children in or collected them, she referred to this. She showed Kim's mother what the school did. Kim's mother was reassured to see the high standard of spelling and large amounts of creative writing many children achieved later in the school. She was interested to see that the writing included stories and poems, descriptions of outings or events, annotations of models children had made and descriptions of experiments they had performed.

In this way, Kim's mother was introduced to different modes of writing. Her concept of 'writing' broadened, but the teacher did not undermine her. She congratulated the mother on teaching Kim the alphabet and especially on starting with the letters of her name. She was pleased that she had taught Kim to be enthusiastic about writing and to feel that she could write. She asked her to write down stories Kim wanted to tell, so that she (as teacher) could make them into a book for Kim. As Kim was not used to 'inventing' spelling with her mother, the teacher worked on this aspect with her in school. In this way, she protected the child–parent relationship from possible failure during what might have been a difficult transition.

Once Kim became confident in her own ability to 'have a go' at spelling, she began to do this spontaneously with her mother. Her mother did not

▷

automatically 'correct' the spelling. She left it unless it was one of the spellings she and the teacher had decided to work on (for example, 'wood' for 'would'). The teacher said, when Kim's mother met her, that she wanted to work on the '-ould' family of words, since Kim consistently spelt this sound '-ood'.

Home and school were working together successfully. Kim's mother had not been asked to abandon her view of how children learn to write. She had broadened it, which had been an exciting rather than an undermining experience. In this partnership, it was the ten minutes before and after school that were of critical importance. Kim's mother also attended any evening 'talks' to parents about different aspects of the curriculum.

Parents who do not bring children to the early childhood setting, nor seek contact with the staff

When this unusual situation arises, it is important for the practitioners working with the family to attempt to make contact with the parents/carers, in a sensitive way. The challenge is how to do this. Three-year-old Jerome's parents did not attempt any contact with the school until the teacher sought it. Indeed, they seemed quite apathetic, and involvement with them required intermediary help from the health visitor. This example is discussed in full in the next section (on multi-agency work) because, as in many instances of complete lack of contact with parents, the support of other professional workers was necessary.

| A network of strategies

Different families have different needs. Having a variety of approaches helps the parent/carer–staff partnership to develop with success, which means that significant people in the child's life are working together for the child.

In the next section, which looks at the ways in which professionals in statutory and voluntary agencies work with parents, the need for early childhood practitioners to work with a variety of adults as well as with parents is emphasised. Being child-centred is too narrow an approach. It is more appropriate to consider the child-in-context, and that includes the various skills and strengths that different professionals and voluntary agencies have to offer in strengthening the child, as a member of a family.

Inter-disciplinary work

In the early stages of the child's life, the GP and health visitor are likely to be key professionals. Health visitors can act as catalysts for family development in co-ordination with other professionals.

One-year-old **JANE**'s family disliked professional workers as they had had a number of unfortunate experiences over the years. The health visitor found it difficult to gain entrance to their flat and yet she and the GP were concerned about Jane's physical growth and weight. She was small for her age, and not eating well. She was too young to attend a playgroup, and there was no parent/toddler group within easy walking distance.

Another of the health visitor's clients had been a nursery teacher until she gave up work to have her child, now a one-year-old. This mother ran a very small parent/toddler group that met three mornings a week. The health visitor put the two mothers in touch. Because the ex-nursery teacher was 'just another mother' with a one-year-old, she was able to work well with the family. Jane and her mother joined the group of four mothers and four children.

Relations with the health visitor improved. She was seen as someone who could help, but not interfere. Visits to a specialist doctor were positive. The father attended the group when his shift work allowed. They all went to a swimming club together, had joint outings and celebrated birthdays together, as well as undertaking joint jam-making and bread-making as part of the parent/toddler group activities. The health visitor was asked to provide information regularly. She organised visits from experts on preventive dentistry, family planning and nutrition, and gave information about nursery provision in the area.

At three years of age Jane attended a larger playgroup so that her mother could work in the mornings. At four years she attended the Reception class of the local school. The health visitor put the playgroup leader in touch with the parent/toddler group leader when a problem arose over Jane's eating. This was quickly resolved.

In this example, the health visitor had co-ordinated and used the different local resources and called upon specialist medical advice in her attempt to help Jane's family. She was sufficiently skilled to use a volunteer worker's skills when her 'professionalism' was acting as a block in the early stages of her relationship with the family. She valued what other workers could offer at every stage. In Jane's case, it was the statutory services that 'led', with the health visitor as the key worker, co-ordinating the GP, volunteer worker, playgroup and teacher.

In the following example, the health visitor again 'led'.

PETRA was born blind. She lived in an area where there was no special education support. Her parents were helped initially by the GP and health visitor, who put them in touch with an educational home visitor from a voluntary agency for the blind. This professional worker helped the family through the first five years of Petra's life, and co-ordinated resources and professional help to such an extent that Petra was able to attend the local primary school. The role of this professional worker was also to offer emotional support to the family, and to act as a bridge between teachers in the school and the family when problems arose, which they frequently did.

There was a gap in statutory services for this family – no advice on how to stimulate and manage Petra in the first five years, and no school for visually impaired children at statutory school age. The LEA bought special school places from the neighbouring authority, but the parents wanted Petra to attend school more locally and to have friends in the community if possible.

The educational home visitor gathered resources for the family with specialist equipment and advice on working with Petra in the earliest years. She supported them in the educational decisions they made and bridged the gap between home and school. She was a highly trained, paid worker, employed by a voluntary agency; she had more impact on this family in the first five years of Petra's life than any statutory worker because of her skill in co-ordinating the medical and educational resources available.

In the following example of Jerome, the specialist nursery teacher was the key worker.

Three-year-old **JEROME**'s parents did not come to school with him on the school bus on the first day. He was 'deaf', but his hearing aid was in his satchel. It would be easy for the teacher at Jerome's special school to draw the conclusion that here was an uncaring family, insensitive to their child's needs. The teacher used a home/school book with each family since children were spread over a large catchment area and were brought to school by bus rather than by their parents. She immediately, on that first day, sent a book home in Jerome's satchel, asking if she could introduce herself to the parents and wondering if they might like to visit the school.

The next day, the book had not been written in. The teacher could not phone the family as there was no phone, so she phoned the GP. He was wary of divulging any information at all, but grudgingly gave the name of the health visitor for the family. Contact with the health visitor revealed that both parents worked and were bewildered by their son, who had seemed to hear and had begun to talk at two years. He had recently been to Jamaica to stay with his grandmother for six months – and while there had stopped talking. On returning home he had been tested and found to have a hearing loss.

The health visitor agreed to find out if the family would like the teacher to visit. Two days later there was a note in the home book suggesting the teacher might like to call one day after school. The health visitor had found that the parents never looked in the satchel, so were unaware of the existence of the home book. The teacher set off on the school bus with Jerome on the suggested day and, at the set-down point, found herself to her surprise at Jerome's childminder's flat. He would be picked up from there an hour later at 5.30 p.m. The childminder was obviously embarrassed about this, and so the teacher said that she had some shopping to do and would go straight to Jerome's flat later, which she did. When she met the parents at 6.00 p.m., a situation potentially damaging to the parent–teacher partnership had arisen. The parents were clearly embarrassed. To them 'after school' meant after work. They had not wanted the teacher to know that Jerome went to a childminder. They clearly thought that a teacher would disapprove of this.

If an atmosphere of trust and mutual respect was to develop, the teacher's training needed to be used. She had received considerable help in working with parents during her specialist training in working with hearing-impaired children. Over tea, she established an atmosphere whereby she made it clear that she was actively seeking the parents' views, and needed their help in order to do her job. The focus was on everyone working for Jerome. The parents admitted their anger that he had been sent to a special school and their perplexity that he had suddenly stopped talking. They talked about their dislike of the hearing aid, which they felt labelled him. They did not want to come to school: they thought they would be upset to see other deaf children. Education to them meant learning to read, beginning with the alphabet, and they supposed that as Jerome was deaf there was no sense in trying to teach him. They just wanted him to be as happy as possible considering his disability. During the visit the teacher listened rather than talked. She also conveyed her delight in teaching Jerome – she wanted them to see that she valued their child.

When parents ask, 'Has he been good?', they are perhaps really asking, 'Do you like my child?' Jerome was pleased to see his teacher, but she made sure that she emphasised how relaxed and purposeful he was at home, what appropriate toys for his age he had, how she worried because he was always so beautifully turned out and his clothes might get spoiled at school.

By the end of the visit, the parents knew that the teacher sympathised with their work pattern and understood the need for a childminder, and that she obviously liked their son and was committed to working with him. They could trust her to be kind to him. She believed he was learning and she thought them caring parents who fed and clothed their child well and stimulated his development with toys. They invited her to visit again.

The partnership developed positively, through home visits. The teacher contacted the ear, nose and throat specialist, who was very helpful in getting a different hearing aid, one that had an automatic volume control. Jerome began to wear it in school. Then the mother took a day off work to come to a coffee morning/talk that the teacher had asked the school's educational psychologist to give. She met other parents and enjoyed it, finding they shared similar experiences and difficulties. At the next home visit, the teacher suggested to Jerome's mother that she might like to visit the classroom in action with one of the mothers she had particularly liked.

In school the mother was struck by Jerome's speech when he was wearing his hearing aid. She watched the teacher working with the children, and took comfort that Jerome was showing off and that her new friend's child was, too. All the adults laughed about it and the atmosphere was relaxed. Gradually the home visits became more focused on Jerome's learning, the curriculum and care of the hearing aid. Ideas for follow-up activities at home were given. The parents told the teacher what they observed Jerome doing, and the teacher shared what happened at school. The parents began to write in the home book. At six years Jerome was beginning to read, talk and lip-read well and was a more relaxed child. He transferred to a partial hearing unit and a year later was integrated successfully into his local primary school, where his parents were able to give him the necessary support.

They trusted his teachers, respecting their knowledge, and felt able to ask for help and information. They felt included in his education, knew that they were important and that the professionals regarded them as good, loving parents.

The key factors in this successful parent–teacher partnership were that the teacher built up the parents' self-confidence and extended what the parents thought education was about, rather than displacing their view with something totally different. The teacher gathered resources and information through a multi-professional approach, working with the health visitor, specialist doctor and educational psychologist.

Where there is little or no contact between professional workers, parents can be left confused and let down. Not all professionals welcomed this contact (in this instance, the GP did not), but the teacher kept going until she found those who also valued a multi-professional approach. Kaplan (1978) talks about the awakening of the unloved self in the parent in the case of a child with a disability (this may well also apply to the parents' relationship with a child at the toddler stage of temper tantrums). Parents need to feel supported, not undermined, by professionals. The teacher put the parents in touch with other parents to form a self-help group, and used an away-from-school setting prior to encouraging the parents into school.

> Two-year-old **JOHN**'s mother cared deeply about his healthy development. He attended a dentist as soon as his teeth came through. The dentist assured her that his thumb-sucking was not a problem. His mouth would need orthodontic treatment at nine or ten years anyway, and he was likely to grow out of it by five or six years. Mother relaxed.
>
> When John started at a playgroup, the staff discouraged him from sucking his thumb during story time. Mother began to worry again when John reported this. She did not like to mention it to the supervisor, who obviously knew more than she did (in her view). At six years of age, John was still sucking his thumb. At eight years, the dentist suggested a visit to the orthodontist in preparation for later treatment. She insisted that the thumb-sucking was no problem. The orthodontist greeted John with, 'And what do you do that you shouldn't do?', and was unpleasant to him about it, saying she would do nothing for him until he gave it up. John's mother ventured to say that she had thought treatment would not begin until he was 10 anyway and that John now sucked his thumb only on going to sleep, or if distressed. The orthodontist gave a smile, but no information.
>
> At the next visit to the dentist, the mother reported this back. The dentist closed professional ranks with the orthodontist, and said, 'Well, he's nearly stopped now, hasn't he?' John's mother felt confused about the conflicting professional views displayed in educational and medical contexts. She worried that as a parent she had failed to do right by John, but felt frustrated and angry because she had tried her best.

Working as a team

When partnerships are strong, the different roles of practitioners complement each other.

Conclusion

This chapter has explored significant people in a child's life – some in the family, some outside it, some chosen by the child, some not. The ways in which adults and children relate to each other are important, and both family and those in contact with the family are critical in the child's development. The more that professional workers in statutory and voluntary agencies concerned with the child's family/carers work together, the better for the child. Meeting a variety of other children is also important, so that the child develops the ability to form relationships, which may be deep or of the kind necessary simply to cope with everyday living together.

Diversity and inclusion

This chapter is about the empowerment of individuals and groups, so that children and adults have access to full lives, whether or not they are in a minority situation. For early childhood practitioners this means helping children to have fulfilling lives, both in their home life and beyond. This involves confronting discrimination and oppression of all kinds. One of the problems educators have always encountered is how to work with children respectfully and value them as unique individuals within a whole group. Even within the family, this can be difficult. A 'one-size-fits-all' approach does not work; children are not all the same.

Policy makers and educational theorists have, over the years, identified particular groups of children whose needs have been significantly ignored. As long ago as the 1960s, studies such as Douglas (1964) alerted practitioners to the fact that working class children were not being successful in the education system. This led to attempts to remedy the situation through compensatory education programmes in the 1960s and '70s (Headstart, Halsey), which focused on cognition. Three useful features emerged from this compensatory movement. Programmes that had lasting impact were found to be those that:

1 worked in partnership with parents and the rest of the family
2 were geared to the individual development and learning of each child within the group
3 were structured in a planned, well thought-through and consistent way.

In these high quality programmes, because the whole family was involved, account was taken of what the child came to school able to do. The child's background and home experiences were valued. Observing the child and using what the child was naturally doing was also valued. Examples of this approach can be seen in Constance Kamii's work in the Ypsilanti Early Education Programme in the USA, the Halsey Studies on Educational Priority in the UK, together with the Leverhulme/Gulbenkian Research Project directed by Chris Athey at the Froebel Institute, London, 1972–77.

All children need individual and sensitive treatment, whether they are spending time with childminders or in group settings.

Guiding principles for early childhood practice

At an Organisation Mondiale pour l'Education Prescolaire (OMEP) conference in London in 1983, Yvonne Conolly set out the following important guiding principles embracing diversity and inclusion, which are adapted for use in this chapter.

Early childhood settings and the individual needs of children and their families

- ○ Children and their families need a sense of belonging and inclusion.
- ○ Promoting a child's sense of well-being and self-worth is essential.
- ○ There is a need to avoid stereotyping.
- ○ There is a need to overcome the natural stranger-fear of people through positive strategies.
- ○ Everyone needs to inspect their own values, assumptions and actions in the way they respect other people.

Inclusion: a sense of well-being and belonging

Everyone needs roots and to feel that they belong to a group.

The inclusive approach can be seen in the need to value and encourage the child's home language where this is different from that used in the school. It is also present in the need to value dialects and accents that relate to class and regional differences. It is present in the need for children of minority ethnic groups to know about their own language, cultural roots and religious ideas, and for the educator to value these. Floella Benjamin (1995: 121), in her book *Coming to England*, says:

> To feel you belong is a most important necessity in life.

Three-year-old **PRATIMA** came to school with her grandmother, who spoke Punjabi. The teacher managed to greet her in Punjabi. Shortly after, Pratima became distressed and fearful. It was clearly something to do with her shoes and shoe-bag. Grandmother could not speak English to explain to the teacher, and the teacher's grasp of Punjabi was too limited. Fortunately, the school was following an inclusive rather than an assimilation approach, and Punjabi was sufficiently valued in the school for there to be a Punjabi-speaking member of staff. She was asked to help and the situation was instantly resolved. Pratima's tears vanished. The wrong shoe-bag was on her peg; hers was quickly found. Pratima's English was developing very well, but in a stress situation she could not use it and it would be inappropriate to expect her to do so. No one uses their latest piece of learning when under stress.

JAMES (two years old) was profoundly deaf; so were his parents. The family used British Sign Language at home and in their friendship circle. With his childminder, who was learning British Sign Language, he was also encouraged to sign. The childminder also used oral language and encouraged the use of a hearing aid.

▷

James's home language was encouraged, but he was also learning about oral language so that he could become bilingual. Like Pratima, James' home language was valued and encouraged, while he was also introduced to English as an additional language (EAL).

Figure 10.1 Children in the school are encouraged to join others in the home corner, often beginning to echo what other children do, such as food-preparation play. Being near an adult with who they have a strong relationship supports them in trying new things, and in concentrating and being focused. Comparing two egg timers is fascinating. So is sharing a book with an interested adult.

For individuals to be included, communities must know about and understand individual and minority group needs.

> Six-year-old **NAHUGO**'s mother took her to school each day. She walked straight past the other mothers; this upset **WILLIAM**'s mother, who felt her smile of greeting was being rejected. A friend had recently returned from Japan and explained to her that in Japan people do not greet each other with a smile in the street. They ignore each other unless there is a verbal greeting. The next day, William's mother verbally greeted Nahugo's mother. She looked a little taken back, but immediately smiled and responded. Thereafter, the two mothers greeted each other each day.

Families need to feel that they can trust those in whose charge they leave their children.

> **JUDITH** was given pork at lunchtime in the early childhood setting. The practitioner who was her Key Person intercepted the meal, asked the dinner helper for an alternative meal without pork and quietly gave it to Judith. 'No one would have known,' was the dinner helper's response. She did not worry that Judith's family practised Reformed Judaism, and that they trusted the staff to apply the dietary stipulations of the religion. On her course, working towards Level 3 qualifications, the helper became more informed and her practice developed.

> Five-year-old **ANTHEA** attended a Church of England primary school. During assembly the head told the children about Doubting Thomas, who had the opportunity to believe in Jesus but did not take it. This placed Anthea in a dilemma. Her mother was agnostic, her father was an atheist. Both had had the opportunity to believe and had rejected it. What did this make her parents in the eyes of the school and Church? Anthea dealt with the situation by keeping secret throughout her education the fact of her parents' rejection of Christianity, as a means of retaining her self-worth at school. In fact, in many respects, she received a sounder spiritual and moral education from her parents than did other children in the school. She experienced with her family a sense of awe and wonder about the universe (her father was a scientist). She learned about celebration at family gatherings, when African music was played and danced to. She learned about 'worthship' in family gatherings, which involved discussion of matters of worth, starvation, poverty, peace, human rights and oppression.

Figure 10.2 The practitioner who leads the 'Play and Stay' session understands the importance of creating a warm and friendly atmosphere. At the end of the session the parents enjoy dancing with their children, and when the children imitate the steps and echo the dance (moving to the centre with enjoyment) it is clear that both parents and children feel valued, their efforts noted and acted upon.

This example demonstrates that organised religion, or belief in revelationary religions, is not the only means by which children are given a sound moral education with ethical values and a desire to lead a good life and contribute to making a better world.

> Six-year-old OVO's family were pantheists, believing in spirits in the trees and plants. He, of all the children in his class, was best able to understand the Native American tribes' relationship with their natural surroundings during a class project on this.
>
> Five-year-old MARGARET was brought up as a Roman Catholic. She could understand that five-year-old Diana wore a Star of David, just as she wore a crucifix.
>
> Four-year-old SADIQ was taken to Westminster Abbey on a school outing. He thought the statues had no clothes on as they were carved in stone, and saw them as rude. His mother was fascinated by the outing and explained to the teacher, who was a Methodist, that in the Muslim mosque there are no statues.

All these children bring different experiences, although it is to be hoped that each will sense awe and wonder, and will celebrate and experience spirituality in some form. Many non-theists (such as atheists and agnostics or free thinkers) do not wish to use the word 'spiritual' to describe their journey through life. Other non-theists (Humanist Quakers, Humanist Unitarians and some Humanists) feel comfortable with the term, seeing the development of understanding of self, others and the universe as a part of their spiritual journey through life. It is difficult to know the emphasis of most non-theists (who comprise 65 per cent of those stating they were of no religion in the last National Census, 2011).

Studying different cultures is a sophisticated, complex and multi-layered process. Everyone eats, however, and likes to present food attractively, uses crockery and equivalent tools with which to eat, sits in a variety of ways. Everyone sleeps, on beds, in hammocks, bunks and so on. Everyone needs protection from heat or cold resulting in a need for clothing, and everyone needs shelter. The different ways in which people tackle these aspects of life then become fascinating and important. They lead to respect for differences through geographical or regional variations, or for historic reasons, which helps in understanding cherished traditions and rituals. This helps children to see that diversity is rich, and to value the things that human beings have in common with each other.

Inclusion does not leave people out; inclusion stresses a sense of belonging

JIM was able to use British Sign Language and oral language. He was profoundly deaf, and chose this description. Labels are often chosen for people with disabilities. Some prefer to be described as hearing impaired. It is part of choosing identity. Jim had attended mainstream schools and was at university – but he had always belonged to groups of deaf people, with whom he had learned to sign. He had friends who were deaf and friends who were not. His bilingualism helped him to develop close friendships with both groups. He said that with hearing people he often became very tired with the concentration and effort required to listen hard and to lip-read, especially in group conversations. He could relax with deaf friends where he could sign. Interestingly, Jim's first remark when he met anyone at the summer school he attended was, 'Are you deaf or hearing?' He was at ease with his deafness. He did not try to deny it; he did not want to. His only bitterness was that hearing people were so insensitive to the needs of the minority group to which he belonged. He felt a privileged member of his group, as he was bilingual. His parents had fought hard to help him succeed in spite of all the obstacles posed by insensitive and inflexible systems.

Encouraging a sense of worth

Self-worth, self-esteem and self-confidence are probably the most important aspects of human development. The way that people feel about themselves, their well-being, affects the way that they seem to others and the way that they behave towards them.

Three-year-old NASREEN was from a Muslim family, but her father was an alcoholic and so her family was disapproved of by the Muslim community. She had been brought to school as usual by her older sister. As the teacher greeted her on arrival, a neighbour brought in his child. He said something in Punjabi to Nasreen and mimed a drinking movement. As he turned to go she stuck out her tongue at his back and went to the practitioner and put her hand in hers. She knew the teacher valued her, and would not be judgemental towards her family.

The practitioner raised this at the staff meeting, and it was agreed that the centre manager would discuss the incident with the neighbour, making it clear that this disrespectful behaviour was unacceptable in this community.

Figure 10.3 When she arrives this little girl sits with the 'anchored' adult, who places herself at a table with Lego, welcoming children and settling them by involving them with the Lego if appropriate. After half an hour the child takes the Lego, on the board, to the carpeted floor area and continues working with the Lego there. Adults join her from time to time, and so do children. After a time, she takes the Lego to the bookcase for display, helped by the boy who shows an interest in what she is doing. An hour has passed, during which time she has shown focused engagement with the Lego.

Four-year-old **KUANG**'s and six-year-old **MING**'s mother was British, their father was Chinese. Their parents helped them to understand Chinese culture through the furniture and decor in the home, the food they sometimes ate, the emphasis on stories and Chinese ideas about health, acupuncture, Tai Chi and herbal medicines. They also knew about the British cultural setting from their mother and from school. Kuang took pride in showing his friends how to write 'mountain' in Chinese. His parents helped him be proud of what he was, half Chinese and half British, of mixed heritage.

There is a tendency in white citizens of the UK to see children of mixed heritage as non-white. This is being addressed by the children of parents of different ethnicities, with the development of hairstyles and fashions in dress that create a feeling of belonging to a group.

Avoiding stereotypes

Knowing who you are and being at ease with yourself is closely linked with self-worth. Part of being able to do this lies in the way children can put themselves into context. 'Who am I?' is an important question, which all people ask of themselves at some point.

If children are labelled by others and stereotyped, this means they are viewed narrowly by others, for example, describing Peter as 'the blind boy', rather than as someone who has as many qualities as any sighted child, or describing Ufoma as black or African, rather than as a child who loves maths and hates gymnastics. Helping children to identify themselves is probably the most constructive thing practitioners can do. It is important to avoid stereotyping people into an identity.

A teacher from Yorkshire attended a course in London. Everyone began to ask her about Yorkshire. 'Oh! You're from Yorkshire.' She began to feel that she was a foreigner. She felt her Yorkshire accent becoming stronger. She found herself wanting to read about the Industrial Revolution and the wool trade. She needed to assert her identity, but it was being chosen for her by others. She was swept along by the way that other people insisted on regarding her; she was being stereotyped as 'the delegate from Yorkshire'. It is important for individuals to assert their own identity so that stereotyping is avoided.

In a music corner, **BETTY** (four years) pretended to be the teacher. She held up a book to show the imaginary children in her class. Her friend **JOANNA** came and sat as a pupil on the floor in front of her. **JOHN** came and tried to join in,

▷

but Betty chased him away, refusing him admittance to the play. She seemed to allow only girls to join this play scenario. John returned, however, but sat at the edge by the entrance to the music corner. He stayed there and gradually moved forward bit by bit until finally he joined the play and was accepted into it by Betty. She had viewed his creeping towards the front with suspicion, but its slowness seemed to help her tolerate his gaining entry to the play.

Overcoming stranger-fear with positive strategies

Mixing with a diverse range of people helps to break down stranger-fear, provided positive strategies are developed that support the situation. Where children do not meet in a positive atmosphere, prejudice based on ignorance and stranger-fear persists and can even be exacerbated. Attitudes to disability are changing as disabled people become more included than they were, although there is still much to do. Discriminatory behaviour based on ignorance and stranger-fear is not to be tolerated, even if it means unpleasantness in public (Siraj-Blatchford, 1994: 69). It is now thought that stranger-fear might be an unhelpful and obsolete survival behaviour, which would have had a purpose earlier in the evolution of humans.

Looking at our basic assumptions, attitudes, values and actions

Practitioners need to examine some of their basic assumptions about the way they introduce children to activities and tune in more sensitively to family styles of learning in order to help individual children in their learning. When children find familiar experiences and share these in conversations they have with the practitioner, relationships develop more easily and the learning is of a deeper quality.

It is important that the staff in early childhood settings meet and discuss issues of equality of opportunity, including ensuring access for every child to become fully included in the group. This will involve everyone together developing and drawing up a policy on diversity and inclusion. It is also essential that every practitioner feels committed to this. Not only this, but the policy then needs to be put into action and regularly reviewed to check that it is being implemented and to make changes as it is developed (Bruce, Meggitt and Grenier, 2010).

Attitudes that promote the guiding principles discussed in this chapter are of no consequence without action. Action requires commitment from people and appropriate resources. Practitioners need varying degrees of additional information, advice, support, special materials and amended environments if they are to work with principles of diversity and inclusion.

For example, the inclusion of a child with a visual disability will mean extra specialist teaching support in the form of peripatetic advisers qualified in the education of visually disabled children; additional technical equipment including braillers; microcomputers with voice output; a special materials service of braille books and audio materials; special lighting; and readiness on the part of the teacher to go for in-service training.

It is the practitioner's responsibility to press for the resources necessary to work inclusively with children so that rich learning environments are developed. It is important that support is given through relevant and effective training (through the Local Authority, Children's Centres and Sure Start, or voluntary organisations with specialist knowledge and expertise). Commercial enterprises that 'put on' training programmes based on making profit need to be carefully scrutinised. Parents need to be informed how to access information and advice and political channels (through their local elected representative).

Margaret Carr (1999) has developed 'Teaching Stories', which help the practitioner to evaluate what is offered to children. This makes a useful way to audit diversity and inclusion for childminders in home settings, and for practitioners working in group settings. It is worded as if it is the child's voice, asking:

- ○ Is this a fair place?
- ○ Is this a safe place?
- ○ Can I trust you?
- ○ Do you know me?
- ○ Do you help me fly?

These make a good starting point for reflecting on practice and thinking through action plans in relation to diversity and inclusion.

Conclusion

The key elements of principles of diversity and inclusion are that communities of all kinds need to create systems that give equality of opportunity, respect and value to all who live within them. Attention must also be given to the various ways in which to empower children and adults as individuals, and also as groups who may be in a minority. This needs to be backed up with policies developed together as a team by those working with young children and their families; these policies must be regularly reviewed.

- ○ Children need a sense of belonging and to feel included; to choose their own identity and have a sense of self-worth.
- ○ Everyone needs to inspect his or her own thinking and actions, and confront assumptions in moving towards diversity and inclusion.
- ○ Fear of 'difference' impedes this process, and needs to be tackled directly.

Early childhood educators are in positions of power for breaking down narrow roles for children, and combating stereotyping of all kinds.

- All people have in common the fact that they are human beings.
- There is much diversity and many differences between people, but this is different from fragmentation of society or cultures.
- It is important to begin with what is common and ubiquitous to all people.
- Differences can be celebrated, respected and valued. Some differences will be unacceptable in the UK, such as inequality between men and women. The UK system of law and justice is the law of the land, and must be adhered to.

Everyone, child or adult, has in common:

- the need for a sense of belonging and inclusion
- the need for a sense of well-being and self-worth
- the need for a full life, not one that is narrowly stereotyped resulting in discriminatory behaviour by others, nor with access denied, restricted or undermined through the creation of an atmosphere that is unwelcoming
- the need to overcome fear of people or situations that are different from what is familiar
- the need to reflect on and look at the values, assumptions and attitudes that influence the way people act towards others.

Every early childhood setting needs a policy on which the whole team has worked and to which they are committed. This needs to be reviewed regularly to make sure it is actively carried out in practice.

Observation that informs assessment, planning and evaluation

11

Planning the development of learning: observation

This book gives a central place to the importance of observation, using a variety of lenses through which to tune in to and understand the child's development and learning. This informs practitioners, working in close partnership with parents/carers, about planning the next steps in learning that are appropriate for the child. It helps practitioners to plan effectively for the individual child, but in ways that ensure the child has a sense of belonging and feels included. The way that the child responds to what is offered helps practitioners to evaluate the appropriateness of what they have provided, which in turn shapes future planning.

- **Assessment** monitors the way the child progresses in the setting, which may be home-based with a childminder, or group-based. It is about tuning in to the child.
- **Evaluation** helps practitioners to interpret, analyse and improve what they have offered and planned for individual children and groups.
- **Reflective forward planning** means we are always looking at what the child has been doing, has been interested in, and has engaged with recently (reflective planning) in order to inform ourselves about how to support and extend the learning and development appropriately (forward planning).
- A **record-keeping** system shows the philosophy (the principles and values) of the setting in action. If the record keeping does not reflect the principles that the practitioners embrace, then there will be confused practice that constantly contradicts itself.

The following principles of record keeping (adapted from Bartholomew and Bruce, 1993; Bruce, Louis and McCall, 2014) help practitioners to make effective links with the principles of the early childhood traditions outlined in this book. They also resonate with the core documents of the four UK countries.

Principles of record keeping that are in alignment with the traditional principles of early childhood practice

Records need to:

1 Keep faith with the bedrock principles of the early childhood traditions.
2 Help partnership with parents/carers and be easy to share with them.
3 Encourage children to reflect on their own learning.
4 Be user-friendly; make efficient, effective use of the time and energy of staff; and be easy to share with multi-agency colleagues and the child's future teachers.
5 Use a variety of techniques for gathering observations – such as written observations, audio and visual recordings, and photography using current technology – to develop portfolios of children's learning.
6 Link assessment of the child with evaluation of what the child is offered.
7 Inform through sharing, planning and organisation, showing progress made and next steps.
8 Link with current requirements.
9 Be flexible and grow formatively.
10 Be capable of fine focus and able to yield specific information.
11 Be easy to review and summarise.
12 Show starting points as well as growth points.

In summary, records are about getting to know the child, what the child is interested in, and what he or she needs next. They show the philosophy and principles in action.

Evaluating the curriculum

Whereas assessment is about how the child makes progress, evaluation helps us to look at what we are offering a group of children, or an individual child, in the curriculum. This will involve practitioners looking at the experiences planned and the materials that they have used, and the way that staff and parents work with children, in groups and alone. Some children find it easier to work in a small group, and on the floor, and free to move around. If sitting at a table is required, they begin to show challenging behaviour.

Assessment and evaluation need to link together

Assessment (how the child is making progress) needs to be linked with evaluation (what the child is offered). When used together in a record-keeping system, the integration of assessment and evaluation by early childhood workers comes about through careful observation of children and informs the curriculum planning. Staff can begin to work out what they will next need to offer to children, either in a large group, a small group or individually.

Figure 11.1 At first the boys do not connect with each other; each is playing alone. One boy is observing what the other two are doing. He moves between the two before joining one. He stays on after one of the boys who initiated the play leaves, having played with him for a time. Is it that he needs another child or adult to start him off with an idea? Children often take up the ideas they see others have. Imitation is a strong factor in developing learning. Once he has, as it were, found a way into a worthwhile play episode he plays in parallel and companionship with the other boy on the mat.

Vicky Hutchin (2010: 43) suggests that there are three kinds of observation:

○ Participant observations occur when the practitioner is involved in the play or the learning experience with the chid.
○ 'Catch as you can' observations arise when something significant is noted, but the practitioner was not directly involved with the child.
○ Narrative observations are planned, and the child is observed across the day/week by all the staff, with the Key Person co-ordinating the observations gathered.

How to make a narrative observation

There are many different forms of observation, but narrative observation has been tried and tested across time since the 1930s, when Susan Isaacs pioneered the method in her school, the Malting House. Her observations are written up in two seminal texts, 'Intellectual Growth in Young Children' and 'Social Development in Young Children'. Observations are as useful today as they were then; the difference lies in their interpretation. Isaacs analysed her raw data (her observations) through a Kleinian psychoanalytic framework. But any theoretical framework could be used. Narrative observations are typically analysed today through the official framework documents of the country. This gives practitioners and parents insights into the child's development and learning. It also deals with the accountability aspect in ways that do not cut across the philosophical base of the record keeping.

Narrative observation involves four steps:

1 The observer writes briefly about the context of the observation.
2 The observer writes down as exact a description as possible of what the child says/does. If other children are involved, the observer writes down enough description of the conversations and actions of the other children to have a clear picture of the target child.
3 The observation can then be analysed and interpreted.
4 The observation can be linked with the observations made of this child by other people. It can also be linked with official curriculum frameworks, research and theory.

This approach discourages value-laden judgements about families and children. It challenges the observer to reflect on cultural differences and to respect children and families, and to take inclusive action in relation to disability, special educational needs, etc. The observer does not 'spoil' the data by analysing throughout. This is because the analysis comes at a later stage, after gathering on-the-spot description.

The description gives enough detail for the observer to be able to analyse this later, without making wild claims that are unsupported by the data. A particular focus can be given for the analysis, such as a focus on play, communication, relationships, mathematics. When the analysis is linked to theory and research, it deepens and gives more illumination. It helps practitioners to understand and work with the child in ways that are right for the child. Photographs and drawings are often included, and sometimes extracts of video.

Formative and summative methods of assessing a child's progress

It is simply not possible to measure most of a child's development or learning. We can catch only glimpses of a child's progress. It is damaging to a child's education if only the learning that is thought to be measurable is given any emphasis in the curriculum. This will bring about a narrowing of the curriculum, whereby children are mainly taught to achieve on formal tests, rather than becoming educated in the real sense. This is sometimes referred to as the 'dumbing down' of the curriculum. It is the difference between helping children to jump through narrow academic hoops, with an emphasis on passive conformity, and expanding their horizons to provide a deep, rich and broad learning. The child will inevitably develop particular interests within this wider framework.

Formative assessment

Formative assessment methods emphasise the learning in which children are involved over time. The emphasis is on the everyday context in which learning takes place rather than on test situations. Formative assessment is about the processes in a child's progress and the way children go through their learning experiences in the curriculum, gradually and over time.

Information is gathered continuously and regularly in natural, non-test situations; for example, by collecting a child's paintings, photographing their models, keeping examples of children's written efforts, and making notes about their dances or singing. The work on documentation in Reggio Emilia in Northern Italy is explored by Edwards et al. (1998: 461–65) through guiding principles for practice, but only in the arts. The Learning Stories developed by Margaret Carr and Wendy Lee in New Zealand are also useful and, in a different way to the Reggio approach, resonate with the early childhood traditions of narrative records built continuously to make a profile or portfolio, and developed in nursery schools in the UK.

Narrative observation notes and photographs taken on the spot while a child is cooking, dancing, doing woodwork, using the climbing frame or hunting for ants in the garden are invaluable. These can be used to inform future planning.

Vicky Hutchin (2010: 47) takes the view that, 'Every observation is likely to have some implications for planning: first, with regard to the individual child and, secondly, for the staff and setting – perhaps changing a routine or introducing something new.' She suggests that, when thinking of the next steps for the child (the planning), it is important to consider what would help the child to extend their skills or understanding in relation to something in which they are observed to be engaged. This might involve creating a learning opportunity, or resources. The way that practitioners participate with the child will be of fundamental importance, too.

Thinking about how to support and extend the learning of one child might mean rearranging and adapting situations and materials, but Vicky Hutchin emphasises that this is likely to open up opportunities for learning for other children as well.

Summative assessment

Summative assessment is about taking stock, pausing and bringing together everything known about the child's progress. Summative assessment can be staff and parents putting together key aspects of a child's progress, for example, physically, mathematically, aesthetically, or in terms of additional needs, diversity and inclusion, or policy review. It is then necessary to decide next steps in what to offer and to evaluate the impact of this on the curriculum. Jan Dubiel (2014) is expert in this field.

Many schools and settings now have a 'special book' for each child, which shows both formative and summative assessment of the child through the child's learning journey. Significant markers in development and learning are entered, with photographs and examples of drawings, etc., and annotations. These show the whole child (not simply their literacy and number learning). Some examples will be gathered because it is realised that they show particular aspects of the learning journey that have been spotted and deemed important to include for that reason. Some are there because parents have thought them significant; some are chosen by the child. There should be contributions from the Key Person, parent/carer and child. But there should not be clutter. Each entry should be there for a good reason, and the reason should be noted and dated.

Every few weeks (more often if the special book also serves as an individual development plan for a child with a special educational need or disability) a summative form will be filled in, which brings together the overall progress made, identifies next steps and addresses any concerns.

Evaluation

Evaluation looks at what children are being offered and how this meets their needs, and it looks at what must be changed, adapted and developed. It involves

Figure 11.2 The profile books are explained in a chart on the wall near the book corner, where parents often sit with their children, sharing a book. This is so that parents are fully informed, in accessible ways and in a simple format, how the record-keeping system works.

a long-term plan and a medium-term plan, which are flexible, adaptable and constantly changing as observation of children informs the planning, and as daily plans emerge out of this. Evaluation occurs regularly when staff reflect together on what children have been offered, and how effective the planning has been, based on evidence from observations informing assessment.

Using assessment, evaluation and planning in linked ways leads to practitioners becoming clear about their intentions and how they will act upon them, and to consider next steps in a child's learning. This means knowing about child development and the early childhood curriculum, and keeping up to date with recent research and thinking. In-service training is an essential aspect of this approach to evaluation and assessment.

Using both formative and summative methods of evaluation and assessment, education in early childhood supports the interactionist approach. Using one or the other method does not, and has severe disadvantages. For example, one of the problems of the kind of summative methods involving formal testing is that what is measured quickly becomes what children ought to know. The problem of 'deriving an ought from an is' is called the Naturalistic Fallacy in philosophy.

Assessment and evaluation are important to children and parents as well as to staff. For example, at open evenings parents/carers often seize upon written work, drawings, paintings or models, or look for sum books. They want to see what their child has done and to compare this with what other children do. Parents enjoy 'performances' of music, drama and dance, because again there is a product to see, a tangible outcome. Outcomes such as these are often the only available means they have of putting their child's achievements, or their anxieties about their child's progress, into any kind of context. The anxieties parents experience about their child's progress cannot be stressed too strongly.

The advantage of using equally explicit formative as well as summative approaches is that parents and others, such as school governors, are included in the process of education, as well as in the outcomes. They are helped to examine the education offered to the child beyond the superficial level, which tends to be entrenched in the education they themselves received. They can be supported in doing so by teachers who are confident and articulate, who constantly seek to improve the service, and are flexible in their thinking, which is based on sound conceptually-based knowledge.

Parents can be helped to see a broader and more wide-ranging picture of their child as it develops over a period of time, based on the continual observations made, often by parents and staff, and on the plans formulated in the curriculum. Their involvement in this process, working with the early childhood worker or teacher, illuminates the process. Parents are then in a position to take pleasure in their child's strengths, and to tackle the weaker areas with support from the school or early childhood setting.

Seeing an individual 'interest book' develop as part of class work, or seeing different paintings displayed on the classroom wall and then made into another kind of interest book are examples of this way of working to make formative assessment more tangible and easier for parents to see in action. Parents are also able to see their child's progress in relation to other children in a more positive way than when suddenly plunged into an open evening, where the differences between their child's achievement and the achievements of others may be startling.

Records need to be kept of all aspects of the child's development. There are multi-professional implications in this. Health records are confidential, but of central importance for those professionals responsible for the child since the aspects inevitably link. Specialists of all kinds (medical, social workers, educational psychologists, educators) need to share and build vital information together with the parent. Building records in a partnership can enable early diagnosis or monitoring of special needs, temporary or permanent, and indicate the level of support a child will need. This approach is particularly helpful in the field of health surveillance, and as a means of offering appropriate help in terms of preventive treatment, remediation or dealing with disability.

The teacher needs to observe and record how often he or she imposes control and discipline on the child, and to what extent children have self-discipline and can curb themselves. This is particularly important where a child has behavioural challenges. Recognising, appreciating and valuing children's efforts increases their self-discipline, and noting progress fosters feelings of self-worth and well-being (Laevers, 1994).

If good narrative observation techniques are in place and formative assessment is thorough, a child's needs and interests can be met through using a wide range of materials. The development and learning of the youngest children is a central part of this. Now, with digital photography, parents and practitioners working with babies and toddlers can develop powerfully informative and useful records of progress and appropriate planning.

Children who have begun to walk might not find drawing at a table appealing. Drawing with a bucket of water and a large brush on the table outside, however, offers very similar learning outcomes. The key is not to make the child come to the drawing table, but to take the drawing possibilities to the child, by building on what the child can do. Sharing such planning with parents makes them part of the team with very positive results for the child's learning.

Narrative observation notes, photography, video recordings and collecting examples of models, painting, drawings and written work, help to capture the processes and outcomes of the development of symbolic behaviour.

It is as important to plot progress in dance choreography, musical composition and performance skill with a bat and ball as it is to see development in a child's written or number work.

A parent at an open day said to **HARRY** (aged three years), 'What a lovely train. You clever boy to do that.' It was a template outline of a steam train that had prints from cotton reels on it. Harry said, 'I only did those' (meaning the cotton reel prints). The teacher had had the idea of making a train to fit a project on transport. She cut out the template and required Harry to print on it. She called this 'personalising' it.

Figure 11.3 Stevie concentrates and is engaged in her Treasure Basket for about 45 minutes. Her mother sits quietly near her, showing quiet interest if Stevie shows her objects. She selects a wooden handle and puts it in her mouth, at different angles and with different positions. She then does the same thing with the wooden bobbin. We saw her in Chapter 8 selecting spheres and circles. These observations help her parents to provide appropriate objects for her Treasure Basket. Chapter 3 examined the interests of three babies using the Treasure Basket developed with Stevie in mind. What suits and interests Stevie is different from what fascinates Cecilia. Maya is older and needs materials that cater for her greater mobility.

Figure 11.4 Several children are using the climbing frame, but one girl is leading the group. She has the skill to stand at the ready preparing to launch herself and swing across to the middle or opposite side, and to land on two feet standing up and not falling over. The adult respects her skill and offers help only to children who need encouragement, but ensures that the girl has the space she needs each time she takes off.

Accurate assessment of children's development is possible only if the work displayed on walls and in books is their own.

All that the case study above illustrates is that Harry can follow a simple instruction and print on an outline – which is a very low-level achievement unworthy of the label 'creative' (Bruce, 2011). Adult-dominated displays, although attractive, reveal a very low level of achievement that seriously underestimates what children can do.

In contrast, displays of work initiated and carried through by children, given adult support, demonstrate what children can do. The children's work can be beautifully mounted by adults and, where appropriate, explanatory notes about the contents or processes of the work can be given (since the result may not be obvious, for example, a blob of paint on a page may represent a ball bouncing).

This method shows the adult's role as supporting and extending what the child can do (Vygotsky's zone of potential development) then sharing this through the classroom display, which illuminates the child's work but does not take it over. Adults who help children to extend what they can do by themselves are more useful to children in the long term than are adults who help them to perform through giving them easy props to lean upon in the short term. Deep down, children know the difference, and their self-esteem is enhanced if they feel real ownership of their achievements. The reward is knowing that 'this is me being able to do this.'

Planning

Instead of making 'plans', which tend to be set in concrete and not changed in light of children's responses (or as is often the case, their lack of response or engagement in relation to 'the plan'), there has been a determination to engage in 'planning'. Planning implies a process, which is ever-changing, and that is exactly how things should be. This is sometimes called flexible, responsive or reflective planning. It means that the staff will map out ideas that, based on observation of children, seem to both respond to the child's interests and at the same time to what they need. The two need to be integrated. If children are not interested in what they are offered, they will not engage with it or learn. It is therefore effective practice to prioritise engaging children in what interests them. They are much more likely to be willing to struggle to learn something they find difficult if this is the case.

There are several things that need to happen, both at the same time and in synchrony when planning the curriculum:

1 Analyse the observations of children across the week and establish what is significant about their interests and needs.
2 Look at the official framework documents in use, and see what is in there that in any way links with point 1.

3 Use large, general points in long-term planning. This might be an emphasis on personal, social and emotional development in the autumn, when many children are new to the setting. This will not need to change very much, because it is more general than specific.

4 Use more specific points for short-/medium-term planning. Many settings now find they do not need both short- and medium-term planning. This is because they make good use of their observations. The child's interests and needs can then become the short-term plan, and can be incorporated into the medium-term planning.

In this way the observations become intertwined with the planning (Bruce, Louis and MCall, 2014), in both the medium and long term. Getting the two together is the key to good planning.

Planning should be undertaken so that children develop and learn in ways that are right for them, at the right time for them. It should also ensure that children learn what they need to know, and are equipped with useful strategies for future learning as well as the dispositions that cultivate this. Planning should help children to find out about and deepen their possibilities to learn more about what interests them, what they need to know in order to function in the world, and what society thinks they ought to know as part of their cultural lives.

Summary

The lenses through which we observe children build on our understanding, so that we can help them to develop and learn as the unique individuals that they are. We can help them to deepen their interests in worthwhile ways, and give them what they need.

The better our observations, the more they inform us and enable us to assess the child's development and learning so that we can identify and plan next steps. Observation also helps us to monitor and evaluate what we offer to children in the learning environment, indoors and outdoors.

The record-keeping systems we devise should be in alignment and resonate with the bedrock principles supporting quality early childhood practice.

The way forward

12

Ten principles of early childhood practice

1 The best way to prepare children for their adult life is to give them what they need as children.
2 Children are whole people who have feelings, ideas, a sense of embodied self and relationships with others, and who need to be physically, mentally, morally and spiritually healthy.
3 Areas of learning, involving the humanities, arts and sciences, cannot be separated; young children learn in an integrated way and not in neat, tidy compartments.
4 Children learn best when they are given appropriate responsibility, allowed to experiment, make errors, decisions and choices, and are respected as autonomous learners.
5 Self-discipline is emphasised as the only kind of discipline worth having. Reward systems are very short term and do not work in the long term. Children need their efforts to be appreciated and valued.
6 There are times when children are especially able to learn particular things.
7 What children *can* do (rather than what they *cannot* do) is the starting point of a child's education.
8 Diverse kinds of symbolic behaviour develop and emerge when learning environments conducive to this are created at home and in early childhood settings, both indoors and outdoors.
9 Relationships with other people (both adults and children) are of central importance in a child's life, influencing emotional and social well-being.
10 Quality in developing children's learning is about three things: the child; the context in which the learning takes place; and the knowledge and understanding that the child develops and learns.

(Bruce, 1987, adapted 2011, 2015)

From these principles, an approach that is consistent, balanced, and supported by an edifice of established and cutting edge theory and research can be developed into the future. Taking account of prevailing practice as well as policy pressures, the following action points are proposed:

○ Adults need to tune in to, listen to and observe children. This requires better understanding of child development and of the different areas of learning.
○ While emphasising the importance of being child-centred, there is also a need to become more family- or carer-centred.

▷

- There is a need for better and more multi-professional exchanges, dialogues and integrated working between health visitors, speech and language therapists, teachers, family workers, etc.
- It is essential to have a better conceptual articulation of what quality early childhood practice is, with appropriate assessment and evaluation that does not cut across its valuable traditions. This requires highly educated, trained, qualified and mature practitioners.

The past leads to the future through the present. Heraclitis said (Collinson, 1987):

You can put your hand in the river once.

You cannot put your hand in the same river twice.

Bibliography and references

Abbott, L., Ackers, J., Barron, I., Johnson, M., Holmes, R., Langston, A., Powell, S., Bradbury, C., Gooch, K. and David, T. 2002 *Birth to Three Matters – A Framework to Support Children in Their Earliest Years*. London: DfES (available from www.dfes.gov.uk)

Abbott, L. and Langston, A. (eds) 2005 *Birth to Three Matters: Supporting the Framework of Effective Practice*. Maidenhead: Open University Press/McGraw Hill.

Abbott, L. and Moylett, H. 1997 *Working with Under Threes: Responding to Children's Needs*. Buckingham: Open University Press.

Ainsworth, M., Behar, M., Wates, E. and Wall, S. 1978 *Patterns of Attachment: Assessment in the Strange Situation and at Home*. Hove: Laurence Erlbaum.

Arnold, C. (2009) *Schema and Emotion*. London: Sage.

Atherton, F. and Nutbrown, C. 2013 *Understanding Schemas and Young Children from Birth to Three*. London: Sage.

Athey, C. 1990 *Extending Thought in Young Children: A Parent–Teacher Partnership*. London: Paul Chapman.

Baker, C. 2000 *A Parents' and Teachers' Guide to Bilingualism*, 2nd edition. Clevedon: Multilingual Matters Ltd.

Baker, M. 2012 Family songs in the Froebelian Tradition. In T. Bruce (ed.) *Early Childhood Practice: Froebel Today*. London: Sage.

Barnes, P. (ed.) 1995 *Personal, Social and Emotional Development of Children*. Oxford: Open University, Blackwell.

Benjamin, F. 1995 *Coming to England*. Harmondsworth: Puffin Books.

Bennett, J. 2004 *Curriculum Issues in National Policy Making*. Paris: Organisation for Economic Cooperation and Development.

Blakemore, S.J. 2000 Early Years Learning. Report no. 140 (June). London: Parliamentary Office of Science and Technology (POST).

Bloch, C., 2012 The Magic and Power of Stories and Play. *Literacy Issue*, 4 December, 1–2.

Bloch, C. 2013 Enabling Effective Literacy Learning in Multilingual South African Early Childhood Classrooms. PRAESA Occasional papers No. 16.

Bowlby, J. 2005 *The Making and Breaking of Affectional Bonds*. London: Routledge.

Bradburn, E. 1989 *Margaret McMillan: Portrait of a Pioneer*. London: Routledge.

Bredikyte, M. 2011 *The Zones of Proximal Development in Children's Play*. Oulu: University of Oulu.

Brennan, C. 2004 *The Power of Play*. Dublin: IPPA/Bernard Van Leer Foundation.

Brehony, K. 2000 English revisionist Froebelians and schooling of the urban poor. In M. Hilton and P. Hirsch (eds) 2000 *Practical Visionaries: Women, Education and Social Progress 1790–1930*. Harlow: Pearson Education.

Brice Heath, S. 1983 *Ways with Words*. Cambridge: Cambridge University Press.

Bronfenbrenner, U. 1979 *The Ecology of Human Development: Experiments by Nature and Design*. Cambridge MA: Harvard University Press.

Brown, S. 2012 The changing of the seasons in the Child Garden. In T. Bruce (ed.) *Early Childhood Practice: Froebel Today*. London: Sage.

Bruce, T. 1976 A comparative study of the Montessori method, and a Piaget-based conceptualisation of the pre-school curriculum. Unpublished MA dissertation, University of London.

Bruce, T. 1978 Side by Side: Montessori and Other Educational Principles. Montessori Society AMI (UK) Third Annual Weekend Conference, February.

Bruce, T. 1984 A Froebelian looks at Montessori's work. *Early Child Development and Care* 14, 151–173.

Bruce, T. 1987 *Early Childhood Education*, 1st edition. Sevenoaks: Hodder & Stoughton.

Bruce, T. 1991 *Time to Play in Early Childhood Education and Care*. London: Hodder & Stoughton.

Bruce, T., Findlay, A., Read, J. and Scarborough, M. 1995 *Recurring Themes in Education*. London: Paul Chapman.

Bruce, T. 1996 *Helping Young Children to Play*. London: Hodder & Stoughton.

Bruce, T. 1997a Adults and children developing playing together. *European Early Childhood Education Research Association Journal* 5, 89–99.

Bruce, T. 1997b Tuning in to Children. A Child's World. BBC/NCB.

Bruce, T. 2004a *Developing Learning in Early Childhood*. London: Paul Chapman/Sage.

Bruce, T. 2009 Learning through play: Froebelian principles and their practice today. *Early Childhood Practice: The Journal for Multi-Professional Partnerships* 10(2), 59–73.

Bruce, T. and McNair, L. 2009 *I Made a Unicorn*. Robertsbridge: Community Playthings.

Bruce, T. (ed.) 2010 *Early Childhood: A Student Guide*, 2nd edition. London: Sage.

Bruce, T., Meggitt, C. and Grenier, J. 2010 *Child Care and Education*, 5th edition. London: Hodder Arnold.

Bruce, T. 2010 *Froebel Today*. In L. Miller and L. Pound *Theories and Approaches to Learning in the Early Years*. London: Sage.

Bruce, T. 2011 *Learning Through Play: Babies, Toddlers and the Foundation Years*, 2nd edition. London: Hodder Arnold.

Bruce, T. 2011 *Cultivating Creativity: Babies, Toddlers and the Early Years*, 2nd edition. London: Hodder Arnold.

Bruce, T. and Spratt, J. 2011 *Essentials of Literacy from 0–7: A Whole-Child Approach to Communication, Language and Literacy*, 2nd edition. London: Sage.

Bruce, T. 2011 All about Froebel. *Nursery World*, 7 April, 15–19

Bruce, T. (ed.) *Early Childhood Practice: Froebel Today*. London: Sage.

Bruce, T. 2015 Endpiece. In J. Moyles (ed.) *The Excellence of Play*, 4th edition. Maidenhead: Open University Press, McGraw Hill.

Bruner, J. 1977 *The Process of Education*, 2nd edition. Cambridge MA: Harvard University Press.

Bruner, J. 1990 *Acts of Meaning*. Cambridge, MA: Harvard University Press.

Bruner, J., Wood, D. and Ross, G. 1976 The role of tutoring in problem solving. *Journal of Child Psychology and Psychiatry* 17, 89–100.

Bunting, J. (ed.) 2003a *'She's not in real life, you know!' Learning Through Imaginative Play at Tachbrook Nursery School*. Centre for Literacy in Primary Education (CLPE)/Tachbrook Nursery School, Westminster Local Authority.

Bunting. J. (ed.) 2003b *Can Write*. Centre for Literacy in Primary Education (CLPE)/Dorothy Gardner Centre, Westminster Local Authority.

Butler, D. 1980 *Babies Need Books*. London: Bodley Head.

Butler, D. 1987 *Cushla and Her Books: The Fascinating Story of the Role of Books in the Life of a Handicapped Child*. Harmondsworth: Penguin.

Carr, M. 1999 Being a learner: five dispositions for early childhood. *Early Childhood Practice: The Journal for Multi-Professional Partnerships* 1, 81–1000.

Carr, M. 2001 *Assessment in Early Childhood Settings: Learning Stories*. London: Paul Chapman.

Christie, J. (ed.) 1991 *Play and Early Literacy Development*. New York: State University of New York Press.

Chukovsky, K. 1963 *From Two to Five*. Berkeley, CA: University of California Press.

Clay, M. 1975 *What Did I Write?* London: Heinemann.

Clay, M. 1992 *The Detection of Reading Difficulties*. Newcastle-upon-Tyne: Heinemann.

Cockerill, H. 1997 Communication through play: non-directive communication therapy. 'Special Times'. Cheyne Centre for Children with Cerebal Palsy, pp.1–23.

Collinson, D. 1987 *Fifty Major Philosophers: A Reference Guide*. London: Routledge.

Conkbayir, M. and Pascal, C. 2014 *Early Childhood Themes and Contemporary Issues: An Introduction*, London: Bloomsbury

Conolly, Y. 1983 Keynote Speech: A Multi-Cultural Approach in Early Education. London: OMEP Conference.

Corsaro, W. 1979 'We're friends, right?' Children's use of access rituals in a nursery school. *Language in Society* 8, 315–336.

Covey, S.R. 1989 *The Seven Habits of Highly Effective People*. London: Simon & Schuster.

Craft, A. 2012 Child-initiated play and professional creativity: enabling four-year-olds' possibility thinking. *Thinking Skills and Creativity Journal* 7, 48–61.

Crown, R. 2004 Children and pets: child's play. *The Blue Cross* 135, winter, 16–17.

Cousins, J. 2003, *Listening to four year olds: How they can help us plan their care and education*. National Early Years Network: London.

Dahlberg, G., Moss, P. and Pence, A. 1999 *Beyond Quality in Early Childhood Education and Care*. London: Falmer Press.

Damasio, A. 2004 *Looking for Spinoza*. London: Vintage/Random Press.

Davies, M. 2003 *Movement and Dance in Early Childhood*, 2nd edition. London: Paul Chapman.

DfES/Primary Strategy KEEP 2005 *Key Elements of Effective Practice*. London: DfES.

Dombey, H. 1983 Learning the language of books. In M. Meek (ed.) *Opening Moves*. Bedford Way Papers no.17. University of London: Institute of Education.

Donaldson, M. 1978 *Children's Minds*. London: Fortuna/Collins.

Douglas, J. 1964 *The Home and the School*. London: MacGibbon & Kee.

Dowling, M. 2010 *Personal, Social and Emotional Development*, 3rd edition. London: Sage.

Dowling, M. 2013, *Young Children's Thinking*. Sage: London

Drummond, M.J. 1993 *Assessing Children's Learning*. London: David Fulton.

Duffy, B. 1998 *Supporting Creativity and Imagination in the Early Years*. Maidenhead: Open University Press.

Dunn, J. 1984 *Sisters and Brothers*. London: Collins/Fontana.

Dunn, J. 1988 *The Beginnings of Social Understanding*. Oxford: Blackwell.

Dunn, J. 1991 Young children's understanding of other people: evidence from observations within the family. In K. Fye and C. Moore (eds) *Theories of Mind*. Hove: Laurence Erlbaum.

Dunn, J. and Plomin, R. 1990 *Separate Lives: Why Siblings Are So Different*. New York: Basic Books.

Dunn, O. and Sage, A. 2003 *Baby Says Bye Bye*. London: Hodder Children's Books.

Edmund, F. 1979 *Rudolf Steiner Education: The Waldorf Schools*. London: Rudolf Steiner Press.

Edwards, C., Gandini, L. and Forman, G. (eds) 1998 *The Hundred Languages of Children: The Reggio Emilia Approach – Advanced Reflections*, 2nd edition. London: Ablex.

Elfer, P. and Dearnley, K. 2007 Nurseries and emotional wellbeing: Evaluating an emotional-containment model of professional development. *Early Years: An International Journal of Research and Development* 27(3), 267–279.

Elfer, P., Goldschmied, E. and Selleck, D. 2011 *Key Persons in the Early Years: Building Relationships for Quality Provision in Early Years Setting and Primary Schools*, 2nd edition. London: Routledge.

Elfer, P. 2012 Emotion in nursery work: work discussions as a model of critical professional reflection. *Early Years Journal of Research and Development* 32(2), 129–141.

EPPE 2003 *The Effective Provision of Pre-School Education Project: Findings from the Pre-School Period*. London: DfES/IoE.

Erikson, E. 1963 *Childhood and Society*. London: Routledge & Kegan Paul.

Fabetti, R. 2005 Eyes and silences. *Early Childhood Practice: The Journal for Multi-Professional Partnerships* 7, 8–12.

Fawcett, M. 2008 The role of the mentor: 5x5x5=Creativity. *Early Childhood Practice: The Journal for Multi-Professional Partnerships* 10, 64–75.

Ferreiro, E. 1997 Reading, Writing and Thinking about the Writing System. Conference Lectures on Literacy: from Research to Practice. Lecture at the Institute of Education, University of London, 13 March 1997.

Ferreiro, E. and Teberosky, A. 1983 *Literacy Before Schooling* (trans. Karen Goodman Castro). London: Heinemann.

Fisher, J. 1996 *Starting from the Child*. Buckingham: Open University Press.

Forbes, R. 2004 *Beginning to Play*. Maidenhead: Open University Press.

Fox, C. 1983 Talking like a book. In M. Meek (ed.) *Opening Moves*. Bedford Way Papers no.17, University of London: Institute of Education.

Froebel, F.W. 1878 *Mother Play and Nursery Songs* (trans. Fanny E. Dwight (songs) and Josephine Jarvis (prose)). Boston, MA: Lee & Shepard.

Froebel, F.W. 1887 *The Education of Man*. New York: Appleton.

Fumoto, H., Robson, S. Greenfied, S. and Hargreaves, D. 2012 *Young Children's Creative Thinking*. London: Sage.

Gardner, D. 1969 *Susan Isaacs*. London: Methuen.

Garvey, C. 1977 Play. The Developing Child Series, J. Bruner, M. Cole and B. Lloyd (eds). London: Collins/Fontana-Open Books.

Gerhardt, S. 2004 *Why Love Matters: How Affection Shapes a Baby's Brain*. Hove, NY: Brunner Routledge, Taylor and Francis Group.

Gesell, A. 1954 *The First Five Years of Life*. London: Methuen.

Gleick, J. 1988 *Chaos*. London: Heinemann.

Gleick, J. (photographs by Porter, E.) 1990 *Nature's Chaos*. London: MacDonald & Co./Sphere Books.

Goddard-Blythe, S. 2004 *The Well-Balanced Child: Movement and Early Learning*. Stroud: Hawthorn Press.

Goldschmied, E. and Selleck, D. 1996 *Communication Between Babies in their First Year*. London: NCB.

Goldschmied, E. and Jackson, S. 2004 *People Under Three*, 2nd edition. London: Routledge.

Goleman, D. 1996 *Emotional Intelligence: Why It Can Matter More Than IQ*. London: Bloomsbury.

Goodman, Y. 1984 The development of initial literacy. In F. Smith, H. Goelman and A. Oberg (eds) *Awakening to Literacy*. London: Heinemann.

Goouch, K. 2015 Permission to Play. In J. Moyles (ed.) *The Excellence of Play*, 4th edition. Maidenhead: Open University Press/McGraw Hill.

Gopnik, A., Goouch, K. and Lambirth, A. (eds) 2007 *Understanding Phonics and the Teaching of Reading: Critical Perspectives*. Maidenhead: Open University Press/McGraw Hill.

Gopnik, A., Meltzoff, A. and Kuhl, P. 1999 *How Babies Think*. London: Weidenfeld and Nicolson.

Goswami, U. and Bryant, P. 1990 *Phonological Skills and Learning to Read*. Hove: Laurence Erlbaum.

Goswami, U. 1998 *Cognition in Children*. Hove: Psychology Press.

Goswami, U. 2007 Learning to read across languages: the role of phonics and synthetic phonics. In K. Goouch and A. Lambirth (eds) *Understanding Phonics and the Teaching of Reading: Critical Perspectives*. Maidenhead: Open University Press/McGraw Hill.

Graves, D. 1983 *Writing: Teachers and Children at Work*. London: Heinemann.

Greenfield, S. 2000 *Brain Story: Unlocking Our Inner World of Emotions, Memories, Ideas and Desires*. London: BBC Worldwide.

Greenland, P. 2000 *Hopping Home Backwards: Body Intelligence and Movement Play*. Leeds: A JABADAO Publication.

Greenland, P. 2010 Physical Development. In T. Bruce (ed.) *Early Childhood: A Student Guide*, 2nd edition. London: Sage.

Gura, P. (ed.) 1992 *Exploring Learning: Young Children and Blockplay*. London: Paul Chapman.

Gura, P. 1996 *Resources for Early Learning: Children, Adults and Stuff*. London: Hodder & Stoughton.

Gussin-Paley, V. 1981 *Wally's Stories*. Cambridge, MA: Harvard University Press.

Gussin-Paley, V. 1986 *Mollie Is Three*. Chicago, IL: University of Chicago.

Gussin-Paley, V. 1990 *The Boy Who Would Be a Helicopter*. Cambridge, MA: Harvard University Press.

Haidt, J. 2006 *The Happiness Hypothesis: Finding Modern Truth in Ancient Wisdom*. New York: Basic Books.

Hakkarainen, P. 1999 Play and motivation. In Y. Engestom, R. Miettinen and R. Punamaki (eds) *Perspectives on Activity Theory*. Cambridge: Cambridge University Press.

Hakkarainen, P. and Bredikyte, M. 2008 The zone of proximal development in play and learning. *Cultural Historical Psychology* 4(4), 2–11.

Hall, N. and Robinson, A. 2003 *Exploring Writing in the Early Years*, 2nd edition. London: David Fulton.

Halsey, A.H. 1972 *Education and Social Change*. Paris: UNESCO.

Harlen, W. 1982 Evaluation and assessment. In C. Richards (ed.) *New Directions in Primary Education*. London: Falmer Press.

Harrison, C. 1996 Family literacy: evaluation, ownership and ambiguity. *RSA Journal CXLIV*, 25–28.

Hawkins, D. 1998 Remarks: Malaguzzi's story, other stories. In C. Edwards, L. Gandini, G. Forman (eds) *The Hundred Languages of Children,* 2nd edition. London: Ablex Publishing.

Holdaway, D. 1979 *The Foundations of Literacy*. Gosford, NSW: Ashton Scholastic.

Holland, P. 2010 *We Don't Play with Guns Here: War, Weapon and Superhero Play in the Early Years*, 2nd edition. Maidenhead: Open University Press.

Holmes, J. 2014 *John Bowlby and Attachment Theory*, 2nd edition. Hove: Routledge.

Hughes, A. 2010 *Developing Play for the Under-Threes: The Treasure Basket and Heuristic Play*, 2nd edition. London: Routledge.

Hughes, A. and Read, V. 2012 *Building Positive Relationships with Parents of Young Children: A Guide to Effective Communication*. London: Routledge.

Hutchin, V. 2010 Meeting individual needs. In T. Bruce (ed.) *Early Childhood: A Guide for Students*, 2nd edition. London: Sage.

Isaacs, B. 2007 *Bringing the Montessori Approach to Your Early Years Practice*, London: Routledge.

Isaacs, S. 1968 *The Nursery Years*. London: Routledge & Kegan Paul.

Jenkinson, S. 2002 *The Genius of Play: Celebrating the Spirit of Childhood*. Stroud: Hawthorn Press.

Kaplan, L. 1978 *Oneness and Separateness: From Infant to Individual*. New York: Simon & Schuster.

Karmiloff-Smith, A. 1994 *Baby It's You*. London: Ebury Press.

Katz, L.G. and Chard, S.C. 1993 *Engaging Children's Minds: A Project Approach*. Norwood, NJ: Ablex.

Kegl, J. 1997 *Silent Children … New Language*. BBC Horizon, 3 April 1997.

Kellmer Pringle, N. 1974 *The Needs of Children* (2nd edition, 1980). London: Hutchinson.

Kenner, C. 2000 *Home Pages: Literacy Links for Bilingual Children*. Stoke-on-Trent: Trentham Books.

Kilpatrick, W. 1915 *Montessori Examined*. London: Constable & Co.

Kitzinger, C. 1997 Born to be good? What motivates us to be good, bad or indifferent towards others? *New Internationalist*, April, 15–17.

Kohn, A. 1993 *Punished by Rewards: The Trouble with Gold Stars, Incentive Plans, A's, Praise and Other Bribes*. Boston, MA/New York: Houghton Mifflin.

Krashen, S. 1981 *First Language Acquisition and Second Language Learning*. London: Pergamon.

Laevers, F. 1994 *The Innovative Project: Experiential Education 1976–1995*. Katholieke Universiteit, Leuven, Belgium: Research Centre for Early Childhood and Primary Education.

Lane, J. 2008 *Young Children and Racial Justice: Taking Action for Racial Equality in the Early Years – Understanding the Past, Thinking about the Present, Planning for the Future*. London: National Children's Bureau.

Lane, H. 1977 *The Wild Boy of Aveyron*. London: Allen & Unwin.

Learning and Teaching Scotland 2005 *Birth to Three: Supporting Our Youngest Children*.

Liebschner, J. 1985 Children learning through each other. *Early Childhood Development and Care* 21, 121–135.

Liebschner, J. 1991 *Foundations of Progressive Education: The History of the National Froebel Society*. Cambridge: Butterworth Press.

Liebschner, J. 1992 *A Child's World: Freedom and Guidance in Froebel's Theory and Practice.* Cambridge: Butterworth Press.

Louis, S. 2012 The importance of schemas in every child's learning, *Early Education,* autumn (68), 4–5.

Louis, S. 2012 Early childhood education in the time of international economic austerity: is it as easy as ABC(D)? *Early Education,* international issue, 66.

Louis, S., Beswick, C., Magraw, L. and Hayes, L. (S. Featherstone ed.) 2013 *Understanding Schemas in Young Children: Again! Again!* London Featherstone Press.

Louis, S. and Miranda, K. 2009 What's their schema? *Early Education,* summer (58), 4–5.

McCormick, C. 2012 Froebelian methods in the modern world: a case of cooking. In T. Bruce (ed.) *Early Childhood Practice: Froebel Today.* London: Sage.

McKeller, P. 1957 *Imagination and Thinking.* London: Cohen & West.

McNair, L. 2007 A development project in the garden: how Froebelian is it? *Early Childhood Practice: the Journal for Multi-Professional Partnerships* 9(1), 26–42.

McNair, L. 2012 Offering children first-hand experiences through forest school: relating to and learning about nature. In T. Bruce (ed.) *Early Childhood Practice: Froebel Today.* London: Sage.

Malloch, S. and Trevarthen, C. 2009 *Communicative Musicality: Exploring the Basis of Human Companionship.* Oxford: Oxford University Press.

Manning-Morton, J. and Thorp, M. 2003 *Key Times for Play.* Maidenhead: Open University Press.

Manning Morton, J. and Thorp, M. 2015 *Two-Year-Olds in Early Years Settings.* Maidenhead: Open University Press/McGraw Hill.

Maslow, A. 1962 *Towards a Psychology of Being.* Princeton, NJ: Van Nostrand.

Matthews, J. 2003 *Drawing and Painting: Young Children and Visual Representation,* 2nd edition. London: Paul Chapman.

Matthews, J. 2011 *Starting from Scratch: The Origin and Development of Expression, Representation and Symbolism in Human and Non-Human Primates.* Hove: Psychology Press.

Maynard, T. and Thomas, N. (eds) 2004 *An Introduction to Early Childhood Studies.* London: Sage.

Meade, A. with Cubey, P. 2008 *Thinking Children: Learning about Schemas.* Maidenhead: Open University Press.

Meek, M. 1985 Play and paradoxes. Some considerations for imagination and language. In G. Wells, and J. Nicholls (eds) *Language and Learning: An Interactional Perspective.* London: Falmer Press.

Miller, L. 1997 A vision for the early years curriculum in UK. *The International Journal of Early Childhood Education: OMEP* 29, 34–42.

Minns, H. 1990 *Read It to Me Now.* London: Virago Education with the University of London Institute of Education.

Montessori, M. 1912 *The Montessori Method.* London: Heinemann.

Montessori, M. 1948 *The Discovery of the Child.* Madras, India: Kalakshetra.

Montessori, M. 1949 *The Absorbent Mind.* Madras, India: Theosophical Publishing House.

Montessori, M. 1966 *The Secret of Childhood.* New York: Ballantine Press.

Montessori, M. 1972 (1939) *Education and Peace.* Chicago: Regnery.

Montessori 1974 (1946) *Education for a New World.* Madras, India: Kalakshetra.

Montessori, M. 1975 *The Child in the Family* (trans. Nancy Rockmore Cirillo). London: Pan.

Moyles, J. (ed.) 2015 *The Excellence of Play,* 4th edition. Maidenhead: Open University Press/McGraw Hill.

Moylett, H. (ed.) 2014 *Characteristics of Effective Early Learning: Helping Young Children Become Learners for Life.* Maidenhead: Open University Press/McGraw Hill.

Murray, L. and Andrews, L. 2000 *The Social Baby: Understanding Babies' Communication from Birth.* Richmond: The Children's Project.

New Zealand Ministry of Education 1996 *Te Whariki: Guidelines for Developmentally Appropriate Programmes in Early Childhood Services*. Wellington: Ministry of Education.

Nicholls, R. (ed.) 1986 Rumpus Schema Extra. Cleveland Teachers, Nursery Nurses and Parents. Booklet based on lectures by Chris Athey.

Nicol, J. 2010 *Bringing the Steiner Waldorf Approach to Your Early Years Practice*, 2nd edition. London: Routledge.

Nicolopoulou, A. Ch 11 The interplay of narrative in children's development: theoretical reflections and concrete examples. pp. 247–73 in *Play and Development: Evolutionary, Sociocultural, and Functional Perspectives* edited by A. Goncu and S. Gaskins 2007 Lawrence Erlbaum, NY, London

Nielsen, L. 1992 Space and Self: Active Learning by Means of the Little Room. Sikon (available from RNIB).

Nutbrown, C. (ed.) 1996 *Respectful Educators – Capable Learners. Children's Rights and Early Education*. London: Paul Chapman.

Nutbrown, C. 2001 *Experiencing Reggio Emilia: Implications for Pre-School Provision*. Maidenhead: Open University Press.

Nutbrown, C. 2006 *Threads of Learning: Young Children Learning and the Role of Early Education*, 3rd edition. London: Paul Chapman.

Ockelford, A. 1996 *All Join In: A Framework for Making Music with Children and Young People Who are Visually Impaired and Have Learning Difficulties*. Peterborough: RNIB.

Ockelford, A. 2008 *Music for Children and Young People with Complex Needs*. Oxford: Oxford Music Education Series.

O'Donnell, M. 2013 *Maria Montessori: A Critical Introduction to Key Themes and Debates*. London: Bloomsbury.

Oldfield, L. 2003 *Free to Learn*. Stroud: Hawthorn Press.

Orr, R. 2003 *My Right to Play: A Child with Complex Needs*. Maidenhead: Open University Press.

Ouvry, M. 2000 *Exercising Muscles and Minds: Outdoor Play and the Early Years Curriculum*. London: National Early Years Network.

Ouvry, M. 2004 *Sounds Like Playing*. London: Early Education.

Ouvry, M. 2012 Froebel's Mother Songs today. In T. Bruce (ed.) *Early Childhood Practice: Froebel Today*. London: Sage.

Oxfordshire Creativity Project in partnership with 5x5x5=Creativity and Early Education, (undated, circa 2009) Evaluation report (available from www.5x5x5creativity.org.uk).

Page, J. 2011 Do mothers want professional carers to love their babies? *Journal of Early Childhood Research* 9(3), 310–23.

Papert, S. 1980 *Mind Storms: Children, Computers and Powerful Ideas*. Brighton: Harvester Press.

Piaget, J. 1962 *Play, Dreams and Imitation in Childhood*. London: Routledge & Kegan Paul.

Piaget, J. 1968 *Six Psychological Studies*. London: University of London Press.

Piaget, J. and Inhelder, B. 1969 *The Psychology of the Child*. London: Routledge & Kegan Paul.

Pollard, A. with Filer, A. 1996 *The Social World of Children's Learning: Case Studies of Pupils from Four to Seven*. London: Cassell.

Powell, S, Werth, L. and Goouch, K. 2013 Mother Songs in daycare for babies. Report to the Froebel Trust Research Committee, Canterbury Christ Church University Research Centre for Children, families and Communities. 9 Sept. 2013.

QCA/DfES 2000 *Curriculum Guidance for the Foundation Stage*. London: DfES.

Read, J. 2012 The time-honoured Froebelian tradition of learning out of doors. In T. Bruce (ed.) *Early Childhood Practice: Froebel Today*. London: Sage.

Riley, J. 2006 *Language and Literacy, 3–7*. London: Paul Chapman.

RNIB 1995 *Play It My Way*. London: RNIB/HMSO.

Roberts, R. 2012 *Self-esteem and Early Learning*, 3rd edition. London: Paul Chapman.

Robson, S. 2010 Self-regulation and metacognition in young children's self-motivated play and reflective dialogue. *International Journal of Early Years Education* 18:3, pp 227–41.

Robson, S. and Rowe, V. 2012 Observing young children's creative thinking, engagement, involvement and persistence. *International Journal of Early Years Education* 20(4), 349–64.

Rogoff, B., Mistry, J., Goncu, A. and Mosier, C. 1993 Guided participation in cultural activity by toddlers and caregivers. Monographs of the Society for Research in Child Development 58, serial no.236.

Rogoff, B., Paradise, R. Arauz, R.M., Correa-Chavez, M. and Angelillo, C. 2003 First-hand learning through intent participation. *Annual Reviews of Psychology* 54, 175–203.

Rousseau, J. 1963 (1762) *Emile* (trans. Barbara Foxley). London: Dent.

Rubin, Z. 1983 The skills of friendship. In M. Donaldson, R. Grieve and C. Pratt (eds) *Early Childhood Development and Education*. Oxford: Blackwell.

Schaffer, H. 2006 *Key Concepts in Developmental Psychology*. London: Sage.

Sherbourne, V. 2001 *Developmental Movement for Children: Mainstream, Special Needs and Pre-school*. London: Worth Publishing.

Smith, F. 1983 *Essays into Literacy*. London: Heinemann.

Spratt, J. 2012 The importance of hand and finger rhymes: A Froebelian approach to early literacy. In T. Bruce (ed.) *Early Childhood Practice: Froebel Today*. London: Sage.

Standing, E.M. 1957 *Maria Montessori: Her Life and Work*. London: Plume Books.

Steiner, R. 1926 *The Essentials of Education*. London: Anthroposophical Publishing Co.

Steiner, R. 1965 *The Education of the Child*. London: Rudolf Steiner Press.

Stern, D. 2002 *The First Relationship*, 2nd edition. Cambridge, MA: Harvard University Press.

Stewart, N. 2011 *How Children Learn: The Characteristics of Effective Early Learning*. London: Early Education/BAECE.

Strathern, P. 1996 *Kant 1724–1804 in 90 Minutes*. London: Constable.

Strathern, P. 1996 *Locke 1632–1704 in 90 Minutes*. London: Constable.

Strauss, M. 1978 *Understanding Children's Drawings*. London: Rudolf Steiner Press.

Tamburrini, J. 1982 New directions in nursery education. In C. Richards (ed.) *New Directions in Primary Education*. London: Falmer Press.

Taylor, D. 1983 *Family Literacy*. London: Heinemann.

Tovey, H. 2007 *Playing Outdoors, Spaces and Places, Risk and Challenge*. Maidenhead: Open University Press.

Tovey, H. 2012 Adventurous and challenging play outdoors, In T. Bruce (ed.) *Early Childhood Practice: Froebel Today*. London: Sage.

Tovey, H. 2013 *Bringing the Froebel Approach to Your Early Years Practice*. London: Routledge.

Trevarthen, C. 1993a Playing into reality: conversations with the infant communicator. *Winnicott Stories* 7, 67–84.

Trevarthen, C. 1993b The function of emotions on early infant communication and development. In J. Nadel and L. Camaioni (eds) *New Perspectives in Early Communicative Development*. London: Routledge.

Trevarthen, C. 1998 The child's need to learn a culture. In M. Woodhead, D. Faulkner and K. Littelton (eds) *Cultural Worlds of Early Childhood*. London: Routledge, Open University Press.

Trevarthen, C. 2002 Origins of musical identity: evidence from infancy for musical social awareness. In R. MacDonald, D.J. Hargreaves and D. Niell (eds) *Musical Identities*. Oxford: Oxford University Press, pp.21–38.

Trevarthen, C. 2003 Infancy, mind. In R. Gregory (ed.) *Oxford Companion to the Mind*. Oxford: Oxford University Press.

Trevarthen, C. 2004 Foreword. In T. Bruce (ed.) *Developing Learning in Early Childhood*. London: Paul Chapman, pp.xi–xiv.

Tumin, S. 1994 Inspecting prisons. *Sunday Times* lecture series, the Royal Geographical Society, Kensington, London, July.

Turiel, E. and Weston, D. 1983 Act–rule relation: children's concepts of social rules. In M. Donaldson, R. Grieve and C. Pratt (eds) *Early Childhood Development and Care*. Oxford: Blackwell.

Vygotsky, L. 1978 *Mind in Society*. Cambridge, MA: Harvard University Press.

Wells, G. 1987 *The Meaning Makers*. London: Hodder & Stoughton.

Whalley, E. 1994 Patterns in play. The use of schemas theory by teachers and parents. *Primary Life* 3, autumn. Oxford: National Primary Centre, Blackwell.

Whalley, M. (ed.) 2001 *Involving Parents in Their Children's Learning*. London: Paul Chapman.

Whinnett, J. 2006 Froebelian practice today: the search for unity. *Early Childhood Practice: The Journal for Multi-Professional Partnerships* 8(2), 58–80.

Whinnett, J. 2012 Gifts and Occupations: Froebel's Gifts (wooden block play) and Occupations (construction and workshop experiences) today. In T. Bruce (ed.) *Early Childhood Practice: Froebel Today*. London: Sage.

Whitebread, D. 2012 *Developmental Psychology and Early Childhood Education*. London: Sage.

Whitehead, M. 2007 *Developing Language and Literacy with Young Children*, 3rd edition. London: Paul Chapman.

Whitehead, M. 2009 *Supporting Language and Literacy Development in the Early Years*, 2nd edition. Maidenhead: Open University.

Whitehead, M. 2010 *Language and Literacy in the Early Years 0–7*, 4th edition. London: Sage.

Whiting, B. and Edwards, C.P. 1992 *Children of Different Worlds: The Formation of Social Behaviour*. Cambridge, MA: Harvard University Press.

Winnicott, D.W. 1974 *Playing and Reality*. Harmondsworth: Penguin.

Worthington, M. 2015 Mathematics and the ecology of pretend play. In J. Moyles *The Excellence of Play*. Maidenhead: Open University Press.

Worthington, M. and Carruthers, E. 2003 *Children's Mathematics*. London: Paul Chapman.

Zuckerman, G. 2007 Child–adult interaction that creates a zone of proximal development, *Journal of Russian and East European Psychology*, 45 (3), pp. 31–58

DVDs

Discovered Treasure: The Life and Work of Elinor Goldschmied 1910–2009: Jacqui Cousins, Anita Hughes and Dorothy Selleck, A Froebel Trust Project (available from www.froebeltrust.org.uk).

Siren Films: these cover a variety of themes, including the recent *The Power of Physical Play*, also the topics of Play, Two-year-olds, Attachment, Toddlers, Outdoor Learning, Early Literacy, Reception Class, and many more (available from www.sirenfilms.co.uk).

Index

Figures in italics refer to diagrams, pictures and tables. Figures in bold are major references.

ability, building on 34–6, 212
Absorbent Mind, The 39
abstract thinking 26, 10, 79
abuse 150, 162, 175
action points, for early childhood education 214–15
active learning 102, 115
adolescence 23
  delinquency 158, 159
  and moral development 159
adult role
  adult/child relationship 23–4, 38–9, 175
  autonomous learning 27–9
  dominating 27, 31, 212
  as educator 21–2, 24, 212
  empiricist view of 3–4
  as extension of child 117
  as helper 39
  and inner life of child 38
  interactionist view of 9
  intervention 26–8, 132
  in literacy 126–30, 132–6, 140
  in moral development 158, 160–3
  nativist view of 5
  in play 27–8, 64–5, 67, 69–71
  in representation 112–13, 117–20
  role modelling 160
  in schemas 80–1, 88
  and self-discipline 30
  setting boundaries 63–4, 160
  see also practitioners
adult/child relationship 23–4, 38–9, 175
adult-directed play 64–5
adulthood, preparation for 21–3
Albon, D. 17–18
alphabet 133, 136, 145–6
  see also literacy; writing
animals 61, 122–3
anxiety
  containing 48, 57
  in parents 208
art see drawing; finger painting
assessment 201, 202, 205–6, 212
  formative 205–9
  summative 206–8
  see also observation
assimilation 9
Atherton, F. 44–5
Athey, C. 74–5, 80–1, 82, 95, 99–100, 130
autism 77
autonomous learning 27–9
babies
  birth order 43
    and books 68, 143
  brain development 45

crawling 57–8
educating 44–58
intellectual lives of 45
language development 45–6
non-verbal communication 122
peer relationships 49–51
play 61
premature 43
reading to 143
role of practitioner 48
sense of self 56–7
singing 56
Treasure Basket 46–54, 87, 210
Baby Room Project 56
balancing 102
bedtime rituals 85
behaviour
  fitting in 161, 162
  formal/informal 159
  unacceptable 95
belonging 190–2
Benjamin, F. 190
bilingual children 123, 125, 144
bio-ecological systems theory 168
biological development 74, 76, 87, 110, 146
  see also child development; nativism
biological pre-programming 5
birth order 43
Blakemore, S.J. 148, 151
blaming 158
block play 82, 93, 100
books
  and babies 68, 143
  choosing 129–30, 143
  see also literacy; reading; stories
boundaries 63–4, 160
Braille 199
brain development 45, 87
breastfeeding 5
Bredikyte, M. 67–8, 69, 73
Brehony, K. 28
Brennan, M. 123
Brice Heath, S. 138
British Sign Language (BSL) 123
Brofenbrenner, U. 168
Brown, S. 65
Bruner, J. 11–12, 102, 104, 116
Buhler, C. 62
Bunting, J. 132
Butler, D. 143
bystander effect 162
capital letters 132–3
carers see parents
Carr, M. 199

Casa dei Bambini   22
cause and effect   77, 155
chemistry   12
child/adult relationship   23–4, 38–9, 175
child-centric environment   22
child development
    biological   74, 76, 87, 110, 146
    cognitive   44
    moral   40, 66, 153–67
    physical   29
    recording   208–9
    social   39–40, 44, 65
    stages of   26, 29, 33–6, 40, 158
    'whole child'   23–25
    see also schemas
child minders   44
childcare provision   44
childhood
    three phases of (Steiner)   22–3
    views of   2–18
Chomsky, N.   5
Clay, M.   131
climbing   94–5
clinging, to parent   178–9
cognitive development   44
comfort zone   149
communication
    babies   122
    conversations   12, 127–9
    deaf children   123–4
    listening   124–7, 130, 144, 146, 161
    non-verbal   122–3
    see also language development
companionship play   69
compensatory education   3
computer work   92
concentration   71
conflict resolution   160–1
Conolly, Y.   189
containing child's anxiety   48, 57
conversations   12, 127–9
cooking play   6, 61
copying   111
    see also imitation
core schema   85–7, 96
Corsaro, W.   170
cortisol   44
Cousins, J.   47, 53
creativity   36
creole language   124
Crown, R.   122
cultural diversity see diversity
curriculum   23, 27
    evaluating   202
    planning   76, 89–93
    spiral   11
Damasio, A.   9, 148
dance   89, 120, 144, 208
De'Ath, E.   175
deaf children   123–4
deficit model, of child   3
delinquency   158, 159
dens   87

development see child development
developmental psychology   18
developmental sequences   34, 35
didactic materials   26, 33, 35
disability   43, 57, 77, 93–4, 198
disablist behaviour   57
disapproval   155
disciplining children   30–1
Discovered Treasure   52
Discovery of the Child, The   34, 39
discrimination   198
    see also inclusion
discussion   26, 30–1
    see also conversations
disembedded tasks   152
displays   212
diversity   2, 57, 134, 189–200
doll's houses   69
Donaldson, M.   152
drama   208
drawing   105–7
    and literacy   142–3
    and schemas   92
    see also images; symbolic behaviour
dressing up   67, 87
Dunn, J.   96, 150, 155
education
    from birth   44
    compensatory   3
    empiricist view of   2–4, 7
    guiding principles of   19–41
    interactionist approach to   8–17
    nativist view of   5–7
    see also curriculum; learning
Effective Provision of Pre-School Education (EPPE)
    12, 16, 129, 138
egocentricity   149
Elfer, P.   53
Elinor Goldschmied Froebel Archive Project   47
embedded tasks   152
embodied self   23, 86
emotional abuse   149
emotions   148, 155
    see also feelings
empathy   5, 148, 149
empiricism   2–4, 7
enactive representation   102–4
envelopment schema   75, 86, 87, 98
environment
    child-centric   22
    and language   5
    outdoor   23–4, 69, 104
    for play   28–9
epigenetics   74, 87
Erikson, E.   5, 158
everyday life play   61, 68
everyday tasks, learning from   152–3
experience
    first-hand   61
    influence of   3
    learning through   104
    and senses   8
extrinsic rewards   165–6

fairy stories 37
family literacy 136–9
feelings
    and language development 130
    of others 148–67
    and schemas 87
    see also emotions
Fein, G. 65
Ferreiro, E. 131, 134–5
finger painting 12, 112
first-hand experience 61
fitting in 161, 162
'flitting' 81
Forbes, R. 48, 49
formal/informal behaviour 159
formative assessment 205–9
Frayn, M. 136
free-flow play 60–74
Freud, A. 62
Froebel, F. 19, 21–42, 55–6, 64, 65–6, 82
Froebel Institute 74–5
functional dependency 77
functional literacy 138–41
garden environment 23–4, 69
gardening play 12–16
Garvey, C. 62
Gerhardt, S. 44, 150, 155
Gesell, A. 5
Gifts 23, 25, 33, 34, 36, 49, 82
Goddard Blythe, S. 162
Goldschmied, E. 46–9, 52–5
Goleman, D. 150, 155
Goouch, K. 137
Gopnik, A. 45
Goswami, U. 144
grandparents, role of 43
Graves, D. 136
Greenland, P. 57
grid schema 81
group play 169–73
group mentality 162
groups 168–73
    large 161–2
    minority 192
    mixed-age 39, 64, 112, 154
    mono-age 64
guilt 158
Gura, P. 93
Gussin Paley, V. 142
habit formation 3
Hakkarainen, P. 67–8
Hall, N. 134, 138
handwriting 131–2
    see also literacy; writing
Harrison, C. 136
health records 208–9
health visitors 183–4, 186
Heuristic Play 47, 52, 88
Hewitt, P. 44
Hodge, M. 43–4
Holland, P. 67
home corner 6, 68, 70–1
Hughes, A. 46–7

'Hundred Languages' of the child 106
Hutchin, V. 206
iconic representation 104
identity 86
    see also sense of self
images, as representation 104, 112
imagination 36–8
imaginative play 68, 164–5
imitation 35–7, 64, 111–12, 139
inclusion 189–200
inner life of child 36–8
integrated learning 25–7
intention 157, 158
inter-disciplinary work 183–8
interactionism 8–17, 31
interest book 208
interest table 104
intrinsic motivation 28, 29, 30, 64, 166
Isaacs, B. 24, 26, 34, 39
Isaacs, S. 47, 65, 204
Jamison, J. 93
jokes 130
justice 5, 26
Kalliala, M. 69
Kant, I. 8, 11
Kaplan, L. 187
Kegl, J. 123–4
Kenner, C. 134
Key Person 48, 52–4, 175–7
Kindergarten 22, 23–4
Kinney, P. 65
Kitzinger, C. 151
knowing-doing gap 156, 158
Kohn, A. 165
labelling 195, 197
language
    and environment 5
    importance of 10
    proto-conversations 12
    and schemas 84
    as symbolic code 104–6
    see also conversations; language development
Language Acquisition Device (LAD) 5, 124
language development 123–31
    adult role 126–30, 140
    in babies 45–6
    correcting 130
leadership 162
learning
    active 102, 115
    adult role in 3–4, 5, 9, 10, 24
    'can do' approach 34–6
    hierarchical model of 24, 26
    integrated 25–7
    mechanisms of 45
    outdoors 23–4, 69, 104
    and repetition 9–10, 26
    stages of 33–4
    views on 2–18
    see also education
'learning by doing' see active learning
learning difficulties, children with 37
Liebschner, J. 21, 40

listening 124–7, 130, 144, 146, 161
literacy
   adult role 126–30, 132–6, 140
   and drawing 142–3
   family literacy 136–9
   and language development 123–31
   phonics-first approach 137
   reading 143–147
   writing 131–43
Locke, J. 2
Louis, S. 44–45
Malguzzi, L. 105
Manning Morton, J. 49
mark-making 93
materials
   for play 26, 28–9, 33, 35, 47
   for representation 118–20
maternity leave 44
mathematics 72, 89, 100
Matthews, J. 80, 92, 117
maturation 40–1
McKellar, P. 130
McMillan, M. 47
mealtimes 152–3
Meek, M. 130, 144
minority groups 192
mixed-age groups 39, 64, 112, 154
mono-age groups 64
Montessori, M. 19, 21–42, 82, 145
moral development 40, 66, 153–67
Mother Songs 23, 36, 39, 55–6, 68
mothers
   as first educators 38
   returning to work 44
   see also parents
motivation
   intrinsic 28, 29, 30, 64, 166
   extrinsic 165–6
   see also self-motivation
Movement Games 23, 36
mud kitchen 68
multilingual children 125
Murray, L. 44
music 68, 92, 120, 208
narrative observation 204–5, 209
nativism 5–7
natural justice 5
Naturalistic Fallacy 208
nature 68–9
   see also outdoor environments
negotiation 63, 155–6, 160
nesting principle 9
Nicol, J. 22, 37
Nielsen, L. 93–4
non-verbal communication 122–3
Nutbrown, C. 44–5, 84
O'Donnell, M. 29
observation 35–6, 48, 77, 98, 117, 201–13
   assessment 201, 202, 205–8, 212
   evaluation 201, 202, 206–9
   formative 205–9
   narrative 204–5, 209

planning 212–13
types of 204
vocabulary of 45, 76
Occupations 23, 33, 34, 36
Ockelford, A. 45, 94
Oldfield, L. 26, 29
only children 43
'original sin' 30
other people, learning about 148–165
outdoor environments 23–4, 69, 104
over-protective parents 178
Papert, S. 84, 87
parents
   anxiety in 208
   over-protective 178
   self-confidence of 175
   working in partnership with 163, 175, 177–88
   see also adult role
partnerships
   between children 154, 173–4
   with parents 163, 175, 177–88
paternity leave 44
peer relationships 39, 49–51, 168–74
performances 120, 208
Persona Dolls 57
personal space 68–9
personality 43
pets 61, 122–3
phonemes 145
phonological awareness 144–5
physical development 29
physical play 61
Piaget, J. 9–10, 62, 64, 83, 110–13, 115–16, 130, 157
picture books 146
pioneer educators 19
planning 212–13
   curriculum 76, 89–93
   reflective 201
play
   adult role in 27–8, 64–5, 67, 69–71
   adult-directed 64–5
   babies 61
   choosing to 64–5
   cooking 6, 61
   dressing up 67, 87
   environment 28–9
   fighting 173
   free-flow 60–74
   imaginative 68, 164–5
   and inner life 36
   as integrating mechanism 73
   materials 26, 28–9, 33, 35, 47
   and moral development 164–5
   and music 68
   physical 61
   pretend 61, 64, 66, 68, 140, 142
   props 63–4, 116
   role play 67
   rules 62–3
   small world play 69
   solitary 68–9
   as spiritual activity 24, 73

superhero play   67
  as work   27
postmodernism   17–18
Powell, S.   55–6
practitioners
  effects of assumptions   198–9
  Key Person   48, 52–4, 175–7
  managers   53
  reflective planning   201
  see also adult role
prejudice   198
premature babies   43
pretend play   61, 64, 66, 68, 140, 142
principles of practice   20–41
problem-solving skills   65
profile books   207
proto-conversations   12
Pugh, G.   175
punishment   31
puppet shows   144
quantity, concept of   83
  see also mathematics
quotity   100
Radcliffe, V.   72
reading   143–147
  phonemes   145
  phonological awareness   144–5
  picture books   146
  synthetic phonics   146
  see also literacy
reciprocity   12
record keeping   201–2, 208–9
reflective behaviour   66, 69, 149
reflective planning   201
Reggio Emilia approach   19, 105, 205
relationships
  with adults   23–4, 38–9, 175
  with other children   39, 49–51, 168–74
religion   194
repetition   9–10, 26
representation   37, 102–21
  adult role   112–13, 117–20
  enactive mode   102–4
  iconic mode   104
  images   104, 112
  and imitation   111–12
  materials for   118–20
  and performance   120
  socio-cultural aspects of   110, 114, 115
  symbolic mode   104–110, 113–16
  and writing   131–4
respect   31
responsibility   27
rewards   30, 165–6
rhyming   145
Rice, S.   98
Riley, J.   135, 136
Roberts, R.   159
rocking behaviour   77
role of adult see adult role
role modelling   160
role play   67

rotation schema   86
Rousseau, J.   5
Rubin, Z.   51, 168
rules of play   62–3
scaffolding   12, 24
schemas   9, 44–5, 74–101
  adult role   80–1, 88
  after childhood   83–4
  in babies and toddlers   87–8
  biological aspects of   76
  configurative aspects of   80, 82–3, 92
  and curriculum planning   76, 89–93
  dynamic aspects of   80, 82, 92
  in everyday life   85–6
  and feelings   87
  historic background   82–3
  and identity   86–7
  and language   84
  socio-cultural aspects of   76, 83, 95
  supporting and extending   99–101
  universal aspects of   93
  and writing   134
Secret of Childhood, The   22
self-confidence   195
self-direction   28–9
self-discipline   30–2, 94, 96, 209
self-esteem   158, 167, 195
self-management   94
self-mastery   39
self-motivation   27–9
self-regulation   9, 31
self-worth   195
sense of humour   130
sense of self   56–7, 161, 197
  see also identity
senses   8, 26, 102
'sensitive period'   33, 34
sensory experiences   102
sensory protection   38
'shared sustained conversations'   129
siblings   43, 61
sign language   123–4
simple-to-complex hierarchical model   24, 26
singing   56, 68
  see also music
Siraj, I.   129
sitting still   161
Skinner, B.F.   3
small world play   69
Smith, F.   142
social development   39–40, 44, 65
socio-cultural context   40–1, 43
socio-cultural influences   74
  on representation   110, 114, 115
  on schemas   76
  on writing   135
solitary play   68–9
sound, awareness of   46
spiral curriculum   11
spirituality   73, 194
  see also moral development
spitting   94

stage theory 33
stages of development, and learning 33–4
Stanley, D. 47
Steiner, R. 19, 21–42, 83
stereotyping 197
stories 66, 144
    see also reading
stranger fear 57, 198
summative assessment 206–8
superhero play 67
SureStart 143
sustained shared thinking 12
syllables 145
Sylva, K. 16
symbolic behaviour 36–8
    and schemas 77
    see also representation
symbolic codes 104–5
symbolic representation 63, 113–16
symmetry 100
sympathy 148
syntax 144
synthetic phonics 146
tabula rasa, child as 3
Tamburrini, J. 143
Taylor, D. 137, 138
technology 139
temperament 32, 43
theatre 120
    see also performances
theory of mind 57, 66, 148, 165, 167
Thorp, M. 49

Time to Play 63
Tovey, H. 24
toys 28, 38
see also play: materials
trajectory schema 77, 81, 84–6, 89, 90–2
tranquillity 31, 37, 39
transformations 67
transitional objects 108–10
transporting schema 78–9, 83, 95–6
Treasure Basket 46–54, 87, 210
Trevarthen, C. 12, 45, 122, 131, 148
trust 52–3
twin studies 74
unacceptable behaviour 95
universal child 17
visual impairment 77
Vygotsky, L. 10–11, 62, 64, 65, 73, 116, 131, 142
well-being 148, 153–4, 190
Whalley, E. 100
Whitehead, M. 84, 125, 146
'whole child' 23–25, 84
Winnicott, D.W. 109–10
working in partnership with parents 163, 175,
    177–88
Worthington, M. 72
writing 131–43
    adult role 132–6, 140
    own name 135
    play scenarios 140
    and representation 131–4
    socio-cultural environment 135
zone of proximal development 10–11, 212